THE SPIRITUAL MAN
Volume III

G. C. KREIS

THE
SPIRITUAL MAN

Watchman Nee

IN THREE VOLUMES

Christian Fellowship Publishers, Inc.
New York

Copyright © 1968
CHRISTIAN FELLOWSHIP PUBLISHERS, INC.
NEW YORK

PRINTED IN U.S.A.
Distributed by Premium Literature Co.
Box 55102
Indianapolis, Indiana 46205

Contents

VOLUME III

EXPLANATORY NOTES   6

PART EIGHT: THE ANALYSIS OF THE SOUL —THE MIND

1. The Mind a Battlefield   7
2. The Phenomena of a Passive Mind   30
3. The Way of Deliverance   45
4. The Laws of the Mind   63

PART NINE: THE ANALYSIS OF THE SOUL —THE WILL

1. A Believer's Will   75
2. Passivity and Its Dangers   90
3. The Believer's Mistake   102
4. The Path to Freedom   120

PART TEN: THE BODY

1. The Believer and His Body   139
2. Sickness   158
3. God as the Life of the Body   196
4. Overcoming Death   213

EXPLANATORY NOTES

Volume III of *The Spiritual Man* is a companion book to Volumes I and II of this series of studies. While many other books have been compiled from his spoken messages, this book translated from the Chinese is the only one of any substantial size which brother Watchman Nee himself ever wrote. Perhaps this will account for the difference in style. At the time of writing it he felt this work might be his last contribution to the church, although since then God has graciously overruled. Long after the book's initial publication in Chinese our brother once was heard to express the thought that it should not be reprinted because, it being such a "perfect" treatment of its subject, he was fearful lest the book become to its readers merely a manual of principles and not a guide to experience as well. But in view of the urgent need among the children of God today for help on spiritual life and warfare, and knowing our brother as one who is always open to God's way and most desirous to serve His people with all that God has given him, we conclude that he would doubtless permit it to be circulated in English. Hence this translation.

Translations used. The Revised Standard Version (RSV) of the Bible has been used throughout the text unless otherwise indicated. Additional translations where employed are denoted by the following abbreviations:

   Amplified—*Amplified Old Testament*
   ASV—American Standard Version (1901)
   AV—Authorized Version (King James)
   Darby—J. N. Darby, *The Holy Scriptures, a New Translation*
   Young's—Young's *Literal Translation*

Soulical and Soulish. The adjectives "soulical" and "soulish" have been used to convey distinctly different meanings. "Soulical" as herein employed pertains to those proper, appropriate, legitimate, or natural qualities, functions, or expressions of man's soul which the Creator intended from the very beginning for the soul uniquely to possess and manifest. "Soulish" appears in these pages to describe that man *in toto* who is so governed by the soulical part of his being that his whole life takes on the character and expression of the soul.

PART EIGHT

THE ANALYSIS OF THE SOUL—THE MIND

1 The Mind a Battlefield
2 The Phenomena of a Passive Mind
3 The Way of Deliverance
4 The Laws of the Mind

CHAPTER 1
THE MIND A BATTLEFIELD

The mind of man is his organ of thought. Through it he is equipped to know, think, imagine, remember, and understand. Man's intellect, reasoning, wisdom and cleverness all pertain to the mind. Broadly speaking the mind is the brain. Mind is a psychological term whereas brain is a physiological term. The mind of psychology is the brain of physiology. Man's mind occupies a large place in his life because his thought easily influences his action.

BEFORE REGENERATION

According to the Bible the mind of man is unusual in that it constitutes a battlefield where Satan and his evil spirits contend against the truth and hence against the believer. We may illustrate as follows. Man's will and spirit are like a citadel which the evil spirits crave to capture. The open field where the battle is waged for the seizure of the citadel is man's mind. Note how Paul the Apostle describes it: "though we live in the world we are not carrying on a worldly war, for the weapons of our warfare are not worldly but have divine power to destroy strongholds. We destroy *arguments* and every proud obstacle to the knowledge of God, and take every *thought* captive to obey Christ" (2 Cor. 10.3-5). He initially tells us of a battle—then where the battle is fought —and finally for what objective. This struggle pertains exclusively to man's mind. The Apostle likens man's arguments or reasonings to an enemy's strongholds. He pictures the mind as held by the enemy; it must therefore be broken into by waging war. He concludes that many rebellious thoughts are housed in these strongholds and need to be taken captive to the obedience of Christ. All this plainly shows us that the mind of man is the scene of battle where the evil spirits clash with God.

Scripture explains that before regeneration "the god of this world (had) blinded the minds of the unbelievers, to keep them from seeing the light of the gospel of the glory of Christ, who is the likeness of God" (2 Cor. 4.4). This verse concurs in what the other verse just quoted said by declaring here that Satan holds on to man's mind by making it blind. Some people perhaps may consider themselves extremely wise in their ability to advance many arguments against the gospel; others may take for granted that unbelief is due to dullness of understanding; but the truth in both cases is that the eyes of man's mind have been covered by Satan. When firmly held by Satan the mind of man becomes "hardened"; man "follows the desires of body and mind (as) children of wrath" and so "is estranged and hostile in mind" because "the mind that is set on the flesh is hostile to God" (2 Cor. 3.14; Eph. 2.3; Col. 1.21; Rom. 8.7).

Upon reading these various passages we can see clearly how the powers of darkness are especially related to man's mind, how it is peculiarly susceptible to Satan's assault. With respect to man's will, emotion and body, the powers of evil are helpless to do anything *directly* unless they first have gained some ground therein. But with man's mind they can work freely without initially persuading man or securing his invitation. The mind appears to be their possession already. The Apostle in comparing men's minds to an enemy's strongholds seems to imply that Satan and his wicked spirits already have established a deep relationship with the minds of men, that somehow they are using them as their bastions in which to imprison their captives. Through man's mind they impose their authority and through the mind of their captives they transmit poisonous thoughts to others so that these too may rise up against God. It is difficult to estimate how much of the world's philosophy, ethics, knowledge, research, and science flow from the powers of darkness. But of one point we are certain: all arguments and proud obstacles against the knowledge of God are the fortresses of the enemy.

Is it strange to behold the mind in such close proximity to the authorities of wickedness? Was not the sin which mankind first committed that of seeking the knowledge of good and evil, and that at the instigation of Satan? Hence man's mind is especially related to Satan. If we were to peruse the Scriptures carefully and to observe the experiences of the saints we would discover that all communications between human and satanic forces occur in the organ of thought. Take, for instance, Satan's temptation. Every temptation with which he entices man is presented to his *mind*. It is true that Satan often uses the flesh to secure the consent of man, yet in each instance of enticement the enemy creates some kind of thought by which to induce the man. We cannot separate temptation and thought. All temptations are offered us in the form of thoughts. Since the latter are so exposed to the power of darkness, we need to learn how to guard them.

Prior to regeneration man's intellect obstructs him from apprehending God. It is necessary for His mighty power to destroy man's arguments. This is a work which must occur at the hour of new birth—and it does happen then in the form of repentance. The original definition of repentance is none else than "a change of mind." Man in his mind is at enmity with God; therefore God must alter man's mind if He would impart life to him. In his unregenerated state man has a darkened mind; at his regeneration it undergoes a drastic change. Because it has been so united with the devil it is vital for man to receive from God a change of mind before he can receive a new heart (Acts 11.18).

AFTER REGENERATION

But even following repentance the believer's mind is not liberated totally from the touch of Satan. As the enemy worked through the mind in former days, so today will he work in the same manner. Paul, in writing to the Corinthian *believers,* confided that he was "afraid that as the serpent deceived Eve by his cunning, your *thoughts* will be led astray from a sincere and pure devotion to Christ" (2 Cor. 11. 3). The Apostle well recognizes that as the god of this world blinds the mind of unbelievers so will he deceive the mind of the believers. Even though they are saved their life of thought is as yet unrenewed; consequently it remains the most strategic battleground. *The mind suffers the onslaughts of the powers of darkness more than any other organ of the whole man.* We should realize that satanic spirits are directing special attention to our minds and are attacking them unrelentingly—"as the serpent deceived Eve by his cunning." Satan did not assail Eve's heart first but rather her head. Similarly today, the evil spirits first attack our head, not our heart, in order to have us corrupted from the simplicity and purity which is towards Christ. They fully understand how it is the *weakest* point in our entire being, for it had served as their fortress before we believed and even now is not yet entirely overthrown. Attacking the mind is the easiest avenue for them to accomplish their purpose. Eve's heart was sinless and yet she received Satan's suggested thoughts. She was thus beguiled through his deception into forfeiting her reasoning and tumbling into the snare of the enemy. Let a believer accordingly be careful in his boast of possessing an honest and sincere heart, for unless he learns how to repulse the evil spirits in his mind he will continue to be tempted and deceived into losing the sovereignty of his will.

Paul continues by telling us from whence this danger comes: "if some one comes and preaches another Jesus than the one we preached, or if you receive a different spirit from the one you received, or if you accept a different gospel from the one you accepted" (v.4). The peril for the Christian is to have false teaching injected into his thought life so as to lead him astray from a sincere and pure devotion to Christ. These are the works the "serpent" is perpetrating today. Satan has disguised himself as an angel of light to lead saints to worship with their intellect a Jesus other than the Lord, to receive a spirit other than the Holy Spirit, and by these to propagate a gospel other than the gospel of the grace of God. Paul pronounces these to be nothing else than the deeds of Satan in the Christian's mind. The adversary translates these "doctrines" into thoughts and then imposes them upon the mind of the Christian. How tragic that few appreciate the reality of these activities! Few, indeed, who would ever think that the devil could give such good thoughts to men!

It is possible for a child of God to have a new life and a new heart but be without a new head. With too many saints, the mind, though their heart is new, is still quite old. Their heart is full of love whereas their head is totally lacking in perception. How often the intents of the heart are utterly pure and yet the thoughts in the head are confused. Having become saturated with a mishmash of everything, the mind lacks the most signal element of all, which is spiritual insight. Countless saints genuinely love all children of God, but unfortunately their brain is stuffed with a hodgepodge of theories, opinions and objectives. Quite a number of God's best and most faithful children are the most narrow-minded and prejudice-filled. Already have they decided what is the truth and what truth they shall accept. They reject every other truth because these do not blend in with their preconceived notions. Their head is not as expansive as their heart. Moreover, there are other children of God whose mind can conceive no thought whatever. No matter how many truths have been heard they can neither remember nor practice nor communicate them to others. These have certainly heard a lot, yet they possess no ability to express any of it. For many years they have received truths, but not even a little can they supply for the needs of others. Perhaps they may even brag how full they are of the Holy Spirit! What creates such symptoms is an unrenewed mind.

Man's head damages people more than man's heart! Were believers to learn how to distinguish the renewal of heart from the renewal of head, they would not commit the mistake of believing in man. Christians ought to realize that even one who maintains a most intimate fellowship with God may nevertheless unknowingly have accepted Satan's suggestions in his mind, which consequently precipitate errors in his conduct, words and viewpoints! Aside from the plain teaching of the Bible no man's words are entirely trustworthy. We must not live by a man's words just because we admire or respect that man. His utterance and conduct may be most holy but his thought may not be spiritual. What we therefore observe is not his speech and behavior but his *mind*. Were we to believe, because of one's life conduct, that what a worker says is God's truth, we would then be making man's word and demeanor our standard of truth instead of the Bible. History is strewn with innumerable cases of sanctified saints who propagated heresies! The simple explanation is that their hearts were renewed but their minds remained old. We will undeniably acknowledge that life is more important than knowledge. Indeed, the former is a thousand times more consequential than the latter. Nonetheless, after some growth in life it is essential to seek the knowledge which proceeds from a renewed mind. We should see how urgent it is for both heart and head to be renewed.

If a Christian's mind is not renewed his life is bound to be lopsided and narrow. Work becomes nigh to impossible for him. The popular teaching nowadays stresses that there should be love, patience, humility and so forth in the Christian life. These traits of the heart are highly significant, since nothing else can replace them. Even so, can we regard these as meeting *all* our needs? They are important but not inclusive. It is equally vital for a person's mind to be renewed, enlarged and strengthened. Otherwise we shall witness an unbalanced life. Many hold that spiritual Christians should not be common sensical, as though the more foolish they are the better. Now except for the fact that such spiritual believers live a little better than the rest, they have no other usefulness and cannot be entrusted with any work. To be sure, we do not advocate worldly wisdom and knowledge, because God's redemption does not call for employing our former sin-stained mind. But He does desire it to be renewed as is our spirit. God wishes to restore our thought life to the excellent state it had when He created it so that we may not only glorify God in our walk but may glorify Him in our thinking as well. Who can estimate the multipled number of God's children who, due to neglecting their mind, grow narrow, stubborn and obstinate, and even sometimes defiled. They fall short of the glory of God. The Lord's people need to know that if they want to live a full life their mind must be renewed. One of the reasons why the kingdom of God lacks workers today is because too many cannot undertake anything with their head. They neglect to seek its renewal after they are saved and hence permit their work to be obstructed. The Bible declares emphatically that we must "be transformed by the renewal of our mind" (Rom. 12.2).

A MIND UNDER THE ATTACK OF THE EVIL SPIRITS

If we carefully examine the mental experiences of a Christian we shall see that not merely is he narrow-minded but that he contains many other defects too. His head, for instance, may be teeming with all kinds of uncontrollable thoughts, imaginations, impure pictures, wanderings and confused ideas. His memory may suddenly fail; his power of concentration may be weakened; he may be obsessed by prejudices which arise from unknown sources; his thoughts may be retarded as if his mind were being chained; or he may be flushed with wild thoughts which revolve unceasingly in his head. The Christian may find he is powerless to regulate his mental life and make it obey the intent of his will. He forgets innumerable matters both large and small. He carries out many improper actions, without knowing why and without so much as investigating the reason. Physically he is quite healthy, but mentally he does not comprehend the explanation for these symptoms. Currently many saints encounter these mental difficulties, but without ever knowing why.

Should a person discover that he manifests the above-mentioned signs, he needs to check out a few matters to determine the origin of those signs. He need only ask himself a few questions: Who controls my mind? Myself? And if so, why can I not control it now? Is it God who manages my mind? But according to scriptural principle God never governs the mind for man. (We shall enlarge on this principle subsequently). If it is neither I nor God who regulates the mental life, who then is in control? It obviously is the powers of darkness who foment these mental symptoms. So whenever a child of God notes that he is no longer able to govern the mind, he ought to perceive at once that it is the enemy who is managing it.

One fact which we must always bear in mind is: man possesses free will. God's intention is for man to control himself. Man has the authority to regulate his every natural endowment; hence his mental processes should be subject to the power of his will. A Christian ought to inquire of himself: Are these *my* thoughts? Is it *I* who am thinking? If it is not I thinking, it must then be the evil spirit who is able to work in man's mind. Since I will not to think (and my mind usually follows my will) then the thoughts which presently arise in my head cannot be mine but rather are those which emanate from another "person" who uses the ability of my mind against my own will. The person should know that in case he has not intended to think and yet there are thoughts arising in his head, he must conclude that these are not of him but of the evil spirit.

To determine whether an idea is of himself or of the wicked spirit, a Christian should observe how it arose. If in the beginning his mental faculty is peaceful and composed and is functioning normally and naturally according to the circumstances he is in, but suddenly a thought or a complete idea (having no bearing on his present circumstances or the work in which he is engaged) flashes across his brain, such inordinate and lightning quick thought is most likely the action of evil spirits. They are attempting to inject their thoughts into the believer's head and thus induce him to accept them as his own. It is unmistakable that the notion which the evil spirits introduce into man's mind is a matter he has not thought about at the moment and which does not follow the trend of his thinking. It is entirely "new"—something he never thought of himself. It has arisen abruptly and all by itself. When one gains this kind of thought it is well for him to inquire: Do I really think in *this* manner? Is it really *I* who am thinking? Do I want to think that way? Or is this something which simply becomes activated in my mind all by itself? The child of God should determine whether or not it is he himself who does the thinking. If he has not originated the idea but on the contrary opposes it, and yet it abides in his head, he then can assume that that idea issues from the enemy. Each thought which man chooses not to think and each one which opposes man's will come not from the man but from the outside.

Oftentimes also one's brain is abounding with sundry ideas which he is helpless to stop. His head is like a thought machine, operated by external force; it continues to think but is impotent to desist. The believer may shake his head repeatedly, yet he cannot shake off the thoughts in his mind. They come to him in waves, rolling unceasingly day and night. There is no way to terminate them. He is not aware that this is but the activity of the evil spirit. He ought to understand what a "thought" is. It is something which his *mind grasps at*. But in the case of these unmanageable thoughts it is not that his mind is grasping at something but rather that *something is grasping his mind*. In the natural course of events it is the mind which thinks about matters; now it is these matters which force the mind to think. Frequently a person wishes to set aside a matter but some external power keeps reminding him of it, not permitting him to forget and forcing him to think on further. This is the perpetration of evil spirits.

To summarize, then, we should investigate every *abnormal* sign. Aside from a natural cause such as sickness, all other abnormal indicators have their source with evil spirits. God never interferes with the operation of man's natural ability; He never abruptly mixes in His thought with man's nor does He abruptly restrict or destroy the functioning of man's intellect. The lightning cessation of all thoughts as though the brain has become a vacuum, the flashing interjection of thought at complete variance with the trend then current in the mind, the hasty severance of memory as if a wire had snapped leaving the mind paralyzed: all these are the results of the operation of the enemy. Because the evil spirit has seized hold of the organ of thought, he is able either to force it to cease functioning or by looosening his grip to let it work again. We must recognize that natural causes can produce only natural symptoms. Flash thoughts or loss of memory are entirely beyond the ability or control of our will and are contrary to natural cause and effect: they must therefore be inspired by supernatural evil forces.

In his letter to the Ephesians Paul is found writing about "the spirit that is now at work in the sons of disobedience" (2.2). It is very important to know that the powers of darkness work not only outside but inside the man as well. When men work they can at most do so with their words, gestures or bodily movements; the evil spirits, however, can work with all these but even more. They can act from the outside in the same way as man acts, but they can work additionally from the inside. This means that they can squeeze themselves into man's thought life and work therein. Man is not capable of doing this: he is unable to enter another man's brain, subtly making many suggestions and confusing this matter of the source of the thoughts; but the evil spirits can. They possess an ability in communication which man does not have. They work initially in man's mind and then reach to his emotion, for mind and emotion are closely knit: they operate first in the mind and from there they arrive at man's volition, because mind and will are intimately joined too.

The manner by which these enemy spirits operate is to plant covertly in man's head notions which they enjoy so as to accomplish their aim, or, conversely, they block thoughts which they do not relish so that man cannot think them through. The Bible distinctly indicates that the powers of darkness are able both to impart ideas to man and to steal them from him. "The devil had already *put* it into the heart of Judas Iscariot, Simon's son, to betray him" (John 13.2). This shows that Satan can put his thought into man's mind. "Then the devil comes and takes away the word from their hearts" (Luke 8.12). This attests that Satan removes whatever word man ought to remember and causes him to forget everything. These two verses reveal the two-fold operation of the evil spirits upon the mind of man, either to add something to, or subtract something from, his mind.

THE CAUSES OF THE ATTACK OF THE EVIL SPIRITS

Why is the Christian's mental life so beset by evil spirits? This can be answered in one sentence: believers afford the evil spirits (or the devil) the opportunity to attack. Let everyone clearly understand that it is possible for one's mind to be assaulted by the devil. This is confirmed by the experience of many saints. And the area primarily assailed by him is the thinking faculty, for it has a special affinity towards evil spirits. It either partially or totally has slipped out from under man's sovereignty and has come under their dictate. Accordingly, these powers can switch one's thoughts on or off according to *their* wishes, completely disregarding the victim's ideas. Although the head is still attached to the believer, his sovereignty over it has been supplanted by another. Regardless how extensively he may protest, little can be corrected. Wherever anyone offers opportunity to wicked spirits, he cannot follow his own will any more but must be obedient to another's. When he gives ground to them in his mind he immediately forfeits his sovereignty over it. This also bespeaks the fact that his mental faculty is now being occupied by evil spirits. Had it not been attacked by them his will would continue to control everything: he could think or stop thinking as he willed without difficulty.

Due to this affinity between the mind and evil spirits, the Christian very often gives way to them. The ground gained furnishes these powers with authority to operate unhampered in the believer's head. Let us be aware of this though: that man's mind belongs to *man;* without his permission the enemy would be powerless to use it. Unless man *voluntarily* delivers (knowingly or unknowingly) his mind to the evil spirits they have no right to encroach on man's freedom. This does not imply that these malevolent forces shall never tempt us in our thought (that is unavoidable in this life), but it does signify that upon exercising our will to oppose the tempting thought, it shall be stopped immediately. The defect in many Christians today is that though they often resist with their will, the thought continues. It ought not be this way. It is a sure indication that the evil spirits are at work.

The most crucial factor in relation to their wicked activity is to have *ground* given to them. Without proper footing they cannot operate. The amount of their activity depends on the amount of space yielded to them. It is in the organ of his thought that the Christian supplies territory to evil spirits and hence there that they operate. Generally speaking, the ground in the mind which may be ceded to the enemy is of six kinds. We shall look at each of these now at some length.

(1) An unrenewed mind. The flesh continually furnishes bases for the enemy's operations. If man's mind is not renewed after his spirit is once regenerated, he exposes a great deal of territory to the machinations of the evil spirit. While many saints do have their mentality changed at the time of repentance, nonetheless the eyes of their heart once blinded by Satan have not yet been enlightened entirely and may still be veiled in many areas. These darkened corners are the old operation centers of the evil spirits: though greatly hindered, they have not been eliminated and thus continue to furnish bases for the operations of the unseen hosts of wickedness.

The devil's armies are most careful to cover up their deeds. If a Christian should remain fleshly they will urge upon him notions which seem to agree with his temperament and measure, prompting him to believe these are naturally the result of his thinking. Aware that this unrenewed mind constitutes their best workshop, the enemy forces employ every artifice to keep the believer in ignorance or to thwart him from seeking the renewal of his mind. The yielding of such ground is quite common among Christians. Were this the only type of ground they relinquish they would not suffer too severely in their intellect and memory; but other kinds are involved.

(2) An improper mind. All sins furnish territory to the adversary. If a child of God cherishes sin in his heart he is lending his mind to satanic spirits for their use. Since all sins derive from the dark powers, he is helpless to resist these powers behind whatever sins he allows to persist in his mind. As long as sinful thoughts remain in the heart, precisely that long do the evil spirits work. All unclean, proud, unkind and unrighteous ideas supply bases of activity to these spirits. Once God's child permits such a notion to stay he finds it harder to resist the next time it emerges, because the powers of darkness already have secured an area in his mind.

Besides the sinful ones there are many other improper thoughts which afford the enemy operational bases. Frequently Satan's hosts will introduce an idea into the believer's head. Should he accept it, then this notion will have acquired a footing in his mind. Each unproven theory, vain idea, unknown thought, word casually picked up by ear, or line inadvertently read—all provide ground to the foe as a future site for operations. The adversary may so fill a person with prejudices as to deceive him into opposing God's truth and embracing many heresies.

(3) Misunderstanding God's truth. The Lord's people rarely are aware that every time they accept a lie from the evil spirits they are furnishing fresh ground to the enemy. Should God's followers misconstrue or misinterpret as being natural or caused by their own selves that which the evil spirits have perpetrated upon their bodies, environments or works, they are yielding up precious territory to them for extending their nefarious deeds. A lie embraced forms the

ground for further activity by the satanic elements. In misunderstanding these phenomena to be the results of their own selves, they unconsciously allow these things to remain in their lives. Although this permission is gained through deceit it nevertheless provides sufficient footing for the evil spirits to operate.

On the other hand many Christians misunderstand God's truths. Being ignorant of the true meaning of co-death with Christ, consecration, the movement of the Holy Spirit, and so forth, they conceive in their hearts certain interpretations of these truths and consequently prejudice themselves. Seizing the opportunity, the evil spirits impart to the saints the same thing which they misunderstand and misconstrue of God's truths. They scheme according to the believer's misunderstanding. The latter judges these things to be of God, unaware that they are but a counterfeit from the evil spirits and founded on his misunderstanding.

(4) Accepting suggestions. Multiplied are the suggestions which Satan's hosts plant in the mind of the Christian, especially ideas concerning his circumstances and future. They enjoy prophesying to him, foretelling what will become of him and what will happen to him. Should he be unconscious of the source of such predictions and permit these to dwell in his mind, the evil spirits, at the appropriate time, will work on his environment to precipitate affairs to happen as prophesied. Perhaps the believer may already expect it to be so, not cognizant that everything has been arranged by the enemy powers. The latter merely put their idea into the form of prophecy, then plant it in his head to see if he will accept it or reject it. Should the will of the believer raise no objection, nay, even approve of the prophecy, the spirits of wickedness have obtained a footing for enacting what they have proposed. The fulfillment of the words of fortune tellers is based entirely on this principle.

Occasionally the adversary interjects prophetic utterances concerning the Christian's body, such as foretelling his weakness or sickness. If he absorbs this thought he will be genuinely sick and weak. He thinks he is actually ill. Those with scientific knowledge conclude it to be a psychological illness, but those with spiritual insight know better that it is solely because the person has received the suggestion of the evil spirit and has hence furnished ground for the latter to fabricate the situation. How many of the so-called natural and psychological illnesses are in reality the machinations of the evil spirits. When a Christian does not repel the thoughts which originate with evil spirits he affords them a base for working.

(5) A blank mind. God creates man with a mind to be used—"he who hears the word and understands it" (Matt. 13.23). God desires man to understand His Word with the intellect, from whence the emotion, will and spirit are reached. A lively head is therefore an obstacle to the work of malevolent spirits. One of their greatest aims is to lead a person's mind into a blank state. Blankness means an emptiness inside, the establishment of a true vacuum. The enemy powers employ either deception or force to transform the Christian's mental faculty into a blank entity. They realize that while his head is empty he cannot think. He has been stripped of all reasoning and sense and will accept without question every one of their teachings, regardless of its nature or consequence.

The Christian ought to exercise his mind, for its exercise constitutes such a disadvantage to evil spirits that they are compelled to exert their entire strength to render it blank. Only as his mind is functioning normally is the Christian fit to *discern* senseless supernatural revelations and various implanted suggestions and recognize their alien sources. A vacuous mind provides a foothold for the evil foe. All revelations and notions received by an empty head emanate from enemy sources. If a Christian should at any time not engage his organ of thought, he will discover how eager they are to help him think!

(6) A passive mind. Broadly speaking, an empty mind differs not too much from a passive one. Strictly speaking, the empty head means not using it whereas a passive one means awaiting some external force to activate it. The latter

is a step beyond the former. Passivity is to refrain from moving by oneself and instead to let outside elements move one. A passive brain does not think by itself but allows a foreign power to do the thinking for it. Passivity reduces man to a machine.

A passive state is most advantageous to the evil spirits for it offers them an opportunity to occupy the believer's will and body too. Just as a darkened mind is easily deceived because it knows not what it is doing and where it is going, even so is a passive mind prone to attack since it has no sensitivity whatsoever. Should anyone allow his head to cease thinking, searching, and deciding and to no longer check his experience and action against the Bible, he is practically inviting Satan to invade his mind and deceive him.

In their desire to follow the leading of the Holy Spirit many of the Lord's people feel they do not need to measure, investigate, and judge by the light of the Bible all thoughts which seemingly come from God. They think being led by the Spirit is being dead to themselves and obeying every notion and impulse of their brain. They follow especially those ideas which arise after prayer; hence they arrange for their mind to be passive during and after prayer. They halt their own thoughts and their other mental activities so as to be ready to receive the "thoughts of God." And the result is that they become hard and obstinate, having no reason and carrying out many harsh, pertinacious and irrational things. They do not know: (1) that prayer will not transform our thoughts into godly ones; (2) that to wait for divine thoughts during and after prayer is to invite counterfeits from the evil spirits; and (3) that God's leading is in the intuition of the spirit and not in the mind of the soul. Not a few saints—ignorant of God's will that He does not wish man to be passive but rather to cooperate actively with Him—spend time training themselves to be of a passive mind. They induce themselves to not think in order to possess God's thoughts. How can they not understand that if they themselves are not using their brain neither will God use it nor put His thoughts into it. The principle of God is for men to control the whole person with their will and to work together with Him. Only the devil would exploit the opportunity of a passive mind and seize its control away from men. God has never wanted men to receive His revelation like a robot; it is the enemy spirits alone who wish it that way. All passivity profits them, for they gladly take advantage of the folly and passivity of God's people to operate in their mind.

PASSIVITY

Any ground ever given to evil spirits invites them to work. Of these grounds the most serious is passivity. Passivity reflects the attitude of the will which in turn represents the total being. Passivity provides the liberty for wicked elements to function, though they habitually do so under cover, trying to deceive the saints. The cause of passivity is the ignorance of the Christian. He misconceives the role of the intellect in spiritual life; He thinks too highly of it but at the same time too lowly of it. Hence he permits his reasoning powers to settle into inertia and welcomes any thought which issues from that inert state. How very necessary, therefore, to clearly apprehend the way God leads.

The passivity of the mind is due to a misconception of the meaning of consecration and obedience to the Holy Spirit. Many take for granted that the thoughts in their head hinder their spiritual walk. They do not perceive that it is a brain which ceases to function or which functions chaotically that hinders spiritual life, whereas one which functions properly is not only profitable but also essential. Such a mind as this can alone cooperate with God. As has been emphasized previously, the normal path of guidance is in the spirit's intuition and not in the mind. An appreciation of this principle is exceedingly necessary and should never be forgotten. The believer must follow the revelation in his intuition, not the thought in his head. He who heeds the mind is walking after the flesh and is accordingly led astray. Nevertheless, we have not said that the mind is utterly useless, that it does not even exercise a secondary role. True, we make a grave mistake if we elevate the mind as *the* organ for direct fellowship with

God and for receiving revelation from Him; yet it *does* have a role assigned to it. That role is to *assist* intuition. Yes, it is by intuition that we come to know God's will, but we additionally need the mind to inspect our inner sense to determine whether it is from our intuition or is a counterfeit of our emotions, whether or not it is of God and harmonizes with the Word. We know by intuition; we prove by the mind. How easy it is for us to err! Without the assistance of the mind we shall find it hard to decide what is authentically of God.

In the normal process of guidance the mind is needed as well. While the guidance of intuition is frequently quite opposite to reasoning, we still must use the head, though not to argue with intuition but to examine whether this thing is really from God. Intuition apprehends the will of God very quickly; however, we require time for the brain to probe and prove whether what we apprehend is truly from our intuition and the Holy Spirit. If it is from God our intuition shall emit an even more accurate sense while under probing, thus effecting in us a stronger faith than before that this thing is in truth from God. The exercise of the intellect in this way—only in the way of *examinaton*—is both beneficial and proper. But should this sensing be of our fleshly thought and feeling, then in the process of examination our conscience will raise its voice of opposition. Consequently, the probing with our mind to *understand* whether a matter is from God or not will not intererfere but will instead give opportunity to intuition to prove itself. If it is of intuition what has it to fear from the probing of the mind? On the other hand, whatever is afraid of being probed is probably out from one's self. The head should never guide or lead, but it unquestionably is needed to probe the authenticity of guidance.

Such teaching is in accordance with the Scriptures: "do not be foolish, but understand what the will of the Lord is" and "try to learn what is pleasing to the Lord" (Eph. 5.17,10). The functioning of the mind cannot be set aside unused. God does not wipe out the various components of man's soul; He renews them first and then uses them. God wants His child to know what he is doing when he obeys. He does not desire a senseless, blind following. It is never His wish that one should follow whatever he hears or feels with a bewildered mind, unaware of what he is about; nor is it ever His way to use any one part of the believer's body without his understanding and consent. God's intention is for the Christian to understand His will and consciously engage the various parts of his body for obedience to God. It is the lazy person who refuses to bear responsibility because he expects to be moved partly or wholly by God only from a passive state. God, however, wants man to examine actively what His will is and next to exercise his own will to obey God. God requires the harmonious working of man's intuition and consciousness.

Even so, a believer, not recognizing this to be God's normal way of guidance, *may* let himself slide into passivity. He may expect God to put His will into his thought; he blindly follows all supernatural leading without employing his intelligence to examine whether it is from God. He even waits for Him to use the parts of his body beyond the sphere of his consciousness; that is to say, he does not engage his mind to understand, or his will to execute in his body, what the will of God is. The consequence of such ignorance is enemy invasion, since passivity is a condition for this phenomenon. (This we shall treat in detail in another place.) If man does not use his intelligence neither will God, because to do so would be contrary to the principle of God's operation. Evil spirits will do so however; they never hesitate to seize the opportunity to use man's mind. It is therefore most foolish for one to allow his mind to sink into a state of passivity because the enemy spirits are on the prowl seeking whomever they may devour.

Let us pursue one step further this matter of passivity as a condition for the operation of evil spirits. We are aware of one class of people who especially relish communicating with these spirits. People usually do not hanker to be demon possessed, but this special class craves to be so possessed. These are the soothsayers, the augurs, the mediums, the necromancers. By accurately observing the cause of their possession we may come to understand the principle of demon possession. These people tell us that in order to be possessed by what they call gods (who actually are demons) their will must present no resistance whatsoever but be favorably disposed to accept whatever comes upon their bodies. To render their will completely passive their mind must first be reduced to blankness. A blank brain produces a passive will. These two elements are the basic requisites for demon possession. Hence a necromancer who is waiting for his "god" to come upon him lets down his hair and shakes his head for a continued period until it is dizzy and his mind completely out of action. As the latter is turning blank his will naturally becomes immobile. At this point his mouth begins to move unconsciously, his body gradually trembles, and before long his "god" descends upon him. This is one way of becoming possessed. Although there may be others, the principle for every spiritist is the same: to achieve passivity of will through a perfectly blank mind; for all spiritists agree that when spirits or demons alight upon them their heads can no longer think and their wills can no longer act. They are unpossessed until this state of an empty mind and an inert will is reached.

Today's so-called scientific hypnotism and religious yogi, which enable people to possess the powers of telepathy, healing, and transforming, are in reality founded upon these two principles. Using the argument that certain methods can be beneficial to mankind, those of this class who perform such techniques as focusing one's attention, sitting silently, contemplating and meditating, are actually employing these devices to reduce their mind to a blank condition and their will to passivity so as to invite supernatural spirits or demons to supply them with many wonderful experiences. Our purpose here is not to inquire whether or not these people realize they are inviting evil spirits to come; we merely wish to observe that they are fulfilling the requirements for demon possession. The consequence is grave; perhaps later they shall awaken to the fact that what they have welcomed are indeed evil spirits.

Our intention here is not a full treatment of this subject. We simply wish to acquaint the Lord's children with the principles behind the practice of the black arts: which are a *blank and passive mind and will*. Evil spirits are overjoyed should these conditions be present, as they can immediately commence to do their dark work.

It is well for every Christian to always bear in mind the one basic and crucially important distinction between the working of evil spirits and that of the Holy Spirit: the Latter works when man fulfills *His* working conditions, while the former work when man fulfills *their* working conditions. If man, even though he may appear to be seeking the Holy Spirit, meets the requirements for evil spirits to operate, God's Spirit will never operate. The wicked spirits wait tirelessly for the opportunity to act. Should anyone be incompetent to distinguish what is truly of God from what is a counterfeit, he need only ask himself one question: what kind of condition was he in when first he experienced such phenomena? If he had fulfilled the prerequisites for the Holy Spirit's activity, it must then have been from God; but had he met the necessary conditions for evil spirits to work, then what he encountered must have been the evil spirit. We do not reject every supernatural phenomenon; what we simply and earnestly desire to do is to separate what is of God from what is of Satan.

The basic distinction between the operating requirements of the Holy Spirit and the wicked spirits can be summarized as follows:

(1) All supernatural revelations, visions or other strange occurrences which require the *total cessation of the function of the mind*, or are obtained only after it has ceased working, are not of God.
(2) All visions which arise from the Holy Spirit are conferred when the believer's mind is fully active. It necessitates the active engagement of the various functions of the mind to apprehend these visions. The endeavors of evil spirits follow exactly the opposite course.
(3) All which flows from God agrees with God's nature and the Bible.

Let us disregard the outward form—it may openly identify itself as devilish or it may disguise itself as divine (such indeed are the terms given)—and simply inquire what the principle involved is. We need to recognize that every supernatural revelation from the powers of darkness demands the cessation of the function of the mind; but that whatever comes from God permits its ability and function to continue as usual without any interference. Both the vision the Israelites beheld at Mt. Sinai recorded in the Old Testament and the vision which Peter saw at Joppa mentioned in the New Testament affirm that these people had complete use of their heads.

By examining every instance in the New Testament where God's supernatural revelation is recounted, we find that everyone there who experiences a revelation does so with his mind functioning and with the ability *to control himself* and use any part of his body. But counterfeit supernatural revelations chiefly require the receiver's mind to be totally or partially *passive*, with the receiver no longer able to employ parts of his body either in part or *in toto*. This constitutes the fundamental antithesis between what is of God and what is of the devil. Where the speaking in tongues is related, for example, the speakers have both control and consciousness of themselves. On the day of Pentecost Peter could *hear* the mocking of the peoples and *answer* them, proving that he and his colleagues were not drunk but were filled with the Holy Spirit (Acts 2). Those who spoke with tongues in the church at Corinth could count the number of two or three, could *control* themselves to speak in turn, and if no interpretation was given could *keep silence* (1 Cor. 14). All retained their consciousness and could restrain themselves. This is because "the spirits of prophets are subject to prophets" (1 Cor. 14. 32). But in counterfeit experience the spirits usually demand the subjection of the prophets to them. Herein can we see which is of God and which is of the devil.

We have written at length on how to differentiate between *special* phenomena given by the Holy Spirit and those given by evil spirits. We shall conclude by briefly observing how they differ in *ordinary* occurrences. Let me only illustrate by using the example of the guidance of God. Now it should be called to mind that the Holy Spirit wants us to be *en-*

lightened and to *know* (Eph. 1.17-18). God's Spirit never treats men as puppets, summoning them to follow Him without any consciousness. He does not even ask them to do good in that way. He usually expresses His thought in the depth of man, in his spirit. Hence His guidance is never confused, vague, puzzling, or compulsory. But not so with the evil spirits. Simply note how they operate: (1) Their thought always invades from the outside, entering primarily via the mind. It does not come from the innermost being, is not a revelation in the intuition, but is a flashing mental thought. (2) Their thought forces, pushes and coerces man to take action immediately. It never affords man time to think, consider or examine. (3) It confuses and paralyzes man's mind so that it can no longer think.

Consequently, we can see that in all the occurrences of a believer's life, whether special or ordinary, everything which proceeds from evil spirits strips the proper functioning from his mind. The Holy Spirit, however, never does.

CHAPTER 2
THE PHENOMENA OF A PASSIVE MIND

IT IS TO BE SORELY LAMENTED that so many Christians, unaware of the basic difference between the activity of evil spirits and that of the Holy Spirit, have unconsciously permitted the enemy to enter and occupy their minds. Let us touch briefly on the phenomena of a mind under the attack of evil spirits.

FLASHING THOUGHTS

After one's mind has sunk into passivity he will receive many thoughts injected from without, notions which are unclean, blasphemous or confused. These pass through his mind in succession. Although he decides to reject them, he is powerless to stop them or alter the trend of his thinking. His mind is like a perpetual motion machine: once begun, it cannot be halted. Regardless if he opposes with his will, he cannot thrust those thoughts from his head. Notions which are counter to the believer's will are given by evil spirits.

Sometimes these ideas flash into the person's brain like lightning. They enable him to understand or to discover special matters. They may arrive in the form of a suggestion, urging him to do this or that. Often they appear to have arisen from the person himself, but upon close examination he *knows* he has not initiated them; they are but the deeds of evil spirits in a passive mind. The child of God ought to resist flashing thoughts which demand action of him because these do not originate with the Holy Spirit. And should he follow them he will realize how worthless they are.

We know that in these latter times evil spirits especially engage in much teaching (1 Tim. 4.1). The Lord's people should guard against such teachings imparted to passive minds. Not a few think they have obtained new light when they search the Scriptures and that they understand matters which their predecessors did not. These individuals should be very cautious, for it is frequently in the time of meditation that wicked powers flash their ideas into a person or stealthily mix some of *their* thought with his. Not aware of the possibility of accepting the teaching of evil spirits in their minds, Christians assume that anything which has suddenly burst upon them while in meditation is their *own* new discovery of faith. They write and preach these ideas as the fruits of *their* research. Upon hearing or reading these teachings, people marvel at the cleverness of these Christians. But do they perceive that many of these doctrines in reality emanate from the bottomless pit? Diverse heresies, numerous so-called "spiritual teachings," sundry interpretations of the Word which tear the church of Christ into pieces originate with these lightning thoughts during Scripture study. We should not be impressed with how excellent such sudden enlightenment may be; rather should we ask *whence* this light came. Was it revealed by the Holy Spirit in our intuition? Did it arise out of our own thinking? Or were these ideas fomented by evil spirits?

Should one's mind be passive, it will be easy for the enemy to inject nonsensical notions into him, for instance telling him: "You are God's special vessel" or "Your work will shake the whole world" or "You are much more spiritual than the rest" or "You should take another course" or "God will soon open a wide door for your preaching" or "You should step out to live by faith" or "Your spiritual usefulness is unlimited." Heady thoughts like these disarm all the vigilance of the saint. He thrives day and night on these ideas—dreaming how great and marvelous he is. Not employing the rationalism of his mind, he fails to realize how harmful and how laughable these notions can be in his spiritual walk. He indulges in them by continuously imagining how glorious his future is going to be.

Some who deliver messages for the Lord are often governed by these bursting thoughts. They preach what has been revealed to them suddenly. They construe their sudden thoughts to be from God and so accept them passively. They do not understand that God neither gives sudden revelation nor imparts it to the mind. Despite the fact such words are sometimes seemingly full of meaning, they nevertheless come from the powers of darkness. Furthermore, occasionally as a believer is preaching, many Scripture verses abruptly swarm into his brain and his thinking; the audience appears to be touched; yet following the meeting no practical help in life is experienced by those who have heard. It is like a dream. This too can be the action of the powers of darkness.

Having yielded territory in his mind to evil spirits, the child of God will realize that they are able to provoke any thought in him. Among fellow-workers, evil spirits often sow a groundless doubt or divisive thought in the mind of one worker so as to separate him from the others. Upon their wicked instigation the worker concludes without foundation that so-and-so thinks such-and-such of him, and so comes the separation. Actually there is no basis for such a thought. If the child of God only knew how to examine the source of such imaginings and how to resist them, there would be no separation. How sad that he regards it as his own thought, not recognizing that the evil spirits have planted it in him.

PICTURES

The adversary also can project pictures onto the screen of a believer's mind. Some are clear and good and are welcomed by him; others are impure and sinful, much detested by his conscience. Whether good or bad, liked or disliked, the sad fact is that he has no strength to prohibit these pictures from entering his head. Against the opposition of his will, there lingers before his eyes past experiences, predictions of future events, and many other matters. This is because his power of imagination has slumped into passivity. He cannot control his imaginative powers but has allowed the evil spirits to manipulate them. The child of God should be aware that whatever does not emerge from his *own* mind proceeds from supernatural enemy forces.

DREAMS

Dreams can be natural or supernatural. Some are inspired by God while others are generated by the devil. Beyond those which are produced by man's physiological and psychological conditions, the rest are supernatural in origin. If one's mind has been open to evil spirits his night dreams become for the most part just another form of the "pictures" he encounters during the day. The wicked unseen powers create pictures in the day and dreams in the night. To determine whether or not his dreams derive from the devil the believer simply should inquire of himself: is my mind *usually* passive? If so, these dreams are untrustworthy. Moreover, dreams and visions which God inspires enable man to be normal, peaceful, steady, full of reasoning and consciousness; but what the evil spirits precipitate are bizarre, rash, fantastic, foolish, and render a person arrogant, dazed, confused, and irrational.

The reason why satanic powers can impart innumerable strange dreams to the Christian is because his mental life is passive. To that one whose mental faculty is already passive none of his dreams proceed from God or from natural causes but are from wicked spirits. At nighttime the brain is not as active as in the day, hence more passive and more liable to being manipulated by the devil. Such night dreams cause him to wake up the next morning with a heavy head and a despondent spirit. His sleep does not replenish his strength because through his passive mind the evil spirits have affected adversely the well-being of the whole man. Anyone who suffers from such night dreams is subject to the nefarious activity of the evil spirits in his mind. If he resists their deeds day and night he shall regain his freedom.

INSOMNIA

Insomnia is one of the common ills of the saints; it is likewise a particularly distinctive work of the enemy in the mind of man. Many find that as they lie in their beds endless thoughts pour into their head. They continue to think about their day's work or to recall past experiences or just to fill their minds with a hodgepodge of unrelated matters. They appear to be considering a thousand different ideas such as what they should do, how they should do it, and what should be the best plan. They think ahead to the affairs on the morrow: how to plan, what might happen, or how to handle a variety of situations. Considerations like these inundate them in waves. Though these people know that bed is the place for sleep and not one for thinking as is a desk, nonetheless their brain revolves incessantly. They appreciate the importance of sleep for the next day's task; they really want to sleep and not think; and yet, due to cause unknown, they cannot. Their mind works relentlessly on and sleep escapes them. Some saints may have suffered the anguish of countless nights of insomnia: as usual when night has fallen they have laid down all concerns and have prepared to rest their minds; nonetheless, no matter how weary they may have been their mind has not been able to rest. For like a machine which cannot be turned off, it continues to operate. Their will has no control over their brain. They are helpless to stop their thinking and can only wait till somehow their mind ceases to work so that they can secure some sleep. In the natural course of events sleep revives one's spirit; but when one has experienced untold nights of insomnia such a believer will come to dread sleep, bed and the night. He has to rest, yet each morning he feels as though he is emerging from a terrible world: his head is heavy, his will is numbed, and he seems to have no energy.

In a situation like this, the child of God is inclined to believe it is due to his physical condition or to the stimulation or overexertion of his nerves. Frequently these reasons are merely suppositional. If they were real, then following rest or some other natural remedy he would experience restoration. But he does not because the evil spirits employ those natural reasons to obscure their unseen activities. Thus when a believer senses thoughts galloping through his head during the night, let him inquire of himself on this wise: where do these thoughts originate? Are they mine or are they foreign? Am I thinking? Do *I* think this way? Could it be from myself when I do not even want to think? Who gives me such multiplied, confused, unclean, oppressive thoughts? Who, indeed, except evil spirits!

FORGETFULNESS

Due to the devil's attack quite a few saints are deprived of their power of memory and suffer from forgetfulness. They forget even what they have just said or done. They cannot locate the article they have just put aside that same day. They forget the promises made not so long ago. They behave as though they are without brain, for nothing seems to remain in their mind. These saints may conclude that their memory is worse than anybody else's, without realizing that their mind is actually under the disturbance of evil spirits. Consequently they must rely on notes. They become slaves to notebooks and memoranda as a means of reminder. Now we are not suggesting that a person should be able to remember everything. We grant that matters can be forgotten after many years or forgotten immediately when they leave no deep impression. Even so, many events which have happened not too long ago and which have arrested one's attention *ought* to be recalled within a certain time limit and under certain appropriate circumstances. Why are they forgotten, lost without leaving any shadow, and beyond recall? The explanation cannot be natural; it must be due to the invasion of malevolent forces. Some matters are quite naturally forgotten, others do not so naturally vanish. All unnatural loss of memory suggests the subtle attack of Satan's hosts. Many Christians undergo this kind of assault. How many endeavors are destroyed by this. And how many jokes are inspired by this forgetfulness. Confidence and usefulness are damaged.

Another phenomenon can be noticed: a believer usually may possess a fine memory, but at various critical moments it unexpectedly fails. His mind seems to have faltered abruptly and he cannot remember anything, plunging him into great difficulties. Such sudden cessation of this function of the mind may appear to be mystifying to him but he may interpret it to be the result of a temporary deficiency in physical strength, something which can happen once in a while. What he does not comprehend is that this is a symptom of his mind undergoing an attack of evil spirits.

LACK OF CONCENTRATION

Satan's minions often interfere with the Christian's power of mental concentration. We acknowledge that different individuals possess varying degrees of this power. Yet from our observations of the experiences of Christians we note that this power in most of them has suffered a greater or lesser degree of loss through the dissipating work of evil spirits. Some appear to be totally powerless to concentrate when trying to think; others are better but their thoughts take flight everywhere after but a few moments of concentration on a particular matter. Especially during times of prayer, Bible reading, or listening to messages do Christians discover their thoughts wandering. Although they will to concentrate, they fail to do so. They may succeed for a short while in arresting their galloping thoughts by their will, but such an effect does not last long. Sometimes they lose all control. It is obviously the enemy who is at work. The reason for the devil's exertions lies in the fact that the believer has made provision in his mind for the evil spirits. What a pity to see a person wasting the power of his mind, accomplishing nothing from dawn to dusk. As the wasting of physical strength is harmful, so the wasting of mental power is damaging too. Today a large number of Christians expend a great deal of time without producing much result. Their minds are assailed by evil spirits and so they cannot concentrate.

Because of the onslaught of these dark forces God's people experience a peculiar kind of inattentiveness. The mind should be focusing on a particular matter, yet abruptly it turns blank and subsequently drifts elsewhere. They are unconscious of what they are doing or what they are reading. They may hold to the opinion that they must have been thinking about other affairs, but can such thoughts be originated by their *own* will? The Christians who all of a sudden cannot hear anything during meetings are numberless. Enemy spirits try to prevent them from hearing what would be profitable, yet not by stopping the operation of their minds but by forcing them to think of other things.

Once the mind has been attacked by the devil believers find it troublesome to listen to others. Oftentimes they miss several sentences or words. To listen attentively they must wrinkle their foreheads, trying to understand what others mean. They frequently fail to comprehend the simplest words; they often misapprehend the teachings given them. All this is due to the disturbances in their minds. With many prejudices have they been stuffed already by evil spirits, and everything has been interpreted already to them. For this reason many a Christian is averse to hearing what others have to say. Before people can finish he is interrupting impatiently, for the evil spirits already have inspired him with countless thoughts and desire him to listen to theirs and then spread them around to others. Such individuals actually are listening both within and without: listening within to the suggestions of the enemy and listening without to people speaking with them. The voice within their minds speaks louder than the one in their ears so that they can barely hear the outside voice. Such symptoms as inattentiveness or heedlessness signify in reality that their hearts are occupied by satanic elements. Believers occasionally experience a sudden state of heedlessness; the fact is, their hearts have been snatched away by the wicked ones. Until they are liberated from the activity of evil spirits they will be powerless to concentrate.

Because of these disturbances in their minds Christians often will shake their heads, trying to rid themselves of these unsettling thoughts. They have to speak aloud to themselves in order to leave an impression on their mind. They must likewise think aloud, else their darkened mind will not understand. They additionally need to read aloud to acquaint themselves with what they have read. All these are consequences of the lack of concentration.

INACTIVITY

Upon being fiercely attacked, the mind of the believer loses its ability to think. It falls almost entirely into the hands of evil spirits so that he himself can no longer use it. He cannot think even should he want to, for he is incapable of initiating any thought of his own. Actually myriads of thoughts over which he has no control pass through his mind; he has no power to halt these and initiate his own. The foreign ideas are too overpowering for him to entertain his own. Occasionally he may locate an opening in his mind through which to insert his thought, but he discovers it is very toilsome to continue thinking. So many voices and so many subjects are there already that these simply squeeze his out. If any person desires to think, he must possess memory, imagination and reasoning power; but the Christian has presently lost these powers, hence is unable to think. He cannot create, deduce or recollect, nor can he compare, judge and apprehend. Therefore he cannot think. And should he attempt to do so he experiences a kind of dazed sensation which stifles any productive thought.

Since his mental process is now under bondage, the believer naturally will develop an inordinately off-balanced viewpoint. A mound looms up before him as a mountain. Everything appears to be as arduous as ascending a stairway to heaven. He is especially fearful of anything which requires thought. He does not like to converse with people because this is too demanding of him. To proceed steadily and diligently at his daily job seems to require his life. He is gripped by an intangible chain which others fail to recognize. He feels as uncomfortable as a slave who wants to revolt but never succeeds.

Thus the Christian lives as in a dream. His time is dissipated, spent without thought, imagination, reasoning, or consciousness. As the mind is assailed the will becomes affected automatically, for the former is the light of the latter. He passively allows himself to be tossed to and fro by his environment and makes no choice for himself. When he is filled with unsettling notions and has no peace, he cannot break through his bondage to emancipation. He seems to be restrained by an unseen impediment. Numerous things he wants to do; yet in the midst of trying to do them he is overwhelmed by an impulsive feeling to stop because all tasks have become impossible in his eyes: to him his life has become nothing but a succession of insurmountable obstacles. How can he ever be satisfied?

Inactivity like this is sharply at variance with the ordinary type. Should one's mind be quiescent he can activate it whenever he wants. But should the inactivity of the brain be due to the oppression of evil spirits, then no matter how much he desires to be active he cannot stir it one iota. He simply cannot think! His head seems to be loaded down by some heavy weight. Such is the phenomenon of a mentality deeply affected by evil spirits.

Many a saint who is continuously worrying contracts this illness of mental inactivity. Yet were we to delve into his environment and position we would inescapably conclude that here is one who certainly ought to be satisfied and happy; but the fact is that he is full of worries and unhappy thoughts. Ask him to give the reason for this and to him nothing whatever can be a sufficient one. Suggest to him to get rid of such thoughts and he finds himself utterly unable. He himself does not understand his plight. He appears to have sunk into a quagmire from which he cannot extricate himself. Hs is so used to worrying that he has no strength to rise above it. This of course is the heavy hand of the enemy. If it were a matter of natural worry there would have to be a *cause of sufficient reason*. All worries without natural cause or sufficient justification are precipitated by evil spirits. The believer has slumped so low because at the beginning he accepted the notions of the wicked ones and now is powerless to free himself. His mind has settled thoroughly into passivity so that it can no longer be active. Such a person is aware of this bondage because he is loaded with burdens. He cannot glimpse the blue sky nor can he comprehend the true picture of anything. He cannot exercise his reasoning power. He is as a prisoner cast into the dungeon, eking out his days in darkness. Evil spirits enjoy seeing men suffer. Everyone who falls into their hands will be so treated by them.

VACILLATION

While the mind of a believer is dominated by enemy powers his thoughts are totally unreliable, since most of them come from the wicked spirits. Few of them are his own. These spirits may generate in him one kind of thought but very shortly afterwards beget an opposite kind. In following such shifting notions the Christian naturally turns into a vacillating person. Those who are with him or work with him consider him unstable in character because he is everlastingly changing positions. Fundamentally though, it is the wicked spirits who change his thoughts and alter his opinions. How frequently we find Christians who say at one moment "I can" but at the next "I can't." They declare in the morning "I want" and shift in the afternoon to "I don't want." The reason is that at first the evil spirits plant in the mind the thought of "I can" and induce him to believe he genuinely can; nonetheless, they next inject into him another and contrary thought of "I can't" and cause him to think he really is unable. So it is not he himself who has altered what he initially declared.

In these numerous shifting attitudes we can detect the adversary at work in the mind of man. Saints may abhor living such a vacillating life, but they have no way to stabilize themselves because they are not their own. If they refuse to follow the alien suggestions the wicked powers shall falsify the voice of conscience and accuse them of not following God. Now to avoid being accused, these saints have no choice but to shift their positions before men. These alternating and unsteady traits all proceed from the same source. In listening in their heads to the suggestions of the evil spirits Christians commence abruptly to undertake many tasks, but as the enemy powers change their proposals the Christians correspondingly shift their labor.

Beyond these occurrences, evil spirits additionally often provoke people to think at inappropriate occasions. They will awaken them at midnight, for example, instructing them to perform such-and-such a matter. If one refuses to obey they will begin to accuse him. Or else in the deep of night they may suggest to him a shift in course, so that an exceedingly important decision is made during a time when the mind is most susceptible to confusion. By tracing the origin of many of these sudden turns of events we will discover evil spirits at work in the mind of men.

TALKATIVENESS

Those of God's people whose minds are assaulted by Satan frequently shy away from conversing with people because they have not the strength to *listen;* for while they are trying to listen to others, thoughts over which they have no control drift through their brains like wind-blown clouds. They are usually most talkative, however. Since their heads are bursting with thoughts, how can their mouths not be abounding with words too? A mind which cannot listen to others but demands that others listen to it is a sick mind. While it is true that some Christians are talkative by nature, nevertheless, unknowingly they may in fact be instruments in the hands of evil spirits. Many Christians are like talking machines which are run by outside powers.

How many there are who cannot restrain their tongues from gossiping, jesting and backbiting. Their heart is clear but they are unable to end or restrict these unprofitable words. It seems that as soon as ideas have moved into their mind and before there has been any opportunity to think them through, they have already become words. Thoughts rush in in waves, compelling the person to speak. The tongue is out of control of the mind and the will. A torrent of words is uttered without *thinking* or choosing. Sometimes they are spoken against the intent and will of the speakers. Later reminded by others, they wonder why they thus spoke. These are all due to the passivity of the mind. Satanic elements can engage man's tongue through man's immobilized mind. They begin by mixing their thoughts with man's thought, and then they proceed to mix their words with man's words.

The Christian must unmistakably understand that all his utterances have to be the result of his own thinking. Any word which bypasses the process of thinking is formulated by the wicked spirits.

OBSTINACY

After a person's mental faculty has declined into passivity and is occupied by the powers of darkness, he categorically refuses to listen to any reason or evidence once he has made a decision. He views any attempt by anyone to make him understand better as an encroachment on his liberty. He deems them most foolish, for they can never know what *he* knows! His concepts may be totally wrong, yet he thinks he has *inexplicable* reasons. Since his mind is entirely immobile, he knows not how to examine, distinguish and judge with reason. He uncritically swallows anything which the evil spirits propagate in his mind, esteeming it to be most excellent. When such an individual hears a supernatural voice he automatically accepts it as God's will; to him the voice already has become his law; it therefore transcends the investigation of reason. Whatever be the thought or voice or teaching he deems it infallible and positively safe. He refuses to test, examine, or consider; he tenaciously holds on to it and is unwilling to heed anything else. No amount of reasoning and conscience of his own or the explanation and evidence of others can move him one bit. Once he believes it to be God's leading, his mind is sealed against any change. And since he does not employ his reasoning power he can be deceived readily by evil spirits. Those who have a little understanding see the danger but he devours it all as candy. To restore such a person as this is certainly not easy.

THE SYMPTOM OF THE EYES

A mind which is passive and assailed by evil spirits can be identified readily through the eyes. Man's eyes reveal his mind more than any other part of his body. If the mind is passive a person reading may look at a book and yet no idea will enter his brain nor make any impression in his memory. While he converses with people his eyes tend to wander around, up and down, flitting in all directions. It is surely a most impolite manner, but he cannot look straight into another's face. On another occasion he may act in the opposite extreme by gazing at another's face without so much as blinking, as though transfixed by some unknown power.

Such gazing can be most serious because the devil uses this means to induct the believer into the attitude of a necromancer. Frequently, upon gazing long at the speaker's countenance the believer begins to listen no longer to what he is saying but is instead intent upon listening to the many thoughts which the malevolent powers at that moment are begetting in him.

We need to observe whether the movement of our eyes follows the consciousness of our minds or acts independently of the intent of our heart. When a mind is passive the person's eyes become dazed. He is apt to behold many unsought and peculiar sights while unable to concentrate on seeing what he wishes to see.

FINALLY

To recapitulate. The phenomena of a Christian's mind under the attack of evil spirits are manifold and various. One principle, however, underlies them all: the person has lost his control. According to the ordering of God, each of man's natural abilities (among which is the thought process of the mind) should be subject completely to man's own rule. But should a Christian unknowingly give ground to evil spirits they may occupy his mental life and take direct action therein, unhampered by the victim's will. Consequently, if ever the Chrisitian discovers any independent action in his mind he should realize he is under the assault of the powers of darkness.

Inactivity in place of activity, disquietude instead of calm, restlessness due to overflowing thoughts, inability to concentrate or distinguish or remember, confusion beyond control, labors without fruit, worklessness during the day and dreams and visions in the night, insomnia, doubts, unwatchfulness, fear without reason, disturbance to the point of agony—one and all are nefariously inspired by the evil spirits.

CHAPTER 3
THE WAY OF DELIVERANCE

WHEN ONE'S MIND HAS fallen victim to the phenomena discussed in the previous chapter, he should seek the way of deliverance. What was described in that chapter were but general symptoms of a passive mind. We cannot set forth everyone's condition in detail because there are variations in the degree of passivity, the extent of the evil spirit's attack, and hence the measure of damage to the mind. Nevertheless it should be stated that as soon as one realizes he has encountered any of the aforementioned phenomena, he must exercise extreme caution because he may have given ground to evil spirits and so is being assaulted. He should look for deliverance.

Few are the believers who are not surprised at their ignorance of the damage done to their mind. It is on the contrary a matter of great surprise to them that they have been unconscious of the fallen condition of their organ of thought. They seem to understand a lot about many matters, but as regards their own mind they know next to nothing. They do not even realize how serious has been the damage inflicted until someone else has pointed it out to them. Why have these not discerned it before? Is it not that this very lack tells us that our mind and the evil spirits possess some special relationship which consequentially weakens our knowledge concerning our mind? Let any who have suffered such damage answer this question.

THE WILES OF THE EVIL SPIRITS

If his eyes have been opened to see his condition, the believer will naturally search for deliverance. Realize, though, that the evil spirits are not going to let their captives go free without a fight. They will apply every ounce of strength upon the person to prevent him from securing deliverance.

The evil spirits will suggest many lies to serve as excuses:

> Those sudden beautiful thoughts of yours are from God.
> Those flashing revelations are the fruits of spirituality.
> That bad memory is due to your ill-health.
> It is natural for you to become abruptly forgetful.
> Your over-sensitiveness is because of your temperament.
> Your weak memory is inherited.
> Insomnia is an outgrowth of sickness.
> You are simply tired.
> You cannot think because you have worked too hard.
> That incessant contemplation at night stems from your mind's overexhaustion in the daytime.
> Impure thoughts arise from your sins.
> You already have fallen.
> You cannot listen to others because of your particular environment and because of their faults.

The evil spirits can manufacture sundry other excuses. Unless God's children realize they are *really being attacked* and have actually fallen from the normal state, the enemy will engage these and other excuses like them to cover up the ground they have gained. But the true reason lies in the fact that the mind is passive and vacuous, and thus occupied by these satanic spirits. Every one of these phenomena is the effect of their pernicious working. We grant the possibility of natural causes being mixed in with these excuses, but the experience of so many saints confirms that the powers of darkness are extremely subtle in operating alongside natural causes so as to deceive the saints into accepting these natural causes—such as temperament, physical condition and environment—as the only explanation, forgetting altogether the subtle mixing in by the evil spirits. The latter are very delighted in hiding their works behind some little natural cause. There is one test which can be brought to bear here, however; and that is, that if the cause is natural the man's condition will be restored to normal once the natural factor is eliminated: but were there something supernatural added to the natural, then the man will not recover even though the natural element is removed. If you have insomnia, for example, the enemy will suggest it is due to your overwork and your mind's overexhaustion. You listen to this and cease working and rest for a period without exercising your mind at all. Nonetheless thousands of thoughts continue to crowd your mind and pass to and fro through your brain during sleep. This demonstrates that your illness is not entirely due to natural cause: a supernatural one is mingled in with it somewhere. If you do not take the time to deal with the supernatural aspect, your removal of the natural element will serve no purpose.

It is of paramount importance that brethren today *examine* the source of these excuses. The wicked powers are highly skilled in misleading people into explaining their evil devices in terms of natural phenomena. They goad them into imagining they themselves are wrong. These individuals thus unconsciously cover up the perpetrations of the evil spirits. Consequently whatever excuse comes into his head the Christian must examine it carefully. Every reason must be scrutinized and every symptom of the mind must be traced. Otherwise, in his mistaking supernatural work to be natural he will cede increased ground to the enemy. Every opinion he entertains about himself needs to be proven, lest he yield new territory to the evil spirits even before the old is recovered.

Because of his long capitulation a person may easily commit the fatal error of defending the malevolent operations of the evil spirits. This must be guarded against, for in so doing he assists them in veiling the true cause of their attack. Although he is in distress, nevertheless he is siding with the evil spirits in preserving their ground.

The devil's hosts at this juncture are inciting the believer's flesh to cooperate with them. Actually the flesh always works together with the devil. For the sake of saving face or for some other reason, the Christian refuses to believe his mind could possibly be occupied by the devil and objects to hearing anything about him or his works. Such distaste of examination for fear that he may lose his "spiritual experience" is a great hindrance to deliverance. He may retort in any one of a number of ways: "I don't *need* deliverance, why should I *want* to be delivered?" or "I have overcome through Christ; He has overcome Satan already, so now I need pay no attention to him but just leave him to God. I focus my attention on Christ." or "I know nothing about satanic matters." or "I concentrate on preaching the gospel, why should I notice Satan?" With these or many other responses the believer dismisses the actions of the evil spirits in him. And to those who try to help him he may even say: "All right, you resist for me and pray for me." He is not speaking with sincerity; he merely desires to live in ease and let others sweat out deliverance for him.

Yet in all this, it should be asked why anyone should object to hearing about Satan and his works? Can it be that his mind has in fact been worked on by Satan and hence is apprehensive about facing the situation once it might be exposed? The truth is that he is familiar with too many things already concerning the devil and does not care to know any thing more. Yet the gospel of Jesus Christ saves people not only from sin but from the devil as well. Why then be afraid if the devil be mentioned when the gospel is preached? Is it not similar to the person who has committed a certain crime and is afraid to have anyone mention that particular crime? Due to his preoccupation with the devil the believer resents people mentioning him. Deep down in his heart he harbors a fear lest his true condition should be revealed. Supposing I am indeed invaded by evil spirits, he gravely muses, then what in the world can I possibly do about it now? Thus he speaks to others as we have indicated above both to cover up and to comfort himself.

But should a believer receive and accept the light and begin to look for freedom, the evil spirits will commence to pour into his mind loads of accusations which charge him with all sorts of errors and which condemn and reprimand him in such a fury that he is left with no energy to recover his lost ground. They know he has obtained light and that they can no longer *deceive* him. They therefore change their tactics to a ceaseless chain of accusations: "You are wrong, you are wrong." During this time the believer, because there is no help in view, feels like sinking into a pit of sin. But if he could recognize this as simply Satan's lie he would rise up and resist. He shall overcome.

Experience teaches us that directly after one apprehends the truth of his having lost the sovereignty over his mind and accordingly begins to seek to regain it, he shall suffer many times over that of previous days. The evil spirits will attempt one final struggle for him. They will employ their customary lying tactic by hinting to him that he cannot possibly regain his freedom since he has sunk too deeply into passivity or that God is not disposed to grant him grace again or that he will fare better if he does not resist or that in any case he can never see the day of deliverance so why bother to strive and suffer anyway. Every child of God ought to know, however, that he should not live by satanic grace. He must have liberty even should he die retrieving it. No one can have fallen into passivity to such an extent that he is beyond deliverance. God is for him and he shall be set free.

Once knowing the truth and acknowledging that his mind has never been released or only partially released from the power of darkness, the child of God naturally will rise up to do battle against the evil spirits in order that their stronghold in him may be overthrown. Then and there he learns that the weapons of war must be spiritual, for fleshly ones avail him nothing. He cannot free himself by making resolutions or by adopting measures to improve his memory or thinking. His mind is captive to supernatural powers that cannot be cast out or destroyed by carnal devices. The believer never dreams that the powers of darkness could have so profoundly usurped his head until he learns the truth for himself and prepares to retrieve the lost territory which these wicked powers will accordingly be stirred to defend. The child of God thus comes to see how dark, dull, passive, and out of control his head truly is. The devil will use every means to torture his mind, threatening him not to take any action to recover the lost territory. This convinces the believer more than ever that his mental life is definitely a stronghold of the enemy and that he has not had complete control over it. He perceives how the enemy attempts to prevent it from understanding truths he desires to learn, for he is able to remember non-essential matters but is totally powerless to comprehend or recall the vital ones. He senses that there is an opposing force in his head which is against the truth to which he already has given consent.

Now begins the war for liberation of the mind. Is the Christian content to remain the stronghold of the evil spirits? If not, then who must solve the problem? God? No, it is man himself. He must choose whether to offer himself wholly to God or allow his thinking apparatus to remain a concession of Satan's. Will the powers of darkness be permitted to utilize his mind? Are they going to be permitted to pour forth their perverted thoughts through the mind of the saved? Will they be allowed to fill his head with the fire from hell? Can they propagate at will their teachings through his mind? Is it henceforth going to be possible for them to resist God's truth by manipulating him in his intellect? Can they harm and torment him via the mind? The Christian himself must decide the issue. Is he willing to be a permanent puppet of the evil spirits? *He* must make the choice, else there can be no possibility of deliverance. To be sure, any decision for God does not then signify he has already overcome. It only indicates whether he is really opposing the attack of the enemy.

THE LOST GROUND TO BE RECOVERED

We will recall that because the believer has given ground to the evil spirits, they have been able to operate on his mind. Earlier we had grouped this lost ground under six headings; now we shall reduce them to three main types:

(1) an unrenewed mind, (2) acceptance of the evil spirits' lies, and (3) passivity. The believer should examine himself carefully to find out which of the three grounds he has furnished to the evil spirits. Is it the unrenewed mind? or the passive mind? or the acceptance of the lie of the evil spirits? Or has he yielded on all three counts? Judging by the experience of Christians, a large number have supplied all three to the devil and his minions. Upon isolating the point or points by which he has ceded territory to the evil spirits, he must set out immediately to recover all the ground he has lost. This is his only salvation. Since he has degenerated into his present state through surrendering this or that foothold to the evil spirits, he will be free solely when these footholds are all regained. The unrenewed mind must be renewed; the lie accepted must be spotted and denied; and passivity must be turned into free action. We shall discuss them one by one.

THE MIND RENEWED

God desires not only a change in the mind of His children at the time of conversion; He desires also a mind that is totally renewed, which is transparent as crystal. We find this commanded in the Word of God. The reason Satan can work is that the Christian has not been liberated entirely from a carnal mind. He may start out with a narrow mentality which cannot tolerate others or a darkened mentality that cannot comprehend deeper truth or a foolish mentality which cannot bear any important responsibility; and afterwards he slips into deeper sins. This is because "the mind that is set on the flesh is hostile to God" (Rom. 8.7). Once knowing the teaching of Romans 6 many Christians see themselves as having already been freed from their carnal mind. What they do not appreciate is that the cross must operate minutely in every area of the man. "Consider yourselves dead to sin" must be followed by "let not sin therefore reign in your mortal bodies" (Rom. 6.11-12). Following the change of mentality there must be the bringing of *"every thought captive to obey Christ"* (2 Cor. 10.5). The mind must be renewed completely, since any residue of its carnality is hostile to God.

For us to have our intellects renewed we must draw near to the cross. This is plainly called for in Ephesians 4. The Apostle Paul describes the darkness of man's carnal mentality in verses 17 and 18; but in verses 22 and 23 he informs us how the mind can be renewed: "Put off your old nature which belongs to your former manner of life and is corrupt through deceitful lusts, and be renewed in the spirit of your mind." We know our old man has been crucified with the Lord already (Rom. 6.6). Here we are exhorted to "put off" so that our mind might be renewed. This brings the cross into view as the instrument for its renewal. A believer should understand that his old brain too is part of that old man which God wants us to put off entirely. The salvation which God imparts through the cross includes not only a new life but the renewal of every *function* of our soul as well. The salvation which is rooted deeply in our being must gradually be "worked out." A serious lack among Christians today is in not perceiving the need for their minds to be saved (Eph. 6.17); they conceive salvation in general and somewhat vague terms. They fail to recognize that God desires to save them to the uttermost in that all their abilities are to be renewed and fit for His use. The mind is one of man's natural endowments. God calls His own to believe that their old man was crucified on the cross; thereafter they need to accept single-mindedly God's judgment towards the old man and exercise their will to resist or to put off its deeds including their old thoughts. They must come to the foot of the cross, willing to forsake their traditional mentalities and trusting God to give them a new mind. Brethren, the old one needs to be thoroughly put off. Yes, its renewal is God's work, but the putting off—the denial, the forsaking—of your old organ of thought is what you must do. If you perform your part, God will fulfill His. And once you put off specifically, you should just as thoroughly believe that God will renew your mind, despite the fact you know not how.

How many of God's children, although hitherto saved and possessed of a new life, still carry about them an old head.

Nothing of their former theories, thought processes, or prejudices has been altered: only a Christian casing has been added. They use their old brain to search, to accept and to propagate spiritual truth. Is it any wonder they fall into countless errors and precipitate endless conflicts in the church? Just as God is displeased with the wicked man who uses his own strength to do the Lord's work, so He is displeased with the wicked man who uses his own mind to apprehend God's truth. An unrenewed mentality is spiritually dead; hence everything which proceeds from it is likewise none other than dead. Many may boast in the depth of their Bible knowledge and in the excellency of their theological tenets, but those with spiritual discernment are aware that it is dead.

Upon recognizing the staleness of his mind and being willing to put it off by the cross, the Christian now should practice denying all carnal thoughts daily. The renewal will otherwise be impossible. For how can God ever succeed in His responsibility of renewing the believer's mind if the latter still thinks according to the flesh?

Patiently and decisively must the Christian examine every one of his thoughts—but in the light of *God*. Whatever is not of Him or is contrary to His truth must be "squeezed" or "pressed" out of his head. Mere mental understanding of truth similarly must be rejected. Paul has mentioned how our unrenewed mind is filled with arguments and proud imaginations (2 Cor. 10.5). These prevent men from arriving at true knowledge of God. Christians must bring all these thoughts captive to obey Christ. The Apostle says "every thought"; consequently one must not allow so much as a single thought to escape such treatment. He should not rest until every idea is brought into subjection to Christ. The examination of his thought should determine whether (1) it comes from his old mind or (2) it emanates from the ground given away, and whether (3) it will yield new ground to the evil spirits or whether (4) it issues from a normal or renewed mind. He should inquire why his thinking is confused, prejudiced, rebellious, or infuriated—why he opposes certain truth before he even examines it—why he is against some Christians whom he has merely heard about (does he have sufficient warrant for so withstanding or does he detest them purely out of a natural mind?). During such a period of investigation every idea and imagination needs to be scrutinized so that those which arise from the old creation may be detected and discarded. To those who live out their days foolishly such a regimen no doubt appears to be unbearable. Being managed by the powers of darkness, their mind is loose and wild. But we must face the fact that a war is on. And unless we fight, how can we retake the fortresses of the enemy which are in the mind? The enemy is very real; how then can we be less vigilant?

LIES DENIED

As the saved one places himself beneath God's light he will discover that often in the past he has accepted lies from the evil spirits which triggered his falling into that condition in which he now finds himself. Sometimes he adopted a wrong *attitude* or *action* due to misunderstanding God's truth by believing in the enemy's lie. For instance, by misunderstanding the relationship between God and man he inadvertently may believe that God dispenses His thought directly to him. So he passively waits and tarries and then accepts those registrations he assumes are from God. The evil spirits are thereby successful in their counterfeit and are able to supply him frequently with innumerable identical thoughts. Or, on another occasion, by appropriating what the enemy has suggested concerning his health or other matters directly involving him, he finds the conditions of his body and related affairs turn out to be exactly as he was told. The evil spirits, for example, may hint to the person's mind that certain things will happen to him. If he does not resist or if he unquestioningly receives the suggestion, he will find before long that whatever the evil spirits have appointed invariably does come to him.

By exercising himself the child of God will uncover many vexations, weaknesses, sicknesses, and other similar phenomena in his life today to be due to his directly or indirectly having accepted lies planted in him in the past by evil spirits. They either are caused directly by believing in these lies or are induced indirectly after believing in them. To secure one's freedom the Christian must experience God's light which is God's truth. Since he formerly lost ground by believing lies, he now must recover this ground by denying all lies. As light dispels darkness, so truth destroys lies. The saint must therefore seek to apprehend every truth concerning himself, God, and the evil spirits. He should pay a price to possess these truths. He should pray singleheartedly for light that he may behold his precise condition (the truth) and thereby know where he has been deceived and has accordingly suffered. He next should scrutinize all his physical and environmental sufferings. Whence does each stem? What has provoked these troubles; was it through believing Satan's lie or by adopting a wrong action through acceptance of any lie? He should trace the source and then *quietly* and *prayerfully* wait to be illuminated by God's light.

The devil abhors light and truth because these remove the ground of his working. Each word of truth has to be fought for in the believer's mind. The evil spirits try to keep from him the truth about their operations. They moreover attempt to disown the *particular* phenomenon which results from accepting a *particular* lie. Their operating principle is ever and anon "to keep them from seeing the light" (2 Cor. 4.4). A Christian must be very thorough in spotting the truth concerning all matters. Truth means at the very least the *true condition.* Even should he be helpless to drive away the enemy, his siding with the truth causes the latter to forfeit his ground. The believer at minimum can declare by his will that he *wants* the truth, that he wants to know and obey the truth. By prayer and by choice of will he ought to resist every satanic lie, whatever form it may take—a thought, an imagination or an argument. In so doing the Holy Spirit is afforded opportunity to lead his darkened mind into the light of God's truth. In practical experience the believer sometimes may spend months before discerning *one* satanic lie. He first must resist in his will every ground of the evil spirits and afterwards overthrow one by one the lies which he *formerly believed but now disbelieves*. In this way he gradually will recover all the surrendered territory. He will not believe, not even in the slightest degree, what the evil spirits say. So shall they lose their power.

NORMALCY RECOGNIZED

If one has plunged into all sorts of vexations due to passivity or believing the lie of the evil spirits, he urgently needs to determine what is normal for him. Except for the unrenewed mind, both passivity and assent to lies furnish such footholds to evil spirits that the Christian's mental state will deteriorate steadily in every direction. His powers of thinking, of recall, of physical endurance, and so forth will all continually fail. If he realizes his danger he ought to rise up and seek liberation. But what should he regard as "liberation"? It is this: he needs to be restored to his *original* state. Hence it is essential for anyone who seeks restoration to determine what his original state was. Each person has his normal condition, that state he had before he fell through the deceit of the enemy. He must be made reaware of his normal state. Upon discovering he is not as he was before, he should ask himself such questions as: What was my former condition? How far am I today from it? How can I be restored to it?

Your former state is your normal state. The condition from which you fell is your measuring rod. Should you be ignorant of what is normal for you, you need to inquire of yourself on this wise: Was my mind born so confused or was there a time when I was not confused? Was my memory habitually so poor or was there a period when I could remember well? Was I usually so sleepless or did I once sleep well? Did I always have so many pictures passing before my eyes like movies on a screen or were there some clear moments? Have I always been weak or was there a time when I was stronger? Is it true I could never control myself or could I once manage myself much better? By answering these questions the person ought to be able to perceive whether he lacks his normal state, is under attack, or has grown passive. He in addition will be helped in delineating what his normal state is.

To define what his original condition was, a person must acknowledge and believe initially that he *does have* a normal state. Though he has fallen today, he nonetheless once experienced a better life. Precisely that is his normal state towards which he should aspire to be restored. Normalcy means nothing but one's normal state. If he finds it difficult to decide what his normalcy is, then let him recall the best experience of his life when his spirit was strong, memory and thought clear, and body most healthy. Let him adopt that as his normalcy. It can afford him a minimum measure to which he ought to attain. He should not be content with any measurement less than that condition. And there is no reason why he should not be able to arrive at that state since he once was there. Yet even that is still not his highest possibility. Consequently he must at least regain his normalcy and refuse to ever again descend from it.

By comparing his present situation to that of his former days the Christian can determine how far he is now from what he once was. He whose mind is being assaulted can now see how weak his memory and thinking have become. And he whose body is being attacked can well appreciate how low his strength today is in comparison with his former strength. Upon realizing he has fallen from his normalcy he immediately should exercise his will to resist the present abnormal condition and strive to be restored to his normal state. Usually the evil spirits will withstand such attempted overthrowing of their strongholds. They will begin to suggest to the believer: You are now old, naturally you cannot expect to have as strong a mind as a youth; man's ability deteriorates according to years. Or, if you are young, they will intimate: Due to an inborn deficiency you of course cannot, like the others, enjoy the blessing of an active mind for long. Or, they will hint to you that you sank into this condition because you worked too hard. They may even grow so bold as to tell you your present state is what you really are, that you are inferior to others because you received a lesser gift. The aim of the evil spirits is to mislead the child of God into believing the explanation for his weaknesses is *natural, necessary* and unsurprising. If God's child neither is deceived nor is passive but is absolutely free, those words perhaps might be worthy of investigation; but should he be deceived and passive, those excuses are utterly unbelievable. He who has been redeemed to enjoy a better life than this poor condition should not allow the powers of darkness to hold him down in a lower state. He decisively should reject their lies.

One point should be noticed: a mind which is weakened through sickness is altogether different from one which is undermined by ceding ground to evil spirits. In the first case, man's nervous system is damaged; in the second, the work of the enemy does not upset the constitution of the nerves but merely inhibits their proper functioning. If a man's mind is not organically damaged but is only temporarily out of normal operation, he can be restored to his former state once the evil spirits are cast out. Many insane people have had their nervous system damaged through natural illness first before they are disturbed by the evil spirits; hence it is more difficult for them to be restored.

PASSIVITY OVERTURNED

After determining what one's normalcy is, the Christian's next important step is to battle for recovery. We should not forget, however, that the adversary will try his best to retain the ground he has won exactly as earthly rulers jealously guard their territories. We cannot expect the powers of darkness to surrender their citadels without a struggle. Quite the reverse, they will fight to the very end. Let us realize that, while it is most easy to cede any ground, it requires an enormous effort to recover it. Yet we should pay particular attention to this observation: that just as each nation has laws and their legal judgments must be absolutely obeyed, so in God's universe there are spiritual laws whose legal judgments are so authoritative that even the devils cannot disobey. If we learn these spiritual laws and act on them the evil spirits will be forced to return what they have taken.

The most basic and consequential law of the spirit realm is that nothing pertaining to man can be accomplished without the consent of his will. It is through ignorance that a child of God accepted the deceit of the evil spirits and permitted them to work in his life. Now he must recover the relinquished territory; and to do so he must exercise his will to overturn his earlier consent by insisting that he is his own master and will not tolerate the enemy manipulating any segment of his being. In such a warfare as this the evil spirits cannot violate spiritual law; and hence they must retreat. At the beginning the believer's mind was usurped by the wicked powers through its passivity; this in turn ushered in the passivity of the will. Now the believer should declare by God's law that his mind belongs to him, that he is going to use it and will not permit any outside force to instigate, employ or control his mind. If he relentlessly retreats from passivity and exercises his mind, the latter gradually shall be liberated till it attains to its original state. (Later we shall have more to say on recovering the ground and its battle.)

In this conflict the child of God must exercise his mind. He must take the initiative in each action and not depend on anyone else. If possible he must make his own decision, not waiting passively for other people or for more conducive environment. He must not glance back at the past nor worry concerning the future but learn to live just for this moment. Prayerfully and watchfully must he proceed step by step. He must exercise his mind and *think*: think what he should do, speak, or become. He must throw away every crutch, not allowing any worldly element or means to be substituted for the ability of the mind. He must use it to think, reason, remember and comprehend.

Because the individual's mental life has been protractedly passive, the battle for freedom likewise requires a protracted period. Let him understand that before he regains his liberty many of his thoughts will not be conceived by him but rather will be inspired by evil spirits who usurp his mind. For this reason he must scrutinize every notion lest he unconsciously furnish new ground to the evil spirits before the old is wholly recovered. During this period, therefore, accusations which arise may not necessarily be due to his faults nor praises be due to his merits. He should not abandon hope if his head is full of despondent thoughts; neither should he be elated if it is filled with exalted ideas.

The believer in addition should assail the lies of the evil spirits. Every suggestion from the enemy must be met resolutely with the truth of the Bible. Answer doubts with the texts of faith; respond to despair with words of hope; reply to fear with words of peace. If he does not know the appropriate verse, let him pray for direction; if he recognizes that something is from his foes then he can say to them, "This is your lie, I will not accept it." Victory is obtained by wielding the Sword of the Spirit.

During the struggle he must never forget the position of the cross. He must stand on Romans 6.11, reckoning himself dead to sin but alive to God in Christ Jesus. He already has died and has therefore been delivered from the old creation. The evil spirits cannot now do anything in his life, for what ground of operation they had has hitherto been taken away on the cross. Each time the Christian exercises his mind and resists the devil he is depending completely on what the cross has accomplished. He perceives that his death with the Lord is a fact; hence he strongly maintains that position before the enemy. He has died; the evil spirits have no authority over a dead person. Pharaoh could not hurt the children of Israel who were on the other side of the Red Sea. Resting on the Lord's death gives the Christian an immense advantage.

FREEDOM AND RENEWAL

As the believer retrieves the ground inch by inch, the effect gradually will be manifested. Although at the beginning situations may appear to turn worse as he attempts to recover, nonetheless if he persists he shall witness the adversary steadily losing his power. Various symptoms will decrease as the territory is increasingly regained. He will detect his mind, with its memory, imagination and reasoning powers, gradually becoming free so that he can use it again. But let him beware of one hazard at this point: he could become self-content and cease to fight to the end, to that point where all lost ground is recovered. And thus he would leave the evil spirits with a foothold for perpetrating some new future action. The believer must continue to restore his sovereignty until he is utterly emancipated. Should he stand on the foundation of the cross and exercise his mind to resist the enemy's usurpation, he shall soon be delivered completely. He shall become master of his own mental life.

Let us briefly recapitulate the process from passivity to freedom:

(1) The Christian's mind was originally normal.

(2) He sank into passivity because he wanted God to use his mind.

(3) He was deceived into thinking he now possesses a new mind.

(4) In point of fact he had fallen below normalcy through the assaults of the evil spirits.

(5) His mind grew weak and powerless.

(6) He battles to regain the lost ground.

(7) His mind seems to become more corrupt and confused than ever.

(8) Actually he is gradually regaining freedom.

(9) He insists on his sovereignty and determines to recover from his passivity.

(10) Passivity is overturned; he is recovered.

(11) By maintaining his will, he has not only succeeded in thereafter retaining his normalcy, but also

(12) His mind is so recovered that he can do what he could not do before.

Let us see that a renewed mind is something deeper than simply a freed one. To regain the strongholds forfeited through passivity and believing the enemy's lie means merely to restore what has been lost; but to be renewed includes not only restoration of what was relinquished but also a coming into possession of something higher than he originally had. To have a mind renewed is to arrive at the highest possibility which God has ordained for his mind. God wants the Christian's mind not just to be unshackled from the power of darkness by becoming wholly self-controlled, but in addition to be *renewed* so that it can cooperate completely with the Holy Spirit. God desires the mind to be full of light, wisdom and understanding, with all its imaginations and reasonings purified and brought to perfect obedience to God's will (Col. 1.9). Let us therefore not be content with but a little gain.

CHAPTER 4
THE LAWS OF THE MIND

WITH HIS MIND RENEWED, the child of God may marvel at its power. He is emancipated from sluggish and non-essential activities. His ability to concentrate becomes much sharper, his understanding more perceptive, his memory more alert, his reasoning more explicit, and his outlook less confined. He works more effectively, thinks more comprehensively, and grasps the thought of others more easily. In addition, he receives spiritual knowledge with an open mind because he is now free from the language of his own petty experience and released into the boundless world of spiritual knowledge. Every prejudice and preconceived notion towards God's work are removed, enabling his mind to undertake the work which before was impossible and to bear responsibility two or three times that which he formerly could bear.

The reason the Christian's mind is ineffective today is because it has not yet been renewed. Yet even once renewed, there is no guarantee that it may not again be harassed by the old mentality. If the Christian does not relentlessly oppose his traditional way of thinking he shall unconsciously turn back to it. As he needs to deny the work of the flesh and daily follow the spirit, so he must resist the old mental way and daily think according to the renewed mind. Such vigilance is absolutely essential; otherwise he will return to his old state. Retrogression is all too possible in spiritual life. Unless a child of God is watchful following his mental renewal, he can still believe in the enemy's lie and once again through passivity give him ground. In order that he may maintain his mind continually in the renewed state, it being renewed day by day, he needs to appropriate its laws. As the spirit has its laws, so the mind has too. We shall mention a few of these, the practice of which will assure victory to the believer.

THE MIND WORKING WITH THE SPIRIT

In analyzing the discerning-understanding-performing process of a *spiritual* Christian, we can identify these steps: (1) the Holy Spirit reveals God's will in one's spirit that he may know what it is; (2) through his mind he comprehends the meaning of this revelation; and (3) with his volition he engages his spiritual strength to activate the body that it may execute God's will. Nothing in a person's life is closer to the spirit than his mind. We know it is the mechanism for learning matters in the intellectual and material realms while the spirit is the component for perceiving realities in the spiritual realm. A Christian knows all things about himself through the intellect whereas he knows the things of God through the spirit. Both are organs of knowledge, hence their relationship is manifestly closer than are others. In walking after the spirit we shall find the mind to be the best helper to the spirit. It is therefore necessary to understand how these two work together.

The Bible speaks most distinctly about the coordination of the spirit and the mind: "that the God of our Lord Jesus Christ, the Father of glory, may give you a spirit of wisdom and of revelation in the *knowledge* of him, having the eyes of your hearts enlightened, that you may *know* . . . " (Eph. 1.17-18). We have explained the meaning of "a spirit of wisdom and of revelation" before; it means that God makes Himself and His will known to us by giving revelation in our spirit. But now we wish to note how the revelation obtained intuitively in our spirit works together with our mind.

"The eyes of your heart" points figuratively to the organ of our reasoning and understanding, that is, our mind. In this passage the word "know" or "knowledge"—used twice—

serves to convey two distinctive notions: the first one is a knowing intuitively, the second is a knowing or understanding mentally. This spirit of revelation is located in the depth of our being. God reveals Himself to our spirit that we may truly apprehend Him by our intuition. Thus far, however, this is but intuitive knowledge; that is to say, the inner man knows while the outer man remains ignorant. The communication to the outward man of what has been known by the inward man is an indispensable step, the lack of which prevents united action by the inner and outer man together. How then can there be this communication? The Scripture informs us that our spirit will enlighten our mental faculty to make it understand the meaning of the revelation in the intuition. Since our outward man depends on the mind in order to comprehend things, the spirit must convey what it knows intuitively to the mind so that the latter can deliver the message to the entire being and enable the child of God to walk according to the spirit.

We first come to know the will of God in our intuition and then our intellect interprets that will to us. The Holy Spirit moves in our spirit, producing in us a spiritual sense; afterwards we exercise our brain to study and to understand the meaning of this sense. It requires the cooperation of both spirit and mind to comprehend fully the will of God. The spirit enables our inner man to know, while the mind causes our outer man to understand. Such cooperation occurs in a second, although it takes longer to describe with pen and ink. They operate like two hands: and in the twinkling of an eye the spirit already has made known to the mind what it has seen. All revelations come from the Holy Spirit and are received not by the mind but by man's spirit, so that man may know by intuition; they are then studied and understood by his mental powers.

We consistently ought to refuse to allow the mind to serve as the prime element for receiving God's will, yet we must not inhibit it from serving as the secondary apparatus for understanding that will. A carnal Christian mistakes the thought of the head to be the criterion for his conduct because he has not yet learned how to walk after the spirit. A spiritual Christian follows the spirit, but he also permits his mind to comprehend what the spirit means. In true guidance these two elements are one. Ordinarily the leading in the spirit opposes what men call reasoning; however, to the person whose rational power has been renewed such reasoning works together with his spirit, thus his guidance seems perfectly logical to *his* reasoning. But the rationality of the person whose inner man has not yet attained this lofty position frequently will withstand the leading of the spirit.

We have observed in Ephesians 1 how the spirit aids the mind. Upon receiving revelation from God the believer's spirit enlightens the intellect. The mind of a spiritual man does not rely upon natural life; it depends instead on the enlightening of the spirit's light. It lapses into darkness otherwise. A renewed mentality needs to be directed by the light of the spirit. This explains why a person may find his thoughts confused and his whole being dissipated if his inner man is blocked by evil spirits. The brain of a spiritual man is sustained by the spirit. Should the latter fall under a seige, its power cannot reach directly to the brain and so the mind immediately loses some control. The preservation of these two elements in their proper relationship requires an alertness lest our spirit be beseiged by the evil spirits and cause our mind to relinquish its normal functioning.

A believer's mind is the outlet of the Holy Spirit. How does He Who dwells in man's spirit express Himself? He is not satisfied with man only believing that He is present in the human spirit. His aim is to manifest Himself through man that others too may possess Him. There are a thousand and one things for which the Holy Spirit requires the cooperation of *man*. It is not enough for Him to *dwell* in man's spirit, He desires additionally to *express* Himself through it. What expresses man's spirit is the mind. Should it be obstructed, the spirit shall be deprived of its means of expression, and then God's Spirit cannot flow from man's inner being to other people. We need the mind, moreover, to read the meaning of our intuitive knowledge, thus opening the way for God to communicate His thought through us. If our mentality is narrow and foolish the Holy Spirit finds Himself unable to fellowship with us in the way He desires.

MIND, THE SPIRIT, AND A SPIRITUAL MIND

The more spiritual a child of God becomes the more he is conscious of the significance of walking according to the spirit and the dangers of walking according to the flesh. But how is he actually to walk by the spirit? The answer given in Romans 8 is to mind the spirit and to possess a spiritual mind: "they that are after the flesh mind the things of the flesh; but they that are after the Spirit the things of the Spirit. For the mind of the flesh is death; but the mind of the Spirit is life and peace" (vv. 5-6 ASV). To walk after the spirit means to have the mind set on the things of the spirit; it also means to have the spirit rule the mind. Those who act according to the spirit are none other than those who are occupied with the things of the inner man and whose mind is therefore spiritual. Walking by the spirit simply denotes that a mind under the control of the spirit sets itself on the things of the spirit. This implies that our mentality has been renewed and has become spirit-controlled and thus qualified to detect every movement and silence of the spirit.

Here we see once more the relationship between these two component parts—"they that are after the flesh mind the things of the flesh; but they that are after the spirit the things of the spirit." Man's head is able to mind the flesh as well as the spirit. Our mental faculty (soul) stands between the spirit and the flesh (specifically here, the body). Whatever the mind sets itself on is what the man walks after. If it occupies itself with the flesh, we walk after that; conversely, if it sets itself upon the spirit, we follow after it. It is therefore unnecessary to ask whether or not we are walking after the spirit. We need only inquire if we are minding the spirit, that is, noticing the movement or silence therein. Never can it be that we set ourselves on the things of the flesh and yet walk after the spirit. On whatever the mind sets itself, that do we follow. This is an unchangeable law. What does our mind think and notice in our daily experience? What do we obey? Are we heeding the inner man or do we obey the flesh? Being occupied with the affairs of the spirit will make us spiritual men, whereas occupying ourselves with the affairs of the flesh will turn us into fleshly people. If our mind is not governed by the spirit, it must be governed by the flesh; if not guided by heaven, it must be guided by earth; if not regulated from above, it must be regulated from beneath. Following the spirit produces life and peace, while following the flesh results in death. From God's point of view, nothing arising from the flesh contains any spiritual value. A believer is capable of living in "death" though he still possesses life.

Why is *minding* the realities of the spirit so important to a life which walks after the spirit? Because that is the most conspicuous condition for securing guidance in the spirit. How many of God's children wait for Him to arrange their circumstances while concomitantly overlooking the need to heed the spirit; that is, they pay no heed to the prompting of their inner depths. Often God Who indwells us already has led us within our spirit, yet because of the dullness of our mental faculty we just do not appreciate it. He has truly given revelation to our intuition, but our intellect is dwelling on a thousand and one matters other than on the movement in the spirit. We are neglecting our spiritual sense. Sometimes our spirit is normal but our mind errs, so we are incapacitated from following the spirit. Whatever is expressed by its intuition is delicate, quiet and gentle; unless we habitually mind its realities, how can we ever know the thought of the spirit and accordingly walk? Our mind ought to be alert like a watchman, always on the lookout for the movement in the inner man so that our outer man may be yielded wholly.

All the leadings of God are transmitted via small delicate sensations in the spirit. God never employs anything like a compulsory, overwhelming feeling to try to force man into obedience. He invariably affords us an opportunity to make our choice. Anything which is forced upon us comes not from God but is a work of the evil spirits. Until we fulfill the essentials for the working of the Holy Spirit, He will not work. Hence it necessitates more than merely waiting for His guidance. Our spirit and mind must function actively together with the Holy Spirit if we expect Him to lead us. We will walk after the spirit if we exercise our inner man to cooperate with the Holy Spirit and use as well our outer man to follow the movement or silence in our spirit.

AN OPEN MIND

Besides experiencing God's direct revelation, we also frequently receive truth through the preaching of the Word by other children of God. Such truth is first received in the intellect before it reaches the spirit. Since we make contact with the utterances or writings of others with the mind, there is hardly any possibility of this kind of truth reaching our life except through the channel of the mind. An open mind is consequently of paramount importance to spiritual life. If our brain is full of prejudice towards the truth or towards the preacher, truth will not enter it nor will it extend to our life. No wonder some believers derive no help—already have they decided what they would like to read or hear.

If a Christian is familiar with the process whereby truth is translated into life he will perceive the significance of a mind being unimpeded. Truth is understood initially by the mind; next it enters and stirs the spirit; and lastly, it is manifested in practical living. A closed mind prevents truth from entering the spirit. A closed mentality is a prejudiced one; it opposes and criticizes any item differing from its idea; its notion becomes the standard of truth; anything contrary cannot be truth. Such a mentality deprives the opportunity for many of God's truths to penetrate into the man; consequently it damages the believer's spiritual life. Many experienced saints can testify to the necessity for an unprejudiced mind in regard to revelation of truth. Oftentimes enough truth has been communicated to us, but we simply have not comprehended it because of the lack of an open mind. How many are the years that God must expend in removing all obstacles before we can accept truth. An unobstructed mentality in conjunction with a free spirit aids us the most in knowing the truth.

If the mind is open the individual will soon perceive the preciousness of a truth which initially appeared rather dull to him but now is illumined by the spirit's light. This is the way a child of God often receives truth: at the beginning it seems quite meaningless; after a while, though, the light of the spirit shines upon his mind and equips him to comprehend the depth of that truth. Although he may not have at his command the proper words to explain it, yet inwardly he has understood perfectly. An open mind lets in the truth, but the illumination of the spirit's light renders the truth profitable.

A CONTROLLED MIND

Every part of the Christian's life needs to be under reins; that includes the mind even following its renewal. We ought not toss the reins to it lest the evil spirits take advantage. Let us remember that *thought is the seed of action*. Carelessness here invariably leads to sin there. An idea sown will eventually grow, however prolonged such growth may require. We can trace all our presumptuous and unconscious sins to those seed thoughts we allowed to be planted before. If a sinful notion is allowed to stay in the head, then after a time, perhaps a few years, it will result in a sinful act. Suppose, for example, we conceive an evil thought against a certain brother. If it is not eradicated and cleansed immediately, it ultimately will produce its unsavory fruit. The Christian must exert his utmost strength to deal with his thoughts. Should his mental life be left uncontrolled, he cannot possibly control anything. Hence Peter exhorts us to "gird up (our) minds" (1 Peter 1.13), by which he means to say that we must regulate all our thoughts and never let them run wild.

God's objective is to "take *every* thought captive to obey Christ." Hence we ought to scrutinize every one of our thoughts in the light of God, not allowing one to escape our observation or judgment. Whatever the notion may be, it must be examined and controlled.

In gaining dominion over his mental life the Christian should not allow any improper thought to remain in him. Every inappropriate item must be driven out. Further, he must not permit his mind to lie idle. Every matter should be weighed carefully so that he may be both a sensible and a spiritual person. He should not allow his mind to drift off at random lest he provide opportunity for the evil spirits to work. It must not be lazy, doing nothing; rather should it always be functioning actively. Even after the Christian has received revelation in the spirit, he still needs to exercise his intellect to examine, to test, and to ascertain whether this is of God or of himself. He also needs to discover whether, by taking any action, he would be following the spirit entirely and according to God's timing, or whether there would be any element of his own mixed in with it. Such mental activity helps the spirit to clarify the revelation received in its intuition as well as to uncover any discrepancy. Any thought which centers on self hinders us from knowing God's will; only whatever disallows self is effective. God never wants us to follow blindly; He insists upon our lucidly apprehending His mind. Anything lacking clarity is unreliable.

When the mind is functioning, beware lest it do so alone, that is, beware lest it operate independently of the spirit's rule. A selfless mind aids the Christian in understanding God's will, but an independent one merely exhibits the corruption of the flesh. For instance, many search the Scriptures with their brain, depending upon their own intellectual ability. Yet the truth they claim to know is but there in their heads. Such independent mental action is quite dangerous, for it accomplishes nothing in the Christian's life other than to furnish some additional information for his thoughts and some additional ground for his boasting. We should sincerely reject all truths which are solely mental, for such knowledge provides Satan with an opportunity to work. We must restrain any desire which seeks mere intellectual knowledge.

The brain ought to function, but it likewise needs to rest. If a believer were to allow it to work incessantly without any occasion for rest, it eventually would become sick just as the body does. He must regulate its activity, forbidding it to grow overactive and go out of control. The defeat Elijah encountered under a broom tree was due to the excessive working of his mind (1 Kings 19).

A Christian should keep his mind in the peace of God at all times. "Thou dost keep him in perfect peace," noted Isaiah, "whose mind is stayed on thee, because he trusts in thee" (26.3). A restless brain is a disturbed brain that is harmful both to spiritual life and to spiritual service. It has led many into numerous errors. An unpeaceful mind cannot operate normally. Hence the Apostle teaches us to "have no anxiety about anything" (Phil. 4.6). Deliever all anxious thoughts to God as soon as they arise. Let the peace of God maintain your heart and mind (v.7). But Paul also exhorts us to put our heads to work and not just let them lie fallow: "brethren, whatever is true, whatever is honorable, whatever is just, whatever is pure, whatever is lovely, whatever is gracious, if there is any excellence, if there is anything worthy of praise, think about these things" (v.8).

The mind is not to be ruled by the emotions. It should rest calmly in God and work by faith. This is the meaning of "a sound mind" which Paul entreats us to cultivate (2 Tim. 1.7 AV). A believer should follow the intuition of the spirit. He must let God's rule of right and wrong judge in all cases.

The head needs to be kept in a humble state. A proud thought easily leads one astray. Any self-righteous, self-important or self-sufficient notion can bring in error. Some have a background of extensive knowledge and yet they fall into self-deceit because they think too much and too highly of themselves. Any who genuinely desire to serve the Lord must do so "with all lowliness of mind" (Acts 20.19 ASV).

He must cast off every self-deceptive consideration and ascertain his place in the body of Christ as appointed by God.

A MIND FULL OF GOD'S WORD

"I will put my laws into their minds," declares God (Heb. 8.10). We should read and memorize more of the Word of God, lest we be unable to find it at the moment of urgent need. If we diligently read the Bible God will fill every thought of ours with His laws. We shall recall instantly what the Bible says when we are in need of light for our way. Many are unwilling to exercise their minds in reading the Word. They like to open the Bible at random following prayer and take whatever is before them as being from God. This is extremely untrustworthy. But if our mind is abounding in His Word, the Holy Spirit is able through our spirit's intuition to enlighten our mind at once by bringing to our remembrance some appropriate verse. We do not require anyone to tell us we should not steal, for we know the Word of God has said so. Such a word is already in our mind. This is true in other matters as well; so if we are united with the Bible in this way, we shall be able to apprehend the mind of God in all regards.

A CRY FOR A CLEANSED MIND

The Christian continually ought to ask God to purify his mental life and keep it fresh. He should request God to root out every evil thought towards Him and all excessive notions as well so that what he believes is completely of God. Pray that you may not only think of Him but in addition think rightly. Pray that no thought will issue forth from your evil nature, but that if it does it will be exposed and disposed of by God's light immediately. Ask God to keep you away from your old pattern of thinking in order that the church of God may not be divided by special doctrines. Ask Him too to check you from accepting any special teaching with your mind which would separate you from His other children. Entreat Him to make you of one mind with the others; and if in any matter this one mind is lacking, then wait earnestly and patiently for it. Beseech Him not to permit you to hold any erroneous idea or teaching in your new life. Implore Him to render you dead not only to this evil nature of yours but also to your evil mentality. Plead with Him that your thought may not in any way be the cause of division in the body of Christ. Beg Him not to allow you to be deceived again. Supplicate on behalf of other children of God that they too may live by Him, no further provoking and no further scattering each other, that all may truly enjoy one life and one mind.

PART NINE

THE ANALYSIS OF THE SOUL—THE WILL

1. A Believer's Will
2. Passivity and Its Dangers
3. The Believer's Mistake
4. The Path to Freedom

CHAPTER 1

A BELIEVER'S WILL

A MAN'S WILL IS his organ for decision-making. To want or not to want, to choose or not to choose are the typical operations of the will. It is his "helm" by which he sails upon the sea of life.

The will of a man can be taken as his real self, for it truthfully represents him. Its action is the action of the man. When we declare "*I will*," it is actually our volition which wills. When we say "*I want, I decide*," again it is our volition which wants and decides. Our volition acts for the entire man. Our emotion merely expresses how we feel; our mind simply tells us what we think; but our will communicates what we *want*. Hence, it is the most influential component of our entire person. It is deeper than emotion and mind. So in seeking spiritual growth the believer must not neglect the volitional element in him.

Many commit the error of treating "religion" as a matter of emotion; they believe that it merely soothes and gladdens men's emotions. Others insist that "religion" ought to be compatible with reason and not overly emotional; only a kind of rational religion is acceptable to these. What both these groups do not know is that true religion *per se* does not aim at emotion or reason but aims to impart life to man's spirit and to lead his will to be completely yielded to God's will. Unless our "religious" experience produces in us a *willing* acceptance of the whole counsel of God, it is very superficial. What can it profit a man if along his spiritual pathway the will exhibits no proper sign of grace? Or if the will is not touched?

True and perfect salvation saves man's will. Whatever is not sufficiently thorough to embrace the salvation of man's volition is but vanity. All pleasant feelings and all lucid thoughts belong exclusively to the external realm. Man may experience joy, comfort and peace in believing God, he may understand His majesty and amass much wonderful knowledge; but does he possess any genuine union with Him if his will is not united with God's? The joining of wills forms the only true union. Consequently, upon receiving life the believer should be attentive not only to his intuition but likewise to his volition.

A FREE WILL

In discussing man and his will we particularly should bear in mind that he exercises a free will. This means that man is sovereign, that he has a sovereign will. What he disapproves of should not be forced on him, what he opposes should not be coerced. Free will signifies that man can choose what he wants. He is not a mechanical toy to be run by others. He is responsible for all his actions; the will within controls all matters both inside and outside him. He is not governed automatically by an external force; rather, he houses a principle within him which determines his acts.

This was the state of man when created by God. The man the Creator fashioned was not something mechanical; for it will be recalled that God said to him: "You may *freely* eat of every tree of the garden; but of the tree of the knowledge of good and evil you shall not eat, for in the day that you eat of it you shall die" (Gen. 2.16-17). How did God command him? God persuaded, prohibited, yet never coerced. If Adam were disposed to listen and not eat the forbidden fruit, it would be *Adam* who so willed. But if he would not listen and would eat, even God would not restrain him. That is free will. God put this responsibility of eating or not eating upon man for him to choose according to his untrammeled will. God did not create an Adam who was incapable of sinning, rebelling or stealing, since to have done so would have been to make man into a piece of machinery. God could advise, prohibit and command; however, the responsibility of hearing or not lay with man. Out of love, God gave the command beforehand; out of righteousness, he would not force man to do what the latter did not wish to do. For man to obey God, it requires a willingness on his part, because God never compels him. He could verily employ sundry means to make man willing; nevertheless, until he gives his consent God will not make His way into the man.

This is an exceedingly vital principle. We shall see later how the Creator never works against this principle, whereas the evil spirits consistently do. By this can we distinguish what is of God and what is not.

THE FALL AND SALVATION

Unfortunately, mankind has fallen. By this plunge man's unfettered volition suffered prodigious damage. We may say that there are two massive contradictory wills throughout the universe. On the one side stands the holy and perfect will of God; on the other is arrayed the defiled, defiling and opposing will of Satan. In between subsists the sovereign, independent, free will of man. When man listens to the devil and rebels against God he seems to render an eternal "no" to God's will and an abiding "yes" to Satan's. Since man employs his volition to choose the will of the devil, his volition falls captive to the devil. Therefore all his acts are governed by Satan's will. Until he overturns his early subjection, man's will remains unquestionably oppressed by the enemy power.

In this fallen position and condition man is fleshly. This flesh—by which his will, together with his other organs, is ruled—is thoroughly corrupted. How can anything pleasing to God ever result from such a darkened will? Even his questing after God springs from the realm of the flesh and therefore lacks any spiritual value. He may invent many ways of worshiping God at this time, yet all are his own ideas, all are "will-worship" (Col. 2.23 ASV), totally unacceptable to Him.

Let us realize, then, that except a man receive God's new life and serve Him therein, every bit of service for God is but the work of the flesh. His intention to serve and even to suffer for Him is vain. Before he is regenerated, his will, even though it may be inclined towards good and God, is futile. For it is not what fallen man intends to do for God but how He Himself wishes man to do for Him that really counts in God's eyes. Man may devise and initiate countless notable works for God; nonetheless, if they do not originate with God they are nothing more than will-worship.

This is true with respect to salvation. When man lives carnally even his desire to be saved is not acceptable to God. We read in the Gospel of John that "to all who received him, who believed in his name, he gave power to become children of God; who were born, not of blood nor of the will of the flesh nor of the *will of man,* but of God" (1.12-13). Man is not regenerated because he wills it so. He must be born of God. Nowadays Christians entertain the incorrect concept that if anyone wishes to be saved and seeks the way of life he undoubtedly will be a good disciple of Christ, for nothing can be better than this desire. God nonetheless affirms that in this matter of regeneration as well as in all other matters related to Him, the will of man is totally nonefficacious.

Many children of God cannot understand why John 1 asserts the will of man to be noneffective whereas Revelation concludes by saying, "Let him who *desires* take the water of life without price" (22.17), as though man himself is entirely responsible for his salvation. And does not the Lord Jesus

Himself give as explanation for the Jews not being saved the following declaration: "You *refuse* to come to me that you may have life" (John 5.40)? Here again, the responsibility for perdition apparently rests on man's will. Can the Bible be contradicting itself? Is there any special meaning behind these apparent inconsistencies? A comprehension of this matter will help us to appreciate what God requires of us in our Christian life.

We will recall that God wishes no one to "perish but that all should reach repentance" because He "desires all men to be saved and to come to the knowledge of the truth" (2 Peter 3.9; 1 Tim. 2.4). No problem arises concerning whom God wants to save or whom He will let perish. The problem before us is, rather, what is the sinner's attitude towards God's will? If he decides to be a Christian because he is naturally inclined towards "religion," naturally contemptuous of the world or naturally influenced by his heredity, environment or family, he is as far from God and His life as are other sinners. If the sinner chooses to be a Christian at the moment of excitement or enthusiasm, he may not fare better than the rest. It all reduces itself to this: what is his attitude towards *God's* will? God loves him, but will he accept this love? Christ calls him, but will he come? The Holy Spirit wants to give him life, but is he willing to be born? His will is useful only in choosing God's will. The question now is, and solely is, how does his volition react towards God's will?

Have we noticed the difference here? If man himself commences the search for salvation, he is yet perishing. Various founders of religions belong to this category. But if man, upon hearing the gospel, is *willing* to accept what God *offers* to him, he shall be saved. In the one case, man originates; in the other, he receives. The one does the willing himself while the other accepts God's will. John 1 speaks of man himself willing, whereas John 5 and Revelation 22 refer to man's *accepting* God's will. Hence no contradiction exists between these two; rather is there a very crucial lesson for us to learn.

God is instructing us that in such a paramount and excellent matter as salvation anything which proceeds from self cannot be accepted but is rejected by Him. Indeed, if we wish to advance in our spiritual development we must understand and bear in mind every vital principle God used in dealing with us at the time of regeneration. These initial principles betoken how we ought to continue in our spiritual life. What we have just now discussed constitutes one of the greatest of these principles. Anything which issues from us, that is from our flesh, is utterly unacceptable to God. Even should we seek such an indispensable and sublime a matter as salvation, our pursuit is nonetheless rejected. What we need unceasingly to remember is that God looks not at the appearance of a thing—whether good or bad, big or small—but looks instead to see whence it originates, from Him or not. In salvation, we are saved not because we want to be saved but because God wants to save us; and so is it to be throughout our lives. We need to see that aside from what God does through us, all other activities, however commendable they may be, are utterly nonefficacious. If we fail to learn this life principle at the initial stage of salvation, we shall encounter endless defeats thereafter.

Moreover, according to the actual condition of man, while he is a sinner his will is rebellious against God. Therefore God must bring men to Himself as well as grant him new life. Now just as the will of man represents the man—for it is the essence of his being, so the divine will personifies God —it being His very life. To say that God will bring man to Himself is to say that He will bring man to His will. No doubt this takes a lifetime to fulfill, but even at the outset of salvation God commences working towards that end. Hence when the Holy Spirit convicts a man of sin, that conviction is such that the man would not have a word to say even should God condemn him to hell. Then when that man is shown by God His definite plan in the cross of Christ he will gladly accept it and express his readiness to receive the salvation of God. Thus do we observe that the first stage of salvation is essentially a salvation of the will. A sinner's faith and acceptance is but his *desire* to take the water of life and be saved. Similarly his opposition and resistance are his *unwillingness* to come to the Lord for life, and accordingly he perishes. The battle whether to be saved or to perish is fought out in the will of man. Man's original fall was due to the rebellion of his will against God's; and so his present salvation is effected by having his volition brought into obedience to God.

Although at the moment of new birth man's will is not yet fully united with God, his fallen will nonetheless is uplifted through his acceptance of the Lord Jesus and his denial of Satan, self, and the world. By believing God's Word and receiving His Spirit, his will is also renewed. After a man is born anew he obtains a new spirit, a new heart, and a new life; his will receives a new master and is henceforth under new management. If his will is obedient it becomes a part of the new life; if it resists, it turns out to be a formidable enemy to the new life.

This renewed will is much more vital than the other parts of the soul. A mind may be misled and emotion can be inordinate, but the will can ill-afford to be wrong. For it to be wrong brings in serious consequences, since it is man's very self and controls all other organs of man. If it is wrong, God's will cannot be realized.

A SUBMISSIVE WILL

What is salvation? It is none other than God saving man out of himself into Himself. Salvation has two facets: a cutting off and a uniting with. What is cut off is self; the uniting is with God. Whatever does not aim at deliverance from self and union with Him is not genuine salvation. Anything which cannot save man from self and join him to God is vanity. A true spiritual beginning involves release from animal life and entry into divine life. Everything belonging to the created one must be relinquished so that the created one will enjoy all things solely in the Creator. The created one must vanish in order that true salvation may be manifested. Real greatness rests not on how much we have but on how much we have lost. Authentic life can be seen only in the abandonment of self. If the nature, life and activities of the created one are not denied, the life of God has no way to express itself. Our "self" is often the enemy of God's life. Our spiritual growth shall be stunted severely if we have no intention nor experience of losing ourselves.

What is self? That is extremely difficult to answer, nor can our answer be fully correct. But were we to say "self" is "self-will," we would not be too far from the mark. Man's essence is in his volition because it expresses what man fundamentally is, desires, and is willing for. Before God's grace has done its work in man all which a man has, whether he be sinner or saint, is generally contrary to God. It is because man belongs to the natural, which is exceedingly antithetical to God's life.

Salvation, then, is to deliver man from his created, natural, animal, fleshly, and self-emanating will. Let us make a special note of this: that aside from God giving us a new life, the turning of our will to Him is the greatest work in salvation. We may even say that God imparts new life in order for us to abandon our will to Him. The gospel is to facilitate the union of our will with God. Anything short of this is failure of the mission. God aims his arrow of salvation not so much at our emotion or our mind but at our will, for once the latter is saved, the rest are included. Man may be united with God in mind to a certain degree; he may agree with Him in his feeling towards numerous things; but the most consequential and most perfect union is that of his will with the divine will. This accord embraces all other unions between God and man. Anything short of the union of wills is inadequate. Since our total being moves according to our will, it is obvious that it constitutes the most influential part of man. Even so noble an organ as the spirit must yield to the rule of the will. (We shall enlarge on this subsequently). The spirit does not symbolize the whole man, for it is but his organ for communication with God. The body cannot stand for man either, because it is only his apparatus by which to communicate with the world. But the will embodies man's authentic attitude, intention and condition. It is the mechanism in him that most nearly corresponds to the man himself. Now unless this will is united with God, all other unions are shallow and empty. Once this ruling will of man is joined completely to God, the man is spontaneously and fully submissive to Him.

Our union with the Lord has two steps: the union of life and the union of will. We are united with Him in life at the time we are regenerated and receive His life. As He lives by His Spirit so shall we thereafter live by the Holy Spirit. This is the bond of life. It indicates we share one life with God. This uniting is an internal one. But what *expresses* that life is the will; consequently there needs to be an external union, one of the will. To be joined with the Lord in will simply denotes that we have one will with Him. These two unions are related, neither is independent of the other. The one of new life is spontaneous, for this new life is the life of God; but the one of will is neither so simple nor spontaneous because our will is clearly our self.

As we have remarked before, God intends to destroy the life of the soul but not its function; so upon being joined with the Lord in life, He launches forth to renew our soul with its various parts in order that our soul may be one with our new life and consequently one with His will. Our will being what it is, God of course daily seeks its union with His will. Salvation cannot be complete until man's will is united entirely with God's. Without that perfect bond *man's self* is yet at odds with Him. He wants us to have His life, but He also wants us to be united with Him. Since our will most closely represents us, our union with Got cannot be complete without the joining of our will to Him.

A careful reading of the Scriptures will yield the fact that a common denominator underlies all our sins: the principle of disobedience. Through Adam's disobedience we perish; through the obedience of Christ we are saved. Formerly we were sons of disobedience; today God wants us to be sons of obedience. Disobedience means to follow one's own will; obedience means to follow God's will. The purpose of divine salvation is to encourage us to deny our will and be united with Him. Right there lies a big mistake among modern Christians. They envisage spirituality to be joyous feeling or profound knowledge. They spend time craving various sensations or questing after mental knowledge of the Bible, for they regard these as highly superior. Meanwhile, acting upon their feelings and thoughts, they go about performing many good, grand and notable tasks which they believe must be quite pleasing to God. They do not comprehend, however, that He asks not how they feel or reason; He only seeks the union of their wills with His. His delight is in having His people desire what He desires and do what He says. Except for a believer's unconditional surrender to God with the believer disposed to accept His will entirely, all else which is labeled spirituality—such as holy and happy feelings or prize-winning thoughts—is but an outward show. Even visions, dreams, voices, sighings, zeal, work, activity, and toil are external. Unless the believer is determined in his volition to finish the course God has set before him, nothing is of any worth.

If we are really united with God in will, we shall cease at once every activity which emerges from ourselves. Hereafter there can be no independent action. We are dead to self but alive to God. No longer do we act for Him under our impulse and according to our way. We act solely after we are moved by God. We are set free from every motion of self. Such union, in other words, is a change of center, a new beginning. In the past all activities focused on self and began with it; today everything is of God. He does not ask the nature of whatever we start; He simply inquires who started it. God discounts every element not yet freed from self, no matter how good it may appear to be.

THE HAND OF GOD

Because many believers are saved but not absolutely yielded to God's will, He uses many ways to effect obedience. He moves His own by His Spirit and touches them with His love that they may obey Him alone, desiring nothing outside His will. But often these do not produce the desired attitude in His children. God consequently must use His hand to lead them to where He desires them to be. His hand is seen primarily in environment. God lays His hand heavily on His people to crush, to break, or to bind—that their wills may be hardened no more against Him.

The Lord is not satisfied until we are thoroughly united with Him in will. To achieve that end He permits many disagreeable things to come to us. He lets us grieve, groan, and suffer. He arranges for many practical crosses to traverse our path that through them we may bow our heads and capitulate. Our volition is naturally exceedingly stubborn; it refuses to obey God until it is heavily disciplined. By submitting ourselves under His mighty hand, willingly accepting His discipline, our will experiences one more cut and is once again delivered to death. And if we continue to resist Him, greater affliction awaits us to bring us into subjection.

God purposes to strip all that is ours away. All believers, after they are truly regenerated, conceive the notion of observing the will of God. Some openly promise such; others secretly entertain this idea. To prove and see whether this promise or thought is real or not, God puts His children through various unpleasant strippings. He causes them to lose material things: health, fame, position, usefulness. What is more, He even causes them to be deprived of joyous feeling, burning desire, the presence and comfort of God. He must show them that everything except His will must be denied. If it is God's will, they should be willing to accept pain and suffering upon their physical bodies. They must be ready to embrace dryness, darkness, and coldness if He seems pleased to so treat them. Even if He should strip them of everything, of even so-called spiritual effectiveness, they must accept it. He wishes His own to know that He saves them not for *their enjoyment* but for His Own will. In gain or loss, joy or sorrow, consciousness of His presence or that of His rejection, Christians must contemplate God's will alone. Suppose it were His will to reject us (which it never is), could we gladly accept rejection? When a sinner first trusts in the Lord his objective is heaven. This is permissible during *that* particular period for him. After he has been taught in God, however, he knows that he has come to believe in Him solely for the sake of His will. Even if, by believing, he were to end up in hell, he would still believe in God. He is no longer mindful of his own gain or loss. If his going to hell would glorify God, he is ready for that. Obviously this is but a hypothetical case. Yet Christians must understand that they live on earth not for themselves but for His will. Their greatest blessing, highest privilege and supreme glory lies in rejecting their corrupt volition of flesh and blood in order that they may be united with God's volition for the accomplishment of His heart's desire. The gain or loss, glory or shame, joy or pain of the created one is nothing to be concerned about. If only the Highest can be satisfied, it matters not to what degree the humble be brought down. This is the only way for believers to lose themselves in God!

TWO MEASURES

Two measures are necessary in being joined to God in will. The first is for God to subdue the activities of our will; the second is to conquer the life of our will. Quite often our volition is subservient to the Lord only in a number of particular matters, which nonetheless prompts us to think that we are fully obedient to Him. Down within us, however, hides a secret tendency which shall rise to the surface when the opportunity is provided. God's intent is not merely to curtail the movement of our will but also to smash its inner tendency so that its very quality seems to be transformed. Strictly speaking, an obedient will and a harmonious one are very different: obedience is related to activity whereas harmony is related to life, nature and tendency. The obedient will of a servant is seen in his executing every order of his master, but the son who knows the father's heart and whose will is one with the father's not only fulfills his duty but fulfills it *with delight* as well. An obedient will puts a stop to one's own activity, yes, but a harmonious will is in addition one heart with God. Only those who are in harmony with Him can actually appreciate his heart. If a person has not arrived at this perfect harmony between his own and God's will, he has yet to experience the summit of spiritual life. To be obedient to the Lord is indeed good, but when grace completely conquers the natural life the Christian will be fully attuned to Him. As a matter of fact, the union of wills is the zenith of anyone's spiritual walk.

Numerous saints conclude they already have lost their wills entirely. Nothing could be farther from reality. When the moment of temptation and trial comes they will discover that an obedient will is not the same as a harmonious one, that nonresistance does not necessarily mean no will of their own self. Who is there who does not care for a little gain, who does not withhold a little something for himself? Who really desires no gold or silver, honor, freedom, joy, advantage, position or whatever? One may think he cares nothing for these items; while he has them he may not be conscious of their hold upon him; but let him be on the verge of losing them, and he shall soon discover how tenaciously he wants to hold on to them. An obedient will may agree with God's will on many occasions, but at some time or other there is bound to be a mighty struggle between the life of the believer's will and the will of God. Unless His grace realizes its fullest work, the saint can hardly overcome.

Obviously from this an obedient will cannot be viewed as perfection. The volition, though broken and deprived of the strength to resist God, has yet to achieve concord with Him. We of course acknowledge that to arrive at the point of being powerless to resist God is itself the fruit of His great grace. And ordinarily we say that an obedient will is already dead in itself. Yet strictly speaking it still possesses a thread of life which is unbroken. There continues to be a hidden tendency, a secret admiring of the former way of life. That is why on certain occasions it finds itself less joyful, less ardent and less diligent in obeying the Lord than at other times. While the will of God is in fact obeyed, there nevertheless remains a difference in personal like and dislike. Had the life of self genuinely and completely been consigned to death, the attitude of the believer towards every part of the will of God would be *exactly the same.* Any disparity in speed, feeling and effort shows a lack of concord in one's will towards God's will.

We may illustrate these two conditions of the will by citing Lot's wife, the Israelites, and the prophet Balaam. The departure from Sodom of the wife of Lot, the exodus of the Israelites from Egypt, and the blessing of Israel by Balaam can all be regarded as obeying the will of God. All these were men and women subdued by the Lord, not following their own opinions; even so, their inward tendencies were not harmonious with Him; hence every one of them ended in failure. How frequently the direction of our footsteps is correct but our secret heart differs with God. And so we ultimately fall.

THE WAY TO SURMOUNT

God never obeys us. He is pleased with nothing but with our obeying Him, that is, obeying his will. However noble, grand and indispensable a thing may be, it cannot be substituted for His will. What He desires us to do is His will. He does it Himself and requires us to do the same. From His view He sees nothing except corruption wherever man's self is present. If acts are performed under the guidance of the Holy Spirit they are good and profitable; but if the same acts are performed by man alone their value is greatly diminished. Consequently the cardinal point is not man's intention nor the nature of the thing, but purely the will of God. This is the first point to keep in mind.

Let us next inquire how man's will can be attuned to God's. How can man effect the transfer from having self-will as his center to having the will of God as his center? It all hinges on the natural life. The measure of our being unshackled from the control of the soul life determines the measure of our union with God, for nothing hinders that union more than the energy of the soul. The more the soul's vitality is crushed the more our will centers on God. The new life in us inclines towards Him, but it is suppressed by the old life of the soul. Committing the soul life to death is therefore the way to mount the peak of spirituality.

The man outside God is lost and the thing outside God is vain. Whatever is outside God comes from the flesh. Any strength or thought other than His is accursed. The believer must deny his own strength as well as his own pleasure. He should disregard himself completely in every respect. Let him do nothing for himself but trust God in all matters. Let him proceed step by step according to His way, waiting for His time, and fulfilling His conditions. Let him receive willingly from God his strength, wisdom, righteousness, and work. Let him acknowledge God as the source of all things. Thus shall harmony be attained.

How this indeed is the "narrow gate" and the hard way! It is narrow and hard because God's will must be the standard for each footstep. It has but one rule: make no provision for self. The least deviation from this rule shall take man out of the way. Nevertheless it is not impossible, for as the soul life is lost by its habits, tastes, desires and longings being gradually broken, there shall remain no more resistance to the Lord. How lamentable that so many Christians have never passed through this gate and walked along this path; while others may have entered, yet do not patiently walk thereafter. Regardless how long or how short that difficult period may be, this alone is the way of life. This is God's gate and God's way. It is true and secure. Anyone who esteems the abundant life must become its pedestrian.

CHAPTER 2
PASSIVITY AND ITS DANGERS

"MY PEOPLE ARE DESTROYED FOR lack of knowledge" (Hos. 4.6) is certainly applicable to our day. Christians nowadays generally are lacking in two kinds of knowledge: (1) a knowledge of the conditions by which evil spirits work; and (2) a knowledge of the principle of spiritual life. Ignorance here is furnishing Satan and his evil spirits an incredible advantage and is inflicting enormous harm on the church of God. What grieves our hearts is that, even as folly is prevailing, Christians continue to boast of their familiarity with the Bible and of the abundance of their experience. They do not realize that their much so-called knowledge is mere human reasoning, quite devoid of usefulness. Humility before the Lord and eagerness in seeking the revelation of God's truths are almost unknown. While boasting in the richness of their knowledge, they themselves sink into the very quicksand from which they can neither extricate themselves nor rescue others. It is indeed a most dreadful scene.

THE LAW OF CAUSE AND EFFECT

For each and every thing God has created there is a law. All actions are governed by laws. Hence evil spirits also operate according to definite laws, one of which is that certain causes will produce certain effects. Now should anyone fulfill the conditions for the working of evil spirits (whether he fulfills them willingly, such as the witch, the medium, or the sorcerer—or unwittingly, such as the Christian), then he has definitely given ground to them to work on him. Notice that the law of cause and effect is involved here. Fire scorches, water drowns: these are laws: none escapes scorching if he falls into fire, nor can any escape drowning if he jumps into water. Likewise everyone who meets the requirements for the operation of evil spirits will be harmed by them. Hence the same law of cause and effect is operative here. It pays no heed to whether one is a Christian or not; once the conditions are met, the evil spirits do not fail to act. Just as a Christian cannot avoid being scorched or drowned if he falls into fire or water, so he cannot escape the danger of being hurt if he ignorantly supplies the prerequisities for the working of evil spirits. The fire scorches everything put into it; the water drowns all who are immersed in it; and evil spirits attack all who give them ground. One will not escape simply because he is a child of God. If he provides the enemy the opportunity, he will not hesitate to assault him. What, then, are the conditions for the working of the enemy? What facilitates this malevolent working? This is the crucial question. The Bible characterizes such conditions as "place" (Eph. 4.27 ASV) or "opportunity" (RSV). It can additionally be denoted as "ground." It means any portion of *empty* space marked off in man for the evil spirits. This place or ground constitutes their foothold. The degree of invasion is determined by the degree of the foothold. The evil spirits will commence to penetrate into any man, be he "heathen" or Christian as soon as he has obtained a footing in him. Whatever affords the evil spirits an opportunity or a foothold by which to attack or invade may be termed as "ground." If ground is given, invasion is unavoidable. The particular cause brings in the particular effect. A Christian who yields ground to evil spirits and yet envisages himself to be beyond attack has been gravely deceived already by the enemy.

Now to put it simply, the ground or territory which the believer furnishes to the evil spirits is sin. Sin includes all the possible grounds. In retaining sin he retains as well the evil spirits that hide behind it. All sin yields territory to them. But there are two kinds of sin, one is positive and the other negative. Positive sins are those which a person commits: his hands perform bad acts, his eyes see evil scenes, his ears hear wicked voices, and his mouth speaks unclean words. These render opportunity to evil spirits in varying degree to take hold of the hands, eyes, ears and mouth of the saint. Whichever part of him sins, that is what invites the enemy to come and occupy it. If occupation stems from *sinning*, the child of God needs to forsake unrelentingly so as to recover the lost territory. Else the evil spirits will increase their hold gradually until the entire person is occupied. *One reason why some who hitherto have accepted the fact of the co-death of the cross find it difficult to lay aside the sin which clings so closely is because aside from the problem of the "flesh" they also have the problem of having been assaulted by supernatural evil powers.*

This kind of positive sin which presents a working opportunity to the evil spirits is by and large understood by most Christians and consequently we shall not enlarge upon it. Let our attention now be focused on the second type, on negative sin. This is largely *mis*understood. Since it is within the scope of the will, we shall discuss it in detail.

The popular notion is that only the positive kind are sins; negative ones are not counted as such. The Bible nonetheless holds that not only all manner of unrighteousness which a man actively *commits* is sin but that "whoever knows what is right to do and fails to do it, for him it is sin" as well (James 4.17). The Word of God treats what man *commits* and what man *omits* both equally as sin. Sin gives footing or ground to the work of evil spirits. And besides the positive sin, the negative kind—that of omission—likewise provides ground for their work.

The particular sin of omission which gives ground to the evil spirits is the believer's passivity. Disuse as well as misuse of any part of one's being is a sin in the sight of God. The Lord endows us with all sorts of abilities none of which are to be misused or go unused. For a person to cease engaging any part of his talent but to allow it to sink into inertia is to provide occasion for the devil and his army to exercise it for him. This is the ground for their sinister operations.

All Christians are aware of sin as a condition for the enemy's assault, but an innumerable number of them are unaware that passivity is also a sin and a condition for his assault. Once place is given, penetration becomes inevitable and sufferings naturally follow.

PASSIVITY

What primarily precipitates the enemy's invasion among the "heathen" and among carnal Christians is willful sin; but "the primary cause of deception ... in surrendered believers may be condensed into one word, passivity; that is, *a cessation of the active exercise of the will in control over spirit, soul and body, or either, as may be the case.*" The organ of volition ceases to choose and decide matters referred to it. "The word passivity simply describes the opposite condition to activity; and in the experience of the believer it means, briefly, (1) loss of self-control—in the sense of the person himself controlling each, or all, of the departments of his personal being; and (2) loss of free-will—in the sense of the person himself exercising his will as the guiding principle of personal control, in harmony with the will of God."* The passivity of a saint arises out of the non-use of his various talents. He has a mouth but refuses to talk because he hopes the Holy Spirit will speak through it. He has hands but will not engage them since he expects God to do it. He does not exercise any part of his person but waits for God to move him. He considers himself fully surrendered to God; so he no longer will *use* any element of his being. Thus he falls into an inertia which opens the way for deception and invasion.

Upon accepting the teaching of their union with God's will, Christians often develop a wrong concept of what this union signifies. They misconstrue it to mean to obey God passively. They think their will must be cancelled out and that they must become puppets. They maintain that they must not employ their own volition any more nor that their

---

*(Mrs.) Jessie Penn-Lewis in collaboration with Evan Roberts, *War on the Saints*, 7th ed. (Bournemouth, England: "Overcomer" Book Room, n.d.), 69, 70. (Hereinafter cited as Penn-Lewis, WOTS)

will should exercise control over any other segment of their body. They no longer choose, decide, or activate with their will. At first it appears to be a great victory, for amazingly "the 'strong-willed' person suddenly becomes passively yielding." (Penn-Lewis, WOTS, 73) He is as weak as water. He holds no opinion on any affair but obeys orders absolutely. He exercises neither mind, nor will, nor even conscience to distinguish between good and evil, for he is a person of perfect obedience. Only when he is moved does he move; a perfect condition (and an invitation too) for the enemy to come in.

By falling into this state of inaction the Christian now ceases from every activity. Indeed, he waits quietly all the time for some external force to activate him. And unless this force compels him to move he shall remain decidedly inert. If such a situation is permitted to continue this one will discover that sometimes when he knows he should act he cannot because the external force has not come upon him. Moreover, even when he wants to act he finds he is unable to do so. Without that outside power he cannot move a step. His will is suppressed and he is bound; he can move only after that alien force has come to move him.

THE BELIEVER'S FOLLY

The evil spirits take advantage of one's inactive state to accomplish their wiles, while he himself persists in esteeming such inertia as real obedience to God and perfect union with His will. He does not realize that God never demands passivity; it is the powers of darkness which have propelled him into this state. Furthermore, God wants His own to exercise their wills actively to cooperate with Him. This is what is implied in such Scriptures verses as: "if any man's *will* is to do his will, he shall know . . ." (John 7.17) and "ask whatever you *will*, and it shall be done for you" (John 15.7). God never disregards our volition.

We human beings enjoy a free will. God never encroaches on that will. While He does expect us to obey Him, He nevertheless respects our personality (note: the word "personality" as employed in this book has always had in view the person of man, not his character). He wishes us to desire what He desires. He will not usurp our desiring and reduce our volition to deathly inactivity. He needs our most positive cooperation. His pleasure is in the created one reaching his summit, that is, perfect freedom of will. In creation God ordains man to an unfettered will; in redemption He recovers that will. Since He did not *create* man to obey mechanically, how could He expect *redeemed* man to be a robot acting under His remote control direction? The greatness of God is certainly manifested in His not requiring us to turn into wood and stone that we might be obedient. His way is to make us obey Him willingly through the working of His Spirit in our spirit. He refuses to will in place of us.

In a word, the *law* that governs the working of God and the working of Satan in man is exactly the same. God delights in seeing man have free will, so He creates him with such a capacity. It means that humanity has the power to choose and decide all matters concerned. Though God is the Lord of the entire universe, yet is He willing to be restricted by a non-encroachment on man's free will. He never forces man to be loyal to Him. And Satan likewise is unable to usurp any part of man without the latter's *consent* granted either knowingly or unknowingly. Both God and the devil require man to be persuaded before operating in him. When man "desires" good, God will accomplish it; but when he "desires" evil, the wicked spirit will fulfill it. This is what we see in the Garden of Eden.

Before regeneration man's volition was enslaved to Satan and therefore not free. But in a regenerated and overcoming Christian the volition is free and therefore able to choose what is of God. Naturally Satan will not let go, so he devises sundry ways to recapture him. He is fully cognizant that he shall never secure permission openly; hence he uses wiles to obtain the necessary consent. Now mark this well: Satan must gain the believer's permission but the latter will never yield it to Satan; the devil is therefore compelled to resort to deception in order to extract this consent from him.

The evil spirits cannot enter without the acquiescence of man's will and they can penetrate only as far as his will approves.

If the believer knows the principle of spiritual life as well as the conditions for the working of evil spirits he will not fall into such danger. It is because he is unconscious both of the advantage the adversary secures through inertia and of the necessity (in spiritual life) of an active will cooperating with God that he allows his volition to be passive. What we must remember always is that God never substitutes His will for man's. Man himself must be responsible for what he does. God does not decide for him.

If the evil spirits do not operate in some passive persons, then most likely the passivity of these individuals in fact amounts to nothing more than laziness or inactivity. Usually those who are inactive in this way (that is, without the working of the evil spirit) *can* become active at any time. However, if they plunge into such a passivity as to be occupied, then they will be unable to be active even if their will *should* desire it.

Here then is the antithesis between the working of God and the working of Satan. Though God wants man to be yielded completely to Him, He also wants him to use every talent he possesses in cooperation with the Holy Spirit. Satan, on the other hand, demands total cessation of man's will and actions that his evil spirits may operate in his stead. The contrast is truly sobering: God calls man to choose actively, consciously and willingly to do His will so that his spirit, soul, and body may be free; Satan coerces him to be his passive slave and captive: God appoints man to be autonomous, free to be his own master; Satan forces man to be his puppet, a marionette altogether manipulated by him: God never requires man to cease his activities before He can work; Satan bids man to be utterly passive and inactive: God asks man to work together with Him consciously; Satan charges man to obey him passively. It is true that God does require man to cease from his every sinful activity without which he cannot cooperate with the Holy Spirit; but

Satan compels him to cease *all* his activities, including the functioning of his soul, so that his minions can act in place of man. Man is thus reduced to a mere piece of machinery without any conscious responsibility.

It is a terrible circumstance that Christians do not know the fact of God's living in them and the principle of His working in them. They think He wants them to be like pawns on a chessboard that He may maneuver them around as He pleases. They feel they must be absolutely passive, possessing no power to choose or decide, but just to be managed insensibly by God. They forget that when God first created man He made him with a free will. God obviously is not pleased if man wills things other than Himself, but neither is He pleased if man were to obey Him mechanically and unconsciously. He is satisfied when a person wills what He wills, and never wants him to become a will-less person. Many matters must be executed by believers *themselves;* God will not do these for them. It is taught that we must hand everything over to God and let Him do it instead of us—that we must not lift our hands nor move our feet—that we must be so surrendered to the indwelling Holy Spirit that He can arrange everything in lieu of ourselves—that we must let God move us. We grant there is some truth in such teaching but the error therein mixed is perhaps more potent than is the truth. (We shall speak more on this point in the next chapter.)

THE DANGERS

A Christian in his ignorance may be deceived by the powers of darkness, may unwittingly tumble into the trap of Satan, and fulfill the conditions for his working. Let us observe the order of this process, for it is highly important: (1) ignorance, (2) deception, (3) passivity, and (4) entrenchment. Ignorance is the primary cause of this process. Satan can deceive because the saint is unfamiliar both with the demand of the Holy Spirit and the principle of satanic working. Were Christians to apprise themselves of how to cooperate with God and what His procedure of working is, they would never accept Satan's deception. But once deceived, they surmise that for God to live and work through them means for them to remain passive; and so they accept as being from God many supernatural manifestations from evil spirits. The deception grows deeper, finally resulting in an entrenchment of alarming proportions.

It is a vicious cycle: each time ground is given, the evil spirits are encouraged to come in; upon entering, they manifest themselves through sundry activities; and if the believer misinterprets these activities, not knowing that they originate with the devil, he will cede even more place to the evil spirits since he has believed already in their lies. This cycle goes round and round, daily augmenting the degree of penetration. Once he descends into passivity by furnishing a foothold to evil spirits, the dangers can easily multiply.

After one has slipped into inertia and ceases to choose for himself, he will passively succumb to whatever circumstance comes to him. He assumes that it is God Who now is deciding everything for him; all that is therefore required of him is but to passively submit. Whatever happens to him is given and arranged by God; it is His will, hence he must silently accept all things. Shortly afterwards the believer loses all power of choice in his daily life; he can neither decide nor initiate anything which falls within his duty. In addition, he is afraid to express his opinions and is even more unwilling to divulge his preference. And so others must choose and determine for him. Such a victim of the enemy is like seaweed adrift in the ocean waves. He very much hopes that others will decide for him or that his environment will be such that only one alternative is open for him to follow, thus relieving him from the responsibility of having to make a decision. He seems to be happy when forced to do anything, for this keeps him from anxiety which would arise from indecision. He would rather be driven by circumstance than be free to choose his circumstance since making a choice is so trying for him.

In such a condition of inertia, to decide a small matter becomes a tremendous chore! The victim looks for help everywhere. He feels quite embarrassed because he does not know how to cope with his daily affairs. He seems hardly to understand what people say to him. Painful is it for him to recall anything; agonizing is it to make a decision; terrifying, to consider any task. His inert will is impotent to bear such a heavy responsibility. Because of its gross weakness he is compelled to wait for assistance through environment or through men. If he is helped by any particular person he rejoices in receiving such help, yet resents beholding the capture of his will. Who can tally up the hours consumed in waiting for outside aid? Are we suggesting that such a passive believer does not like to work? Not at all; for when compelled by an external force he is able to work; but just have the compulsion terminate and he will halt right in the middle of his labor, feeling himself insufficient in strength to carry on. Innumerable unfinished jobs form the sad testimonials of a passive will.

How inconvenient must this state of inaction be! A believer has to rely on multiplied notes to help him remember; he has to talk aloud to concentrate; he has to devise hundreds of "crutches" to assist him along in life. His senses gradually grow dull until finally he unconsciously develops many idiosyncrasies and queer habits such as not looking straight while talking, bending while walking, exercising little or no mind in any undertaking, either attending too much to physical needs or excessively suppressing bodily requirements, and so forth.

In his foolishness the Christian does not perceive that all these symptoms flow from passivity and invasion but instead believes that they are merely his natural weaknesses. He comforts himself with the thought that these are not too surprising since he is not as gifted or well-endowed as others. He fails to discern the lies of the evil spirits and allows himself to be further deceived. He dare not undertake any task nor do any work because he is so afraid, so nervous, so inarticulate, so dull in mind, or so weak in body. He has never examined why other believers fare so differently. People less talented than he can do far more. And even he himself was much better before. How then can he attribute these symptoms to heredity, natural temperament, and so forth? Know that these are caused by the evil spirits whether one perceives it or not.

Being well acquainted with the believer's current condition, the powers of darkness will foment many troubles in his environment to disturb him. Because his will is passive already and powerless to work, the evil spirits usually will maneuver him into a situation where the exercise of volition is necessary so as to embarrass him and subject him to derision. During such a time, the victim is being harassed by the evil spirits as they please, just like a caged bird that is teased at will by naughty boys. They instigate many difficulties that these may wear out the saint. How distressing that he has not the strength to protest and resist. His circumstances wax worse. He has the authority to deal with the evil spirits, yet he cannot utter a word. The powers of darkness have gained the upper hand, all because their victim has fallen from ignorance to deception, from deception to passivity, and from passivity to the sufferings of deep entrenchment. Nevertheless, he has not yet discerned that such a situation has not been given by God; and so he continues on in his passive acceptance.

When the Christian has sunk into such a state he unconsciously *may even rely upon the help of the evil spirits*. He cannot will anything by himself, hence looks for outside forces to help him. He is troubled often by the evil spirits, yet he innocently expects these same spirits to come to his aid. This is the reason why they desire to make him passive. Holding in their hands the various talents that a believer possesses, they are able to express themselves whenever these talents are exercised. They like to do the willing in place of the person. And the evil spirits certainly are not going to hesitate to exert themselves wherever they are so welcomed. They delight in enticing a person to follow outside revelation blindly without using either thought or will; they therefore often impart a host of strange and supernatural phenomena to men.

The Christian, unaware of the principle of God's working, assumes he is being obedient to *God* when actually he is a prey to deception. Let us be advised of this verse in Romans 6: "Do you not know that if you yield yourselves to anyone as obedient slaves, you are slaves of the one whom you obey . . .?" (v.16) If we offer ourselves in name to God but in actual practice are yielding to the evil spirits we cannot escape being the latter's slave. True, we are deceived; even so, we have yielded openly to the false one and are consequently responsible. The Christian should realize that if he does not commune with God in accordance with the proper conditions for divine fellowship but instead fulfills the requirements for the working of the evil spirits, he will then be enslaved by them.

We ought to review one final time this process culminating in entrenchment. As a person is coveting the physical sensations of God's presence and other similar experiences (as earlier described in Parts Three and Seven) he may be deceived by evil spirits and accorded many counterfeit workings. He naïvely accepts these as from God and accordingly gets himself into a state of passivity. He concludes that he must not make any move, for is it not God Who will move him? He terminates all actions, believing God will act in place of him. But God never does so because He wants man to cooperate actively with Him. However, the believer unwittingly has fulfilled the conditions for the operations of the evil spirits and they do not hesitate to step in and act. Man himself does not act, neither does God act, so the evil spirits act for him. Let the Christian mark this well that once he has perceived the will of God in his spirit's intuition his whole being needs to be employed actively in executing God's will. He should not be passive.

CHAPTER 3
THE BELIEVER'S MISTAKE

We must not fall under the misapprehension that those believers who are deceived by evil spirits must be the most defiled, degenerate, and sinful. They are on the contrary oftentimes fully surrendered Christians spiritually more advanced than ordinary believers. They strive to obey God and are willing to pay any cost. Unwittingly do they stumble into passivity because of the fact that although they are wholly consecrated they know not how to cooperate with God. Those who are less serious about spiritual matters do not face the danger of passivity, for how could anyone sink into inactivity and eventually into the grip of the enemy when, though professing to be utterly consecrated, he persists in living according to his own ideas? He might give ground to evil spirits in other respects but certainly not in the matter of yielding to God's will by delivering a passive ground to the enemy. Only those committed ones who disregard their own interests are open to passivity. Their will can easily slip into this state since they are most eager to obey all orders.

Many will wonder why God does not protect them. Is not their motive pure? How can God permit such faithful seekers of His to be deceived by evil spirits? Many people will contend that He ought to safeguard His Own children under any circumstance; they do not realize that to enjoy God's protection one must fulfill His conditions for protection. Should a person fulfill the conditions for the working of the evil spirits God cannot forbid the latter to work, for He is a law-abiding One. Because the Christian intentionally or unintentionally has surrendered himself to the evil spirits God will not hinder them from the right to control that one. How many hold to the idea that a pure motive safeguards them from deception! Little do they realize that the people most deceived in the world are those with good intentions. Honesty is no condition for not being deceived; but *knowledge* is. Should the believer neglect the teaching of the Bible, failing to watch and pray even though trusting his pure motive to keep him from deception, he shall be deceived. How can he expect God to protect him when he is providing the prerequisites for the working of evil spirits?

Countless saints consider themselves beyond deception because they have had frequent spiritual experiences. This very element of self-confidence betrays the deception they are in already. Unless they are humble enough to acknowledge the possibility of being deceived, they shall be deceived perpetually. Deception is neither a matter of life nor of intention but one of knowledge. It is difficult for the Holy Spirit to point out the truth to that person who has absorbed too many idealistic teachings in the early stages of his Christian experience. Equally hard is it for others to supply him with necessary light if he already has developed a prejudiced interpretation of the Scriptures. The danger of such false security is to give opportunity for the evil spirits to work or to continue to work.

We saw earlier how ignorance is the cause of passivity and passivity, the cause of entrenchment. The latter condition would never occur if a Christian had the right knowledge. Actually passivity is a *mistaken* obedience or consecration. It may additionally be said to be an *excessive* obedience or consecration. Had he recognized how the evil spirits require man's inertia for their working he would not have allowed himself to descend into passivity. Had he realized that God does not reduce man to a marionette in order to work, then he would not wait passively to be moved. Ignorance accounts for today's tragic plight among the saints.

A Christian requires knowledge in order to distinguish God's working from that of Satan's. He should know the principle of divine operation as well as the condition for satanic operation. He who possesses such knowledge guards himself from the powers of darkness. Since Satan assails the believer with lies, he must be met with the truth. Because he intends to keep the believer in darkness, he must be countered with light. Let us learn by heart that the principle governing the working of the Holy Spirit and that of the evil spirit are diametrically opposite. Let us also remember that each operates *according to his respective principle*. Although the evil spirits are skillful in a variety of camouflages, their working principle remains the same. By examining the inward principles we are able to differentiate what is of the Holy Spirit from what is of the evil spirit, for each invariably acts in accordance with his particular principle.

Let us now consider in some detail a number of erroneous conceptions which Christians more than not commonly hold.

A MISTAKEN NOTION CONCERNING CO-DEATH WITH CHRIST

The conditions for passivity in a believer may come about through a wrong interpretation concerning the truth of "death with Christ." Paul says that "I have been crucified with Christ; it is no longer I who live, but Christ who lives in me; and the life I now live in the flesh I live by faith in the Son of God, who loved me and gave himself for me" (Gal. 2.20). Some misconstrue this to connote self-effacement. What they deem to be the summit of spiritual life is "a loss of personality, an absence of volition and self control, and the passive letting-go of the 'I myself' into a condition of machine-like, mechanical, automatic 'obedience'." (Penn-Lewis, WOTS, 86)* They thereafter must harbor no feelings; they should instead renounce all consciousness of personal wishes, interests and tastes. They must aim at self-annihilation, reducing themselves to corpses. Their personality must be totally eclipsed. They misapprehend the command of God to mean a demand for their self-effacement, self-renunciation and self-annihilation so they may no longer

---

*See previous Chapter for full bibliographical citation.

be aware of themselves or their needs but may be conscious only of the movement and operation of God in them. Their misconception about being "dead to self" means for them the absence of self-consciousness. So they endlessly deliver their self-consciousness to nought till they sense nothing but the presence of God. Under this mistaken notion they assume they must practice death; on each occasion therefore when they become aware of "self" or are conscious of personal wants, lacks, needs, interests or preferences they consistently consign these to death.

Since "I have been crucified with Christ," they argue, then *I* no longer exist. And since it is "Christ who lives in me," then *I* no longer live. *I* having died, I must practice death—that is, I must not harbor any thought or feeling. Because Christ is alive within me, He will think or feel in my place. My personality is annihilated, therefore I will obey Him passively, permitting Him to think or feel for me. Unfortunately these people overlook what Paul further said about "the life I now live in the flesh." Paul died, and yet he has not died! This "I" has been crucified, nevertheless "I" still lives in the flesh. Paul, upon having passed through the cross, still declares of himself that "I now live"!

This confirms that the cross does not annihilate our "I"; it exists forever. It is "I" who will one day go to heaven. How can salvation ever benefit *me* if somebody else goes instead of me? The true purport of our accepting co-death with Christ is that we are dead to sin and that we deliver our soul life to death; even the most excellent, most righteous and most virtuous soul life we deliver to death. God beckons us to deny the desire to live by our natural power and to live instead by Him, leaning upon His vitality moment by moment for the supply of every need. This does not in anyway imply that we are to destroy our various functions and settle into passivity. Quite the reverse is true: such a walk with God requires us to exercise our will daily in an active, consistent and believing manner for the denial of our own natural energy and the appropriation of divine energy. Just as neither the death of today's physical body means annihilation nor the death of the lake of fire suggests extermination, so co-death with Christ in the spirit cannot denote effacement. Man as a person must exist; his will must continue: only his natural life must die. This is the teaching of the Holy Scriptures.

The consequences of a misconception of the truth such as this are (1) the believer himself ceases to be active; (2) God cannot use him because he has violated His operating principle; therefore (3) the evil spirits seize the opportunity to invade him since he unwittingly has fulfilled the prerequisites for their working. Due to his misinterpretation of the truth, and his practicing of death, he becomes a tool of the enemy who has disguised himself as God. Alas and alack, this misapprehension of the teaching connected with Galatians 2 has come to be in many cases the prelude to deception.

After such a "death" as this the individual is deprived of any feeling. He cannot feel for himself, nor can he feel for others. He gives those around him the impression of being like iron and stone, utterly devoid of feeling. He does not sense the suffering in others nor is he sensitive to how much pain he has given people himself. He has no ability to sense, to distinguish or to discern things within or without. This person is totally unaware of his own manner, attitude, and action. He speaks and acts without exercising his will and knows not from whence his words, thoughts and feelings originate. Without having made any decision through his own volition these words and feelings nonetheless flow like a river. All his actions are mechanical; no knowledge has he of their sources; he is only spurred on by an alien power. Strange to say, however, unconscious of self as he is, yet is he most sensitive to the treatment accorded him by others. He tends to misunderstand and hence to suffer. In any case, this "unconsciousness" forms both the condition and the consequence of the enemy's penetration. By it the evil spirits are enabled to work, to attack, to suggest, to think, to press or to suppress without the slightest resistance from the believer who is completely unaware of anything.

Let us consequently keep in mind that what people commonly term "death to self" in essence signifies death to the life, power, exercise and activity of self; in no way does it refer to the death of one's personality. We must not efface ourselves and render our personalities non-existent. This is a distinction we must comprehend. When we say without self, we mean without any self-activity, not without self-existence! If a Christian accepts the interpretation which envisages a loss of personality and refuses to think, feel or move, he shall live as one in a dream. Though he conceives himself to be truly dead, entirely selfless, and intensely spiritual, his consecration is not towards God but is as to the evil spirits.

GOD'S WORKING

Another text easily mishandled is Philippians 2.13: "it is God who worketh in you both to will and to work, for his good pleasure" (ASV). To some this passage seems to teach that God performs both the willing and the working; that is, that He puts into His child what He has willed and worked. Since God wills and works instead of him, he himself need not do so. The believer has become a kind of superior creature having no need to will and to do work now that God has done so for him. He is like a mechanical toy which exercises no responsibility of its own to will and do. These saints do not see that the correct substance of this verse is that God works in us up to the point of our readiness to will and to work. He undertakes only to that point and no farther. He never wills or acts in place of man. He merely endeavors to bring man to the position of being disposed to will and to do His excellent will.

Man himself must perform the willing and the working. The Apostle carefully states, "*you* both to will and to work" —not God wills and works, but *you;* your personality continues to exist and hence you yourself must will and act because the responsibility is yours. God is indeed at work, but never does He substitute Himself for us. To choose and to do belong to the man. God wants to move us, melt us and encourage us, so that our hearts may bend towards His will, yet he does not will instead of us to do His will. He turns us towards His desire, then leaves us to make up our will. What the Word teaches here is that one's volition requires the support of God's power. How ineffectual and fruitless are deeds done according to one's own volition apart from Him. God does not will in man's stead, but neither does He desire man to will independently. He calls him to will in His power, which is to say, to will according to His working in man.

Not comprehending the correct meaning of this passage the believer surmises that he need not will. He thus allows another volition to control his being. He dare not decide any issue, choose any action, or even resist any power, but passively waits for the will of God to come to him. When an external volition decides for him he passively accepts it. He quenches whatever proceeds from his own volition. And the result: neither he himself uses his volition nor God uses it to choose and decide for him, since He requires active cooperation. But the evil spirits seize his passive will and act instead of him.

We need to see the difference between God willing for us and our volition cooperating with God. If He were to choose and decide *in lieu* of us we would have no real connection with the act or deed done because our hearts would not have been exercised towards it. And when we come to ourselves afterwards we would know that it was not done by *us*. But if we exercise our volition and actively cooperate with God, *we* undertake to do the thing ourselves though in the divine power. A person under deception may consider himself the doer, speaker and thinker, but when enlightened by God he realizes he does not really want to so do, speak and think. He knows he has no connection with these acts because they were performed by the enemy.

It is not God's purpose to annihilate our volition. If we say we henceforth shall have no volition of our own but shall let His will be manifested in our body we have not offered ourselves to God; instead, we have covenanted with the evil spirit since God never substitutes His will for ours. The right attitude is this: that I have my own will, yet I will the will of God. We should put our volition on His side—and even this is to be done not by our own strength but by the life of God. The truth of the whole matter is that the life which formerly energized our volition has now been committed to death so that now we engage our volition in the energizing life of God. We do not eliminate our will; it is still there; only the life has changed. What has died is our own life; the function of the will continues although renewed by God. Hereafter the volition is energized by the new life.

THE WORK OF THE HOLY SPIRIT

Those believers are numberless who have plunged into passivity and enslavement because of not understanding the work of the Holy Spirit. What follows are some of the most common misunderstandings.

1. *Obey the Holy Spirit.* Believers think Acts 5.32 suggests that they must obey the Holy Spirit—"the Holy Spirit whom God has given to those who obey him." But they fail, according to the command given in the Bible, to test all the spirits to see if they are of truth or of error (1 John 4.1,6). They instead accept as being the Holy Spirit every spirit which comes to them. They think this obedience must be highly pleasing to God. What they do not know is that the Scripture here does not teach us to obey the Holy Spirit but to obey God the Father through the Spirit. In verse 29 of Acts 5 the Apostles when under questioning by the council replied that they "must obey *God.*" Should anyone make God the Spirit his object of obedience and forget God the Father he tends to obey the spirit in him or around him instead of obeying through the Holy Spirit the Father Who is in heaven. This will set him on the road to passivity and in addition provide the evil spirits the chance for counterfeit. Overstepping the bounds of the Word of God ushers in countless perils!

2. *The Rule of the Holy Spirit.* We will recall from our past discussion how God rules our spirit through the Holy

Spirit and how our spirit rules our body or the entire person through the soul (or will). This may sound simple, yet the spiritual implication is enormous. The Holy Spirit influences our intuition alone to make His will known. Only our spirit does he fill and nowhere else. *Never does He control or fill our soul or body directly.* This point should be carefully underscored. We should *not* therefore expect God's Spirit to think through our mind, feel through our emotion, or decide through our volition. He makes His will known to our spirit's intuition in order that we ourselves may think and feel and act according to His will. It is a grave blunder to think we must offer our mind to the Holy Spirit to let Him think through it. The truth is He never uses man's mind directly instead of man. He never asks him to offer himself passively to Him. What God wishes is cooperation with him. He does not work for man, because even His movement in working for him could be quenched by the believer. He never forces anyone to do anything.

The divine Spirit does not directly control man's body either. If man desires to speak he has to engage his *own* mouth—to walk, his *own* feet—to work, his *own* hands. The Spirit of God never interferes with man's freedom of will. Aside from working in man's spirit (which is God's new creation), He does not use any part of man's body apart from the consent of the latter's own volition; nay, even if man is willing, He does not exercise any of his bodily parts for him. Man should be his own master. He must exercise his own body. This is God's law which He will not violate.

We often say that "the Holy Spirit rules over man." By this we mean He works in us to make us obedient to God. But if we should mean that He directly controls our total being we are in complete error. We can distinguish right here between the work of the Holy Spirit and that of evil spirits. The Holy Spirit indwells us to witness that *we belong to God* whereas evil spirits manipulate people to reduce them to robots. God's Spirit asks for our cooperation; evil spirits seek direct control. Hence it is plain that our union with God is in the spirit and not in the body or soul. Should we misunderstand the truth and expect God to move our mind, emotion, volition, and body directly, we open wide the door to the counterfeit of evil spirits. While a Christian should not follow his own thought, feeling or preference, nevertheless after he has received revelation in his spirit he ought to *execute* with his mind, emotion and will this charge which has come to his spirit.

SPIRITUAL LIFE

Among the various misconceptions relating to spiritual life can be found the following.

1. *Speaking.* The text used is Matthew 10.20: "it is not you who speak, but the Spirit of your Father speaking through you." Christians often assume that God will speak for them. Some imagine that while delivering a message in a meeting they must not employ their mind and will but simply offer their mouths passively to God, letting Him speak through them. Needless to say, however, the words of Jesus recorded in this particular passage are to be applied only to the time of persecution and trial. It does not suggest that the Holy Spirit will speak instead of the believer. The experience of the Apostles Peter and John in the council fulfills this prediction.

2. *Guidance.* Text: "And your ears shall hear a word behind you, saying, 'This is the way, walk in it' " (Is. 30.21). Saints do not perceive that this verse refers specifically to the experience of God's earthly people, the Jews, during the millennial kingdom when there shall be no satanic counterfeit. Unaware of this fact they view supernatural guidance in a voice to be the highest form of guidance. They esteem themselves more spiritual than the rest and hence receive supernatural guidance of this type. They neither listen to their conscience nor follow their intuition; they merely wait in a passive manner for the supernatural voice. These believers hold that they do not need to think, ponder, choose or decide. They simply need to obey. They permit the voice to be substituted for their intuition and conscience. And the consequence is that "(a) he does not use his conscience; (b)

God does not speak to him for automatic obedience; (c) evil spirits take the opportunity and supernatural voices are substituted for the action of the conscience." (Penn-Lewis, WOTS, 121) The outcome is that the enemy gains more ground in the believer. And "from this time (forward) the man is not influenced by what he feels or sees, or by what others say, and he closes himself to all questions, and will not reason. This substitution of supernatural guidance for the action of the conscience explains the deterioration of the moral standard in persons with supernatural experiences, because they have really substituted the direction of evil spirits for their conscience. They are quite unconscious that their moral standard is lowered, but their conscience has become seared by deliberately ceasing to heed its voice; and by listening to the voices of the teaching spirits, in matters which should be decided by the conscience in respect to their being right or wrong, good or evil." (Penn-Lewis, WOTS, 121-22)

3. *Memory*. Text: "But the Counselor, the Holy Spirit, whom the Father will send in my name, he will teach you all things, and bring to your remembrance all that I have said to you" (John 14.26). Christians do not grasp that this verse means the Counselor will enlighten their mind so that *they* may remember what the Lord has spoken. They instead think it instructs them not to engage their memory because God shall bring all things to their minds. They accordingly allow their memory to degenerate into passivity; they do not exercise their wills to remember. And what is the outcome?— "(a) the man himself does not use his memory; and (b) God does not use it, because He will not do so apart from the believer's co-action; (c) evil spirits use it, and substitute their workings in the place of the believer's volitional use of his memory." (Penn-Lewis, WOTS, 121)

4. *Love*. Text: "God's love has been poured into our hearts through the Holy Spirit which has been given to us" (Rom. 5.5). Believers misconstrue this to signify that they are not themselves to love but to let the Holy Spirit dispense God's love to them. They petition God to love through them

that His love may be supplied abundantly so as to fill them with divine love. They no longer will love for hereafter it is God Who must make them love. They cease to exercise their faculty of affection, permitting its function to sink into total paralysis. With the result that (a) the believer himself does not love; (b) God will not bestow supernatural love upon him in disregard of the man or the operation of his natural affection; and so (c) evil spirits substitute themselves for the man and express their love or hate through him. And once he has abandoned the use of his will to control his affection the evil spirits put their counterfeit love in him. Thereafter he behaves like wood and stone, cold and dead to all affections. This explains why many saints, though holy, are scarcely approachable.

"You shall love the Lord your God with all your heart, and with all your soul, and with all your mind, and with all your strength," says the Lord Jesus (Mark 12.30). Now *whose* love is this? Exactly whose heart, soul, mind and strength is brought into view here? It is of course ours. Our natural life needs to die, but these natural endowments and their functions remain.

5. *Humility*. Text: "Not that we venture to class or compare ourselves with some of those who commend themselves" (2 Cor. 10.12 ff.). Believers misjudge this long passage from verse 12 to 18 as signifying a call to hide themselves to the extent that they are left without a proper self-regard, one which God unquestionably permits us to have. Not a few instances of self-abasement are essentially a disguise for passivity. Consequently: (a) the believer effaces himself; (b) God does not fill him; and (c) evil spirits exploit his passivity to render him useless.

When the Christian is self-abased under the enemy's penetration his surroundings appear entirely dark, hopeless and desolate to him. He gives the impression of being deadly cold and dishearteningly melancholic to all who are in contact with him. He himself easily faints and is discouraged. At critical moments he deserts the fight and withdraws, thus embarrassing others. God's work is not too important to him.

In speech and work he tries hard to hide himself, but this only manifests his self the more—to the great sorrow of the truly spiritual. Due to his excessive disregard for himself he stands by watching when there is such great need in the kingdom of God. He exhibits perpetual inability, hopelessness, and wounded feelings. While he may envisage this to be humility he does not realize it is but the work of the evil spirits. True humility is able to look at God and proceed on.

GOD'S ORDERING

We know that besides man's will there are two other totally antagonistic wills in the world. God calls us to obey Him and to resist Satan. Twice in the Bible do we find these two sides mentioned together: (1) "submit yourselves therefore to God," exhorts James, and then he follows immediately with "resist the devil" (4.7); (2) "humble yourselves therefore under the mighty hand of God," enjoins Peter, and continues by charging his readers to "resist (the devil), firm in your faith" (1 Peter 5.6,9). This is the balance of truth. A believer certainly must learn to submit himself to God in all matters, acknowledging that what He orders for him is the best. Though he suffers, yet he heartily submits to the will of God. This, however, is just *half* the truth. The Apostles understood the danger of being lopsided; hence we find them right away warning the Christian to resist the devil once he submits to God. This is because there is another will besides His, that of Satan's. Frequently the devil counterfeits the will of God, especially in the things which happen to us. If we are unaware of the presence of a will other than God's, we can easily mistake Satan's to be God's and so fall into the devil's trap. For this reason God wants us to resist the devil when we submit to Him. Resistance is done by the *will*. Resistance means our volition opposes, disapproves, and withstands. God wishes us to exercise our volition, therefore He exhorts us to "resist the devil." He will not resist for us; we ourselves must do so. We have a will; we should use it to take heed to God's Word. So teaches the Bible. Thinking that God's will is revealed in His orderings, the Christian may accept anything which comes to him as His will. In that event he naturally will not employ his volition to choose, decide or resist. He just quietly accepts everything. This sounds good and appears right, but it contains a serious fallacy.

Now we do acknowledge the hand of God behind everything, and we do confess we must submit fully under His hand. But the point at issue here is more one of attitude than of conduct. If what happens to us is the direct will of God, would we object to it? This is a matter of our heart intention. But after we are assured of our obedience to God we should inquire further: does this emanate from the evil spirit or is it but God's permissive will? If it is His commanded will, we have no objection; if otherwise, we will resist it together with God. Hence this never implies that we should submit to our environment without daily examination and testing. Our *attitude* remains the same at all times but our *practice* comes only after we are sure of God's will, for how could we submit to Satan's will?

A Christian ought not act as one who is without a brain, passively driven by his environment. He actively and consciously should examine the source of every item, test its nature, understand its meaning, and decide the course to take. It is important to obey God, but not blindly. Such active investigation is not a sign of rebellion against God's ordering, because our heart's intent continues to be one of submission towards God. We only wish to be sure that in our submission we are verily obeying *God*. A definite lack in an obedient attitude exists among believers today. Though they perceive God's will, they nevertheless fail to yield. Contrariwise, those who have been broken by God run to the other extreme by unquestioningly accepting whatever occurs to them. The truth lies in the center; *obey* in heart and *accept* after being assured of the source.

How sad, though, that many fully consecrated believers do not discern this difference. Such a Christian therefore passively submits to his environment, surmising that *everything* happens to him by the order of God. He gives ground to the evil spirits to torment and hurt him. These spirits provide environment (their snares) by which to trap the saint into performing their will or raise up circumstances to trouble him. Believers may misunderstand this to be what Matthew 5.39 enjoins when it says "do not resist one who is evil," not recalling that God summons them to struggle against sin (Heb. 12.4). By overcoming environment they are ovecoming the spirit of this world.

The factors in such a misapprehension of God's ordering are that (a) believers do not use their will to choose and decide; (b) God certainly does not oppress them with environment; and (c) the evil spirits utilize the environmental circumstances as a substitute for their passive will. Rather than obeying God these believers actually are obeying the evil spirits.

SUFFERINGS AND WEAKNESSES

Having fully surrendered to God the Christian naturally concedes that he should walk in the way of the cross and suffer for Christ's sake. He additionally acknowledges the futility of his natural life and is willing to be weak in order that he may be strengthened by the power of God. These two attitudes are commendable but they can be utilized by the enemy if they are not rightly understood.

Having recognized that there is something of great profit in suffering, the Christian following consecration may submit passively to whatever comes to him without question. He simply believes he is suffering for the Lord and that therefore it is both profitable and rewarding. Little does he understand that, unless he intentionally exercises his will both to accept what God allots and to resist what the enemy dispenses, his passive acceptance of *all* suffering will surely afford an excellent opportunity to the evil spirit to torment him. Suffering at the hand of the evil spirit while believing the satanic lie that his suffering emanates from God merely gives the enemy the right to prolong the assault. The person is unaware that his suffering does not arise from God but arises out of his fulfilling the conditions for the working of evil spirits. He still pictures himself as suffering for the church that he may complete what is lacking in Christ's afflictions for the sake of His body. He conceives himself a martyr whereas in fact he is a victim. He glories in these sufferings, yet they constitute but symptoms of the adversary's entrenchment.

We should notice that all these afflictions which flow from the work of the evil spirits are meaningless—positively fruitless and purposeless. Apart from the fact that one is suffering, there is no sense to it. The Holy Spirit does not bear witness in our intuition that this proceeds from God.

Should the believer investigate a little he may discover that he did not encounter such experiences before he offered himself to the Lord and *chose to suffer*. Having made the choice, he automatically accepted all sufferings as from God, although most are triggered by the power of darkness. He has surrendered ground to the evil spirits; he has believed their lies; and his life is consequently marked by unreasonable and ineffectual sufferings. Knowing the truth concerning the deep workings of the evil spirit helps the individual not only to overcome sins but to eliminate unnecessary afflictions as well.

The child of God may hold this same erroneous concept concerning weakness. He thinks he should maintain a condition of weakness if he is ever to possess God's strength. For has not the Apostle Paul asserted that "when I am weak, then I am strong" (2 Cor. 12.10)? He accordingly *wills* to be weak that he too may be strong. He does not observe that the Apostle has not *willed* to be weak but that he is merely relating to us his experience of how the grace of God strengthens him in his frailty for the accomplishment of God's purpose. Paul has not desired this infirmity; yet he is strengthened by God in that infirmity. Paul is not to be found persuading a strong believer to *purposely choose* weakness in order that God may strengthen him afterwards. He simply is showing the *weak* believer the way to strength!

Choosing weakness and choosing suffering both fulfill the requirements for the operation of evil spirits since by so doing man's will is placed on the enemy's side. This explains why countless children of God who enjoyed good health in the beginning find themselves weakened daily after they have chosen to be weak. The strength they expect does not emerge: they soon become a burden to others: they are useless in God's work. Such a choice does not draw down God's power; rather does it furnish the evil spirits ground for attack. Unless these saints persistently resist this debility they shall encounter prolonged weakness.

THE VITAL POINT

What we have described may be applied primarily to serious cases; many other people have not gone to such an extreme. The principle involved is nonetheless the same for all. The devil does not fail to act whenever there is *passivity of will* or a *fulfillment of his working conditions.* Although some Christians may not specifically choose suffering or weakness, they nevertheless *unwittingly* allow themselves to sink into passivity, thus ceding place to the enemy and falling into a perilous situation. Let anyone who has the above experience ask himself whether he has fulfilled the operating requirements of the evil spirits. This will save him from many counterfeit occurrences and unnecessary sufferings.

We know the enemy makes use of the truth, yet he overextends it beyond its bounds. Which of the following is not of truth: self-denial, submission, waiting for God's ordering, suffering, and so forth? Even so, evil spirits exploit the believer's ignorance of the principle of spiritual life to divert him into fulfilling their operating requirements. If we fail to judge the underlying principle of any teaching, as to whether it meets the conditions of the Holy Spirit or that of evil spirits, we shall be deceived. Any overextension of the truth is most precarious. Let us be very cautious in this regard.

By now we should be acquainted fully with the basic distinction between the working of God and that of Satan: (a) *God wants the believer to cooperate with Him by exercising his will and using all his abilities in order that he may be filled with the Holy Spirit;* but that (b) *to facilitate his* work the evil spirit demands the believer to be passive in his will and to deny the use of either part or all of his abilities. In the first case, God's Spirit fills the spirit of man and imparts life, power, release, enlargement, renewal, and strength to the man that he may be free and unshackled. In the second case, Satan occupies man's passive organs and, if undetected, proceeds to destroy his personality and will by reducing him to a puppet, subduing his soul and body, and leaving him bound, oppressed, ravaged and imprisoned. The Holy Spirit enables the believer to know the will of God in his intuition so that he may understand it afterwards with his mind and carry it out later by freely exercising his will. The satanic spirit, however, so puts the person under the oppression of an external power that it appears to him to represent God's will and compels him to act like a machine devoid of thought or decision.

Today many of God's children have fallen unknowingly into passivity: their will and mind cease to function; hence they experience untold sufferings. All simply happens according to law. Just as there is a law to everything in the natural realm, so is there also a law to everything in the spiritual realm: certain actions produce certain results. God Who establishes these laws is Himself law-abiding. Whoever violates one of these laws, willfully or unintentionally, must reap the corresponding consequence. But if man exercises his will, mind and strength to cooperate with God, His Spirit will then work, for this too is a law.

CHAPTER 4
THE PATH TO FREEDOM

IT IS POSSIBLE FOR a consecrated Christian to be deceived into passivity for some years without ever awakening to his dangerous plight. The degree of inactivity will increase in scope until he suffers unspeakable pain in mind, emotion, body and environment. To present the true meaning of consecration to these ones thus becomes vitally important. The knowledge of truth is absolutely necessary for deliverance from passivity, without which freedom is *impossible*. We know that a believer falls into passivity through deception but this latter in turn is caused by a lack of knowledge.

THE KNOWLEDGE OF TRUTH

The very first step to freedom is to know the truth of all things: truth concerning cooperation with God, the operation of evil spirits, consecration, and supernatural manifestations. The child of God must know the truth as to the source and nature of the experiences he may have been having if he expects to be delivered. Since his descent was (1) deception, (2) passivity, (3) entrenchment, and (4) further deception and passivity, then the way to release will be initially the uncovering of deception. Once the early deceit is dissolved, passivity, entrenchment and further deceit will disintegrate. Deception unlatches the gate for the evil spirits to rush in; passivity provides a place for them to stay; and the result of these two is entrenchment. To dispossess them requires an ending of passivity which in turn needs the exposure of deception, and this is brought about by nothing else save the knowledge of truth. Knowledge of truth is therefore the first stage towards freedom. Only the truth can set people free.

We have cautioned our readers repeatedly about the danger of supernatural experience. We are not suggesting that every such manifestation must be categorically resisted, forsaken and opposed: this would be at variance with Biblical teaching since the Scriptures record numerous supernatural acts of God. Our purpose simply has been to remind Christians that there can be more than one source behind supernatural phenomena; God can perform wonders, but so can evil spirits imitate! How crucial for us to distinguish what is of God from what is not of God. If one has not died to his emotional life but earnestly seeks sensational events, he will be easily duped. We do not urge people to resist all supernatural manifestations, but we do exhort them to resist every supernatural occurrence which derives from Satan. So what we have tried to point out throughout this Part of the book has been the basic differences between the operation of the Holy Spirit and that of the evil spirit so as to help God's children discern which is which.

It can be stated that present day Christians are particularly susceptible to trickery in supernatural matters. Our earnest hope is that in their contact with supernatural phenomena they shall first undertake the task of discriminating lest they be beguiled. They must not overlook the fact that when the supernatural experience is authored by the Holy Spirit they are still able to engage their own mind; it is not required that they be totally or partially passive before they obtain such an experience. And afterwards too they are still able to exercise their conscience freely to distinguish good and evil without the least inhibition. But should the experience be authored by the evil spirit, then the victims must settle into passivity, their mind be blank, and their every action be performed under outside compulsion. Such is the essential difference. The Apostle Paul mentions in 1 Corinthians 14 various spiritual gifts among which are revelation, prophecy, tongues and other supernatural manifestations. He acknowleges these gifts as flowing from the Holy Spirit, yet he defines the nature of these God-given gifts in these words: "the spirits of prophets are subject to prophets" (v.32). If what the prophets (believers) receive is from the Holy Spirit, then the spirits they receive will be subject to them. This means that the Holy Spirit Who bestows diverse supernatural experiences upon men will not infringe on their rights by manipulating any part of their bodies against their wills. They continue to retain the power of *self-control*. Only that spirit which is subject to the prophet or believer is from God; any spirit which demands the prophet to be subject to it is not from God. Although we should not oppose all supernatural elements, we nonetheless should judge whether these supernatural spirits require a man's passive subjection or not. The workings of the Holy Spirit and those of the evil spirit are fundamentally opposite: the Former wishes men to be sovereignly free; the latter requires him to be altogether passive. The believer should judge his experience by this criterion. Learning whether he has been passive or not can be the solution to all his problems.

Should the child of God desire freedom his folly must be removed. In other words, he must know the truth. He needs to appreciate the real nature of affairs. Satanic lies bind, but God's truth unshackles. Naturally the knowledge of truth is going to be costly, for it will shatter the vainglory one has assumed due to his past experiences. He looks upon himself as far more advanced than others, as being spiritual and infallible. How hard hit he will be if he confesses the possibility of his being invaded or if he is shown to have been so invaded! Unless God's child sincerely adheres to all the truth of God, it becomes very rough for him to accept this kind of painful and humiliating truth. One encounters no difficulty in accepting that truth which is agreeable; but it is not easy at all to take in a truth which blasts one's ego. To acknowledge himself as liable to deception is relatively easy; whereas to confess that he is entrenched by the enemy already is most difficult. May God be gracious, for even after a person has known the truth he may yet resist it. The acceptance of truth is thus the first step to salvation. The child of God must be willing to know all the truth concerning himself. This requires humility and sincerity. Therefore let him who vehemently opposes such truth beware lest unknowingly he actually be enslaved.

The roads to truth are many and various. Some are awakened to their true state upon discovering that they have lost their liberty in all respects through their protracted and serious satanic bondage; others whose experiences may be ninety per cent of God and only ten per cent impurity come to know the truth when they begin to doubt their experience; still others are brought to a knowledge of their condition through the truth given them by other believers. In any event, the Christian should not refuse the first ray of light which shines upon him.

Doubting is the prelude to truth. By this is not meant to doubt the Holy Spirit or God or His Word but to doubt one's own past experience. Such doubt is both necessary and scriptural because God commands us to "test the spirits" (1 John 4.1). Believers often embrace a wrong idea: they are afraid to examine the spirits lest they sin against the Holy Spirit. But it is He Himself Who desires us to make the test. Now if it turns out to be the Holy Spirit He can stand the test; if however it is the evil spirit its true nature will accordingly be exposed. Is it God Who has in fact caused you to fall into today's position? Does the Holy Spirit ever work contrary to His law? Are you really infallible in all matters?

Having received some light as to the truth, the believer next can readily admit that he is susceptible to deception. And this affords the truth a working opportunity. The worst fallacy one can ever commit is to reckon oneself infallible. To maintain that others may be wrong but never he is to be duped to the very end. Only after he is self-abased will he be able to see that he is genuinely deceived. By comparing the principle of divine working against the conditions of satanic working, he concludes that his past experiences were obtained through passivity. He had fulfilled the requirements for the working of the evil spirits, hence was given those many strange manifestations which made him happy initially but which pained him ultimately. He had not cooperated actively with God but had instead passively followed that will which he had taken for granted must be God's. Both his happy and painful experiences must have originated with evil spirits. He consequently now admits how deceived he has been. The child of God not only must accept the truth but in addition must admit his condition in the light of that truth. In this way the lie of the enemy shall be annulled. Thus one's experience here is to (a) acknowledge that a *believer* is open to deception; (b) admit that *he* too is subject to duplicity; (c) confess that *he* is deceived; and next (d) further inquire as to why he was beguiled.

THE DISCOVERY OF GROUND

We may now infer that ground must have been furnished the evil spirit. But what is the ground which a believer supplies? Before he considers what ground he has given, let him first review exactly what ground is.

The believer ought to realize that besides sin there are other elements which can afford ground to evil spirits: the acceptance of a counterfeit, passivity of will, and assent to the enemy's flashing thought. For the present we focus our attention on passivity, that is, on allowing our mind or body to sink into a coma-like state, ceasing to exercise conscious control over the mind, and inactivating the proper functions of the will, conscience and memory. Passivity, though there are various gradations of it, forms the principal ground. The scope of the enemy's penetration is determined by the degree of passivity. As soon as the person becomes aware of an inert condition—whatever its degree—he must recover that ground at once. Firmly, intently and persistently he should oppose the enemy's attempt to maintain any footing in him, especially in the areas where he has been deceived. It is indispensable that he know the ground and recover it.

Upon realizing he has been deceived, the believer should next seek light concerning the ground he has lost and try to recover it. Since evil spirits maintain their position on the territory surrendered to them, they shall leave once that area is cleared away.

Because the Christian has fallen into passivity and deception by not using his will in self-control, he now must exercise his will actively to resist through the power of God the powers of darkness in every temptation and suffering and to cancel his earlier promises to them. Since passivity came in gradually, it will be eliminated gradually. The measure of one's detection of his inertia is the measure of that one's emancipation. If the duration of his inactivity has been long, the longer will it take to be delivered. To descend a mountain is always easier than to ascend it; in like manner, to become passive is easy but to regain freedom is painstaking. It requires the cooperation of the total man to retake all forfeited ground.

The child of God definitely should ask God to show him where he has been deceived. He must sincerely desire to have *all* the truth about himself revealed. Generally speaking, whatever the believer fears to hear will probably pertain to the ground given the enemy. What he is afraid to deal with is the very item he should dispense with, for nine out of ten times the enemy has established his footing right there. How necessary that the Christian beseech God to shed light on his symptoms and their causes so that he may recapture the lost territory. Enlightenment is a "must"; without it the believer tends to interpret the supernatural as being something natural, the spiritual (of the evil spirits) as being something physical. And so he provides ground for the enemy.

THE RECOVERY OF GROUND

One common principle underlies the way all ground is relinquished to evil spirits: it is through passivity, the inactivity of the will. If lost ground is ever to be recovered it is mandatory that the volition be reactivated. The Christian henceforth must learn (a) to obey God's will, (b) to resist the devil's will, and (c) to exercise his own will in collaboration with the will of the other saints. Responsibility for recovering ceded territory rests chiefly on the will, It is the volition which became passive, hence it must be the volition which dispels passivity.

The first measure the will undertakes is to *resolve*, that is, to set itself towards a definite direction. Having suffered much at the hands of evil spirits but now enlightened by the truth and encouraged by the Holy Spirit, the child of God is led naturally to a new position of abhorring those wicked spirits. He accordingly resolves against all their works. He is determined to regain his freedom, be his own master, and drive off his enemy. The Spirit of God so works in him that his fury against the evil spirits gathers momentum. The more he suffers the more he hates; the more he ponders his plight the more furious he becomes. He resolves to experience a complete emancipation from the powers of darkness. Such a resolve is the first step towards the recovery of lost ground. If this resolution is real he will press on towards the goal no matter how fierce a fight the enemy may put up. The entire man supports his resolve to henceforth oppose the adversary.

The Christian also should engage his will to choose, that is to decide the future he desires. In days of spiritual battle this choice can be very effective. He should ever and anon declare: I choose freedom; I want liberty; I refuse to be passive; I will use my own talents; I insist on knowing the wiles of the evil spirits; I wish for their defeat; I will sever every relationship with the powers of darkness; I oppose all their lies and excuses. Such a declaration of the will is highly beneficial in warfare. It expresses his *choice*, not simply his resolve, on these particular matters. The powers of darkness pay no attention to one's resolve, but should he choose with his will to oppose them through the power of God then they most certainly shall flee. All this is related to the principle of the freedom of man's will. Just as in the beginning the believer permitted the evil spirits to enter, so now he chooses the very opposite, the undercutting of any footing of the enemy.

During this period of conflict the Christian's will must be engaged actively in various operations. Beyond resolving and choosing, he also ought to *resist*. That is to say, his will must exert its force to contend with the evil spirits. He moreover should *refuse*—shut the door against—the entry of the enemy. By resisting he prohibits the evil spirits from further working; by refusing he cancels the former permission he had granted them. Refusal in addition to resistance practically immobilizes all the perpetrations of the enemy. Resisting is our attitude regarding what lies ahead of us; refusing is our position regarding what lies behind. For instance: by proclaiming that "I will to have my freedom" we are refusing the evil spirits; yet we need as well to resist, that is, to exert strength in combating the enemy so that we may keep the freedom we have just obtained through refusal. Both refusal and resistance must be continued until complete emancipation is won.

To resist is truly a battle. It requires all the strength of the spirit, soul and body. Nevertheless, the main force is the will. To resolve, choose and refuse are primarily questions of attitude; but to resist is a matter of overt practice. It is a conduct expressive of an attitude. It is wrestling in the spirit, which is to say, that the will through the strength of the spirit *pushes* the evil spirits off the ground they presently occupy. It is an assault against the enemy line. In resisting, one employs one's will power to drive, push and chase off. The enemy spirits, even should they perceive the believer's hostile attitude against them, will not budge an inch from the ground they occupy. They must be driven out with real force. The child of God must mobilize spiritual power to immobilize and remove the enemy. He must *exercise* his will to chase them away. A mere declaration of intention is insufficient. It needs to be coupled with practical measures. Resistance without refusal is similarly ineffective, because the ground originally promised to the enemy must be recovered.

In retaking surrendered territory the believer must use his will on the one side to resolve, choose and refuse and on the other to resist. He should resolve to fight, choose freedom, refuse ground, and resist the enemy. He must contend for his sovereignty. This element of free will should never be lost sight of. God has granted us an unhampered volition that we may be our own masters, but today the evil spirits have usurped our members and talents. They have become man's master; he has lost his sovereign rights. To oppose this the believer enters the fray. He continually declares: I am not willing to let the evil spirits encroach on my sovereign rights; I will not allow them to invade my personality; I will not permit them to possess me; I will not follow them blindly; I will not consent to their manipulating me; I will not, I verily am unwilling; I intend to be my own master; I know what I do; I resolve to control myself; I prefer to have my entire being subject to myself; I resist all the works of the wicked ones as well as their right to work on me. In resolving, choosing and refusing with our will we arrest any further working of the enemy. Thereafter we must resist with our will.

The believer commences his life anew following the recovery of his ground. The past is over, and now marks a new beginning. What was offered to the evil spirits has all been reclaimed. The spirit, soul and body of the whole person are retrieved from the enemy's hand and are rededicated to God. Every inch of the territory surrendered through ignorance has today, one upon another, been recovered. The sovereign power of man is once again returned to him. And how is this done? By rejecting what once was accepted; disbelieving what once was believed; withdrawing from what once he drew nigh to before; destroying what once was erected; canceling what once was covenanted; retrieving what once was promised; dissolving what once was joined; resisting what once was obeyed; uttering what once went unspoken; opposing what once was cooperated with; and denying what once was given. Every past consideration, counsel, and permission must be overthrown; even past prayers and answers must be denied.

Without a doubt every one of these dealings runs directly against the evil spirits. Formerly an intimate association had been formed with these spirits through mistaking them for the Holy Spirit; presently, with the newly added knowledge, all which was yielded to them in ignorance must be retrieved. Just as each ground *one after another* was ceded, so now all must be reclaimed *specifically*. The greatest hindrance to complete liberty is the believer's unwillingness to recover all territory carefully: point by point, one after another. He tends to exercise his will in a general, vague and inclusive way to retake all ground. Such general opposition merely indicates the correctness of the believer's attitude. To be set free he must restore everything specifically. This may seem laborious but if he genuinely wills to be released and prays for God's light, the Holy Spirit gradually shall reveal the past to him. By resisting them one by one, all eventually shall be dissolved. By patiently pressing forward he shall experience deliverance in one area after another. He is on his way to freedom. To resist in a general way shows we do really oppose the evil spirits; but only resisting in specific fashion can force them to desert the ground they occupy.

Step by step the will of the Christian had descended downhill till it became totally passive. Now he must reverse the process and step by step ascend to freedom. He must retrace all the stages by which he descended, only this time his direction will be upward. Previously he was deceived into passivity by degrees; he now needs to reactivate his will in the same manner. All his earlier passivity must be restored one by one. Each movement upward bespeaks some regaining of ground. Whatever was most recently lost to the evil spirits is usually the first ground to be recovered, just as in climbing stairs we ascend the last step of our descent first.

The child of God must reclaim all footholds until he arrives at the freedom he first enjoyed. He should know *from where* he has fallen since it is to that place that he must be restored. He ought to understand what was hitherto normal for him—how active his will and how clear his mind were in the beginning—as well as what his current condition is. By comparing these two states he will be able to ascertain how far he has descended into passivity. Whatever his normal state was, that must he now set before himself as the minimum standard or goal of his ascent. He should not be satisfied until his will is restored to its original state, that is, until it actively controls every part of his being. He should never deem himself free before his normalcy has once more been regained.

Hence the child of God needs to recover completely every function of his being which has toppled from normalcy into passivity—whether that function be to think, to recall, to imagine, to discern right from wrong, to resolve, to choose, to refuse, to resist, to love, or whatever. Everything over which he has relinquished control must be restored to his personal sovereignty. He should exercise his volition to oppose inertia as well as to make use of all these functions of man. When he tumbled into passivity the evil spirits seized upon his passive organs and used them instead of him. The attempt to reclaim lost areas and regain personal use of his organs may be exceedingly difficult for the believer. This is due to the facts that (a) his own will is necessarily weak yet and hence powerless to direct every portion of his being; and (b) the evil spirits contend against him with their full strength. If for example he has been passive in the matter of decision he will now cancel the ground given and forbid the evil spirits to work any more. He is determined to decide for himself without any of their interference. But he finds (a) that he cannot decide and (b) that the evil spirits do not let him decide and act. When the believer refuses them permission to control him, they will not allow their captive to act without their permission.

Right here must the believer choose: is he going to be forever passive, is he going to let the evil spirits act forever for him? He of course will not permit them to manipulate him any longer. Though temporarily he is unable to decide anything, he nonetheless will *not allow* the evil spirits to control his power of decision. The battle for freedom has now been joined. This is a contest of the *will*, for it is through its passivity that all the parts of the man have fallen into the hands of the evil spirits. Hereafter the will must rise up to (a) oppose the rule of the evil spirits, (b) recover all lost ground, and (c) work actively with God for the use of every part of his person. Everything hinges on the volition. The evil spirits will withdraw if the believer's volition withstands them and forbids them to occupy his organs any further.

Every foot of surrendered territory must be recaptured; each bit of deception must be uncovered. The child of God needs to contend patiently with the enemy over each and every matter. He must "fight through." All ground is not necessarily removed at the moment of refusal. The evil spirits will yet mount their last struggle; the children of God must be strengthened through many battles. "The refusing must therefore be reasserted, and the believer refuse persistently, until each point of ground is detected and refused, and the faculties are gradually released to act freely under the will of the man. The faculties let go into passivity should regain their normal working condition, such as the operation of the mind kept to true and pure thinking so that any subject being dealt with is mastered, and does not dominate beyond control. So with the memory, the will, the imagination, and the actions of the body, such as singing, praying, speaking, reading, etc." (Penn-Lewis, WOTS, 193)* The will must be engaged as the master of the entire man. All talents must be able to function properly according to one's normal condition.

In addition to refusing any ground to the powers of darkness, the child of God will have to refuse all their operations. If by his volition he maintains this antagonistic attitude the endeavors of the enemy will be spoiled. He should ask God for light on the enemy's exertions so as to resist them one by one. Since the operation of the evil spirits in the child of God is (a) to act in place of him and (b) to influence him to act according to their will, he must (a) refuse to let them act for him and (b) resist their influence on him. He needs to re-

---

*See Part Nine, Chapter 2 for full bibliographical citation.

fuse to let in the enemy spirits as well as refuse any ground that will maintain them in him. As he resists, the foe shall contend in every way. He must therefore battle with *all his strength* until he is restored to his normalcy and freedom. When he first begins to fight he may find himself temporarily incapacitated; but if he struggles on with all his might, his volition will turn from passivity to activity and control his whole being. Thus shall passivity and the enemy's entrenchment be destroyed in battle.

"The 'fighting through' period is a very painful time. There are bad moments of acute suffering, and intense struggle, arising out of the consciousness of the resistance of the powers of darkness in their contest for what the believer endeavors to reclaim." (Penn-Lewis, WOTS, 194) In exercising his volition to (a) resist the rule of the evil spirits and (b) reinstate his own office, the Christian shall meet stiff opposition from his enemy. Initially he may not be aware of the depth to which he has fallen; but once he commences, point by point, to fight his way back to a normal state, then does he discover how far he has plunged. Because of the resistance of the enemy he may find at the initial stage of combat that his symptoms grow *worse* than before, as though the more he fights the less strength his will has and the more confused becomes the particular area over which the engagement is being fought. Such a phenomenon is nonetheless the sign of *victory!* Though the believer does feel worse, in reality he is better. *For it demonstrates that the resistance has had its effect: the enemy has felt the pressure and is consequently making his last stand. If one continues to exert the pressure the evil spirits will depart.*

During the battle it is positively essential that the believer stand on Romans 6.11, acknowledging himself as *one* with the Lord: the Lord's death is his death. Such faith releases him from the authority of the evil spirits since they can have no power over the dead. This position must be firmly taken. In conjunction with such a stand as this there must be the use of God's Word against all the lies of the enemy, because at this juncture the adversary will lie to the saint by suggesting that he has fallen beyond any hope of restoration. If he listens to this guile he will surely tumble into the greatest peril of all. He should remind himself that Calvary has destroyed Satan and his evil hosts already (Heb. 2.14; Col. 2.14-15). The work of salvation is finished that all may experience deliverance out of the powers of darkness into the kingdom of the Son of God's love (Col. 1.13). Suffering for the sake of recovering ground assures a person of that which the enemy is afraid of, and how urgent that the ground be recovered. Consequently, whenever the wicked powers inflict new and greater afflictions upon the believer, let him perceive that these are from the enemy and then let him refuse and disregard them, neither worrying nor talking about them.

If the Christian patiently endures temporary discomforts and courageously exercises his volition to recapture surrendered territory, he shall find himself progressively being freed. Little by little as the ground is refused to the enemy and restored to the believer the degree of penetration will correspondingly decrease. If he does not cede any *new* ground to the enemy the latter's power to harass him shall diminish as the ground dwindles. While it may require some time before he is set free completely, even so he is now on the road to liberation. He begins to be conscious of himself, his need for food, his appearance, and other such elements of awareness which were relinquished through the enemy's attack. But he must not misconstrue these to be a retrogression in his spiritual life. On the contrary, the restoration of consciousness is evidence that the former invader has departed from his senses. Thus at this stage he should proceed faithfully until full freedom has been restored. He should be wary of contentment with a little gain; he should not stop until his normalcy is recovered entirely.

TRUE GUIDANCE

We need to comprehend the true way by which God leads man, and the relationship between man's will and the will of God.

The obedience of the Christian to God ought to be unconditional. When his spiritual life reaches the summit his will shall be perfectly one with God's. This does not imply, however, that he has no more volition of his own. It is still there; only the fleshly control of it is gone. God always requires man's volition to cooperate with Him in fulfilling His will. By beholding the example of our Lord Jesus we can be assured that the volition of anyone fully united with God is still very much with him. "I seek not my *own* will but the will of him who sent me"; "not to do my *own* will but the will of him who sent me"; "nevertheless not *my* will, but thine, be done" (John 5.30, 6.38; Luke 22.42). Here do we see the Lord Jesus Who, though one with the Father, yet possesses His *Own personal* will apart from that of the Father. He has His Own will but neither seeks nor does that will. The implication is obvious that all who truly are united with God should place their will alongside His. They should not annihilate their organ of volition.

In true guidance the Christian is not obligated to obey God mechanically; instead he must execute God's will *actively*. God takes no pleasure in demanding His own to follow blindly; He wants them to do His will in full and conscious exercise of their total beings. A lazy person would like God to act for him so that he can simply follow passively. But God does not desire His child to be lazy. He wishes him to prepare his members actively and obey actively after he has spent time in examining the will of God. Wherefore in the practice of obedience the believer goes through the following steps: (a) *willingness* to do God's will (John 7.17); (b) *revelation* of that will to his intuition by the Holy Spirit (Eph. 5.17); (c) strengthening by God to *will* His will (Phil. 2.13); and (d) strengthening by God to *do* His will (Phil. 2.13). God never substitutes Himself for the believer in carrying out His will; consequently, upon knowing the will of God he must will to do it and then draw upon the power of the Holy Spirit to work it out.

Why must the Christian draw on the power of the Holy Spirit? Because standing alone his will is very weak. How true are those words of Paul: "I can will what is right, but I cannot do it" (Rom. 7.18). One must be strengthened by the Holy Spirit in the inner man before he can practically obey God. Hence *God* first works in us to will and then works in us to work for His good pleasure (Phil. 2.13).

God reveals His will in our spirit's intuition and there supplies strength to us both to will and to work out His will when our volition is united to Him. He demands that we be one with Him, but He never uses our will for us. The purpose of God's creation and redemption is to give man a perfectly free volition. Through the salvation accomplished by the Lord Jesus on the cross we Christians now can choose freely to do the will of God. All the charges in the New Testament concerning life and godliness are to be either chosen or rejected as we so wish and will. Such charges would mean nothing if God were to annihilate the operation of our volition.

A spiritual Christian is one who has full authority to exercise his own volition. He always should choose God's will and reject Satan's. While at times he is uncertain whether something is from God or from the devil, yet he is able to choose or reject. He can declare: Even though I know not if this is of God or of Satan, yet I choose what is God's and reject what is Satan's. He may continue to be uninformed but he can continue to maintain the attitude of wanting what is God's and rejecting what is the devil's. A child of God ought to exercise this right of choosing or rejecting in all respects. It does not matter too much if he is unaware, as long as he decides to choose the will of God. He may say: whenever I know what God's mind is, I shall do it; I always choose God's will and reject Satan's. This attitude affords the Spirit of God opportunity to work in him until his will against the devil daily grows stronger and Satan daily loses his influence in him. In this way God secures another faithful servant in the midst of a rebellious world. By persistently maintaining the *attitude* of rejecting the enemy's will and continually beseeching God to prove what is of Him, the believer begins before long to appreciate the great effectiveness of such an attitude of will in spiritual life.

SELF CONTROL

The summit of a Christian's spiritual walk is self-control. What commonly is spoken of as the Holy Spirit ruling in us does not mean that He directly controls any part of man. Any misunderstanding of this can result in either deception or despair. If we know that the aim of the Holy Spirit is to lead man to the place of self-control, we shall not fall into passivity but shall make good progress in spiritual life.

"The fruit of the Spirit is . . . self-control" (Gal. 5.22-23). The work of the Holy Spirit is to bring the believer's outward man into perfect obedience to his self-control. The Holy Spirit rules the believer through his renewed will. When a child of God walks after the flesh his outward man is rebellious to the spirit and so he becomes a disintegrated person. But when he walks in the spirit and produces spiritual fruit he manifests the power of self-control as well as love, joy, kindness and so forth in his soul. The outward man, once dissipated and confused, is now thoroughly subdued and perfectly submissive to the man's self-control according to the mind of the Holy Spirit. What the Christian must therefore control by his will are:

(a) his own spirit, maintaining it in its proper state of being neither too hot nor too cold. The spirit needs the control of the will just as do the other parts of man. Only when one's volition is renewed and is filled with the Holy Spirit is he able to direct his own spirit and keep it in its proper position. All who are experienced agree that they must engage their will to restrain the spirit when it becomes too wild or to uplift it when it sinks too low. Only so can the believer walk daily in his spirit. This is not contradictory to what we mentioned before about man's spirit ruling over the whole person. For when we say the spirit rules the total man we mean that the spirit, by knowing the mind of God intuitively, *governs* the whole being (including the volition) according to God's will. Whereas in stating that the will controls the man we mean the will *directly controls* the entire man (including the spirit) according to the will of God. In experience these two perfectly agree. "A man without self-control is like a city broken into and left without walls" (Prov. 25.28).

(b) his own mind and all the rest of his soul's abilities. All thoughts need to be subjected fully to the control of the will; wandering thoughts must be checked one by one— "take every thought captive to obey Christ" (2 Cor. 10.5). And "set your minds on things that are above" (Col. 3.2).

(c) his own body. It ought to be an instrument to man, not his master by virtue of unrestrained habits and lusts. The Christian should exercise his volition to control, discipline and subdue his body in order that it may be entirely submissive, ready to do God's will and hindering not. "I pommel my body and subdue it" (1 Cor. 9.27). Once the believer's volition has achieved a state of perfect self-control he will not be hindered by any part of his being, because the moment he senses God's will he immediately performs it. Both the Holy Spirit and man's spirit need a will under self-control by which to execute God's revelation. Hence on the one hand we must be united with God and on the other hand subdue our whole being so as to render it obedient to us. This is imperative to spiritual life.

PART TEN

THE BODY

1 The Believer and His Body
2 Sickness
3 God as the Life of the Body
4 Overcoming Death

CHAPTER 1
THE BELIEVER AND HIS BODY

We should know what place our physical body occupies in the purpose and plan of God. Can anyone deny the relationship between the body and spirituality? In addition to a spirit and a soul we also have a body. However healthy may be the intuition, communion and conscience of our spirit and however renewed the emotion, mind and will of our soul, we can never develop into spiritual men and women—never be perfected but continually lacking in some way—if our body is not as sound and restored as are our spirit and soul. We should not neglect our outer shell while attending to our inner components. Our life shall suffer if we commit this blunder.

The body is necessary and important; otherwise God would not have created man with one. By accurately searching the Scriptures we can discover how much attention God pays to man's body, for the Bible has a lot to say about it.

Most singular and awesome of all is the fact that the Word became flesh: the Son of God took upon Himself a body of flesh and blood: and though He died He wears this garb forever.

THE HOLY SPIRIT AND THE BODY

Romans 8.10-13 unfolds to us the condition of our body, how the Holy Spirit helps it, and what ought to be our right attitude towards it. If we appropriate these verses we will not misunderstand the place of a believer's body in God's plan of redemption.

"If Christ is in you, although your bodies are dead because of sin, your spirits are alive because of righteousness" (v.10). Initially both our body and spirit were dead; but after we believed in the Lord Jesus we received Him into us to be our life. The fact that Christ by the Holy Spirit lives in the believer forms one of the essential tenets of the gospel. Every child of God, however weak, has Christ dwelling in him. This Christ is our life. And when He enters to make His abode in us, our spirit is made alive. Formerly both the spirit and the body were dead; now the spirit is quickened, leaving only the body dead. The estate common to *every believer* is that his body is dead but his spirit is alive.

This experience produces a wide disparity between the Christian's inward and outward state. Our inner being is flowing with life while the outer man is still full of death. Being full of the Spirit of life we are very much alive, yet we exist in a shell of death; in other words, the life of our spirit and the life of our body are radically unalike. The former is life indeed, but the latter is verily death. This is because our physical frame is still the "body of sin": no matter how advanced a Christian's spiritual walk is, his flesh is nonetheless the "body of sin." We have yet to possess a resurrected, glorious, spiritual frame; "the redemption of our bodies" (Rom. 8.23) awaits us in the future. Today's body is just an "earthen vessel," an "earthly tent," a "lowly body" (2 Cor. 4.7, 5.1; Phil. 3.21). Sin has been driven out of the spirit and the will but it has not been expunged from the body. Because sin remains there, it is therefore dead. This is the purport of "your bodies are dead because of sin." Simultaneously, however, our spirit is alive. Or to phrase it more correctly, our spirit receives life because of the righteousness which is in Christ. When we trust in Him we receive Him as our righteousness and we also are justified by God. The former is Christ imparting to us His very Self (a substantive transaction); the latter is God justifying us for Christ's sake (a legal transaction). Without the impartation there can be no justification. The moment we receive Christ we obtain the legal position of being justified before God and additionally the practical experience of having Christ imparted to us. Christ comes into us as life so that our dead spirit may be made alive. This is the import of "your spirits are alive because of righteousness."

"If the Spirit of him who raised Jesus from the dead dwells in you, he who raised Christ Jesus from the dead will give life to your mortal bodies also through his Spirit which dwells in you" (v.11). Verse 10 explains how God quickens our spirit; this verse tells us how God gives life to our body. The tenth verse speaks of the spirit being made alive, with the body still dead; the eleventh verse goes further by saying that after the spirit is made alive the body too may live. The first part announces that the spirit lives because of Christ dwelling in us; this part declares that the body will live because of the Holy Spirit abiding in us. The Holy Spirit will give life to our bodies.

The body is dead not in the sense that this outer shell is, but in the sense that it is traveling towards the grave; spiritually speaking it is counted as dead. According to man's thought the body possesses life; yet according to God even that life is death because it is abounding with sins—"your bodies are dead because of sin." On the one hand, although there is strength in the body we must not permit it to be manifested. It should not have any activity, for the activation of its life is but death. Sin is its life, and sin is spiritual death. The body lives by spiritual death. On the other hand, we know we should witness, serve and labor for God. These require bodily strength. Now inasmuch as the body is spiritually dead and its life is nothing but death, how then can we ever engage it to respond to the demands of spiritual life without concomitantly drawing upon its death-life? It is obvious that our body cannot and will not do the will of the Spirit of life within but will oppose and fight against Him. How can the Holy Spirit therefore induce our body to answer His call? He must Himself give life to our bodies of death.

The One "who raised Christ Jesus from the dead" is God. Why is He not directly named? It is to emphasize the *work* which God did in raising the Lord Jesus from the dead. It aims at calling the attention of believers to the feasibility of God raising their *mortal* bodies since God hitherto has raised the *dead* body of Jesus. The Apostle indirectly says this Spirit of God is the Holy Spirit, Who also is the Spirit of resurrection. He again employs the word "if"—"if the Spirit of Him . . . dwells in you he . . . will give life to your mortal bodies." He is not doubting that the Holy Spirit is in the believer, for he mentions in verse 9 that anyone belonging to Christ has the Spirit of Christ. What he means is: you have the Holy Spirit indwelling you; therefore your mortal bodies should experience His life. This is the privilege shared by all who possess the indwelling Spirit. He does not wish any saint to miss this blessing through ignorance.

This verse in reality teaches that if the Spirit of God abides in us, then through this indwelling Power God also gives life to our mortal bodies. It is not speaking of a future resurrection because that is not the subject here. It simply compares the resurrection of the Lord Jesus with our receiving life today in our body. If the verse were touching upon resurrection it would use the term "the body of death"; but only the mortal body is in view here, one which is subject to death *though not yet died*. The believer's body is spiritually dead, for it marches towards the grave and must die. This is quite distinct from one already deceased in the literal sense. Just as the Holy Spirit indwelling us is an ever current affair, so the Holy Spirit giving life to our mortal bodies must be a current experience too. We should realize further that it is not speaking of our regeneration here either, for the Holy Spirit is not imparting life to our spirit but is instead giving life to our bodies.

By this verse God informs His children of their bodily privilege, which is life to their mortal frames through His Spirit Who indwells them. It does not assert that the "body of sin" has become a holy body or that our "lowly body" has been transformed into a glorious one or that this mortal body has put on immortality. These cannot be realized in this life. The redemption of our earthen vessels must wait till the Lord comes and receives us to Himself. To change the nature of our body in this age is impossible. Therefore the real meaning of the Holy Spirit giving life to our bodies is that: (1) He will restore us when we are sick and (2) He will preserve us if we are not sick. In a word, the Holy Spirit will strengthen our earthly tents so that we can meet the requirements of God's work and walk in order that neither our life nor the kingdom of God will suffer through the weakness of the body.

This is what God has provided for all His children. Yet how many Christians day by day genuinely experience this life given by His Spirit to their mortal bodies? Are there not many whose spiritual life is endangered by their physical condition—many who fall because of their physical weakness —many who cannot work actively for God because of the bondage of illness? The experience of Christians today does not correspond to God's provision. Various reasons of course account for this discrepancy: some refuse to accept God's provision for they maintan it has nothing to do with them; while others know and believe and desire this provision but have not presented their bodies a living sacrifice. These hold instead that God has furnished them strength to live through themselves. But those who truly wish to live for God and claim this promise and provision by faith shall experience the reality of the fullness of life in the body as given by the Holy Spirit.

"So then, brethren, we are debtors, not to the flesh, to live according to the flesh" (v.12). This verse fully describes the proper relation between the believer and his body. Countless brethren are slaves to their fleshly frames. The spiritual life of many is totally imprisoned in their bodies! They exist as two different persons: when they withdraw to the inner man they have a feeling of being spiritual, nigh to God and abounding in life; but when they live in the outer flesh they feel fallen, carnal and alienated from God because they are obeying their bodies. Their body becomes a heavy burden to them. A little physical discomfort can alter their life. A slight illness or pain will perturb them and flood their hearts with self-love and self-pity. Under these circumstances it is impossible to follow a spiritual course.

The Apostle in using the words "so then" is merely continuing beyond what he has enunciated before. We believe this verse directly follows upon verses 10 and 11. The tenth declares the body is dead; the eleventh states the Holy Spirit gives life to the body. On the basis of these two bodily conditions, the Apostle can consequently conclude by saying: "so then, brethren, we are debtors, not to the flesh, to live according to the flesh." First, since the body is dead because of sin, we *cannot* live by following the body. To do so would be to commit sin. Second, because the Holy Spirit has given life to our mortal frames we *need not* live according to the flesh, since it has no authority any longer to bind our spiritual life. By this provision of God's Spirit our inner life is competent to directly command the outer frame without interference. Previously we seemed to be debtors to the flesh—incapable of restricting its demands, desires and lusts—and lived according to the flesh by committing many sins. But now we have the provision of the Holy Spirit. Not only the lusts of the flesh have no control over us, even its weakness, illness and suffering have lost their grip.

Many argue that we should fulfill the legitimate desires and demands of the flesh, but the Apostle contends we owe nothing to it. Beyond preserving our earthly tents in a proper condition as God's vessels, we owe the flesh nothing. Naturally the Bible never prohibits us from taking care of the body, else we would have to allot even more time and attention to it because of unnecessary sickness. Clothing, food and lodging are requisites; rest is also necessary. Nonetheless, what we stress is that our life should not be occupied solely by these concerns. True, we should eat when hungry, drink when thirsty, rest when weary, clothe ourselves when cold. Yet we must not permit these affairs to penetrate so deeply into our hearts that we make them partial or total objectives in our life. We must not love these necessaries. They should come and go according to *need*: they should not stay in us and become desires within. Sometimes for the sake of God's work or some other overriding need, we must pommel our body and subdue it despite its own requirement. The Disciples' love of sleep in the Garden of Gethsemane and the Lord's endurance of hunger by the well of Sychar present a contrasting picture of defeat and victory over the legitimate requirement of the body. Because we are debtors to the flesh no longer, we ought not sin according to its lusts nor slacken in spiritual work due to physical weakness.

"For if you live according to the flesh you will die, but if by the Spirit you put to death the deeds of the body you will live" (v.13). Should Christians reject God's provision and live by the flesh instead, they certainly will be punished.

"If you live according to the flesh you will die." This word "die" and the word "live" in the next clause have several meanings. We will mention only one, which is the death of the body. According to sin our body is "dead"; according to consequence it is a "body of death"—that is, it is doomed to death; if we live by the flesh this body of death shall become a dying body. In following the flesh we on the one side are unfit to receive the life given to the body by the Holy Spirit, while on the other we shorten the days of our life on earth because all sins are harmful to the body. All sins manifest their effectiveness in the flesh, and that effect is death. Through the life given to our body by the Holy Spirit we should resist the death which is in it; if not, death will quickly complete its work there.

"But if by the Spirit you put to death the deeds of the body you will live." We should receive the Holy Spirit not only as the Giver of life to our earthen vessel but also as the Executor of its deeds. How can we expect to have Him give life to our fleshly frame if we neglect the work of putting to death its deeds? For only by putting to death its deeds through the Holy Spirit can we *live*. For the body to live its doing must first be put to nought, or else death shall be the immediate result. Herein do we discover the mistake of many. Christians assume they can live for themselves—using their fleshly frames for the things they wish to do—but at the same time expect the Holy Spirit to give life to their frames so that they can be healthy and without infirmity. Would He give life and strength to men to empower them to live for themselves? How utterly ridiculous! The life God gives to our body is for the purpose that we may thereafter live for Him. If the Holy Spirit were to grant health and strength to us who have not offered ourselves wholeheartedly to God, would that not bolster us to live more energetically for ourselves? Innumerable Christians seeking the Holy Spirit as life for their mortal frames should now see that they do not have this experience because they have neglected this essential point.

We cannot ourselves control our body, but through the Holy Spirit we can. He will empower us to put to death its many deeds. Believers have all experienced their lack of strength to deal with the fleshly lusts which provoke the members of the body to perform deeds gratifying to the flesh. But by the Holy Spirit they are fit to cope with the situation. This is very important to know. It is useless to try to crucify one's self. Today many grasp the truth of being crucified with the Lord on the cross, yet few exhibit its reality. The truth of co-crucifixion is but a teaching to many saints. This is essentially due to a lack of clear understanding concerning the place of the Holy Spirit in the scheme of salvation. They do not apprehend how the Spirit moves together with the cross. We must realize that the cross without God's Spirit is absolutely ineffective. *Only the Holy Spirit can take what the cross has accomplished and make believers experience it. If we hear the truth of the cross but do not allow Him to work this truth into our lives, then we know nothing but a theory and an ideal.*

A recognition "that our old self was crucified with him so that the sinful body might be annulled" (Rom. 6.6 Darby) is indeed good; but we remain shackled by fleshly deeds if "by the Spirit" we have not "put to death the deeds of the body." We have seen too many saints who understand most lucidly the truth of the cross and have accepted it yet in whom it is not one whit effective. They begin to wonder whether the reality of the *practical* salvation of the cross can ever be experienced in their lives. But they should not be surprised at all since they have forgotten that only the Holy Spirit can translate the cross into experience. He alone can substantiate salvation, nonetheless they forget Him. Unless believers abandon themselves and trust completely in the power of the Spirit to lay to rest the deeds of the body, the truth they profess to know will persist as mere theory. Only a putting to death by the power of the Holy Spirit will give life today to our mortal frame.

GLORIFY GOD

The passage in 1 Corinthians 6.12-20 sheds additional light on this matter of the believer's body. Let us consider this passage verse by verse.

"All things are lawful for me, but not all things are helpful. All things are lawful for me, but I will not be enslaved by anything" (v.12). As substantiated by the verses following, the Apostle Paul is here writing about the body. He judges all things to be lawful because according to nature every demand of the body—such as eating, drinking or sex—is natural, reasonable and lawful (v.13). Yet he further judges that not every one of them is necessarily helpful nor should any enslave man. In other words, according to man's natural existence the Christian may be permitted to do many things with his body, but as one who belongs to God he is additionally able *not* to do these things for the glory of God.

"Food is meant for the stomach and the stomach for food —and God will destroy both one and the other. The body is not meant for immorality, but for the Lord, and the Lord for the body" (v.13). The first half of this verse corresponds to the first half of the preceding verse. Food is lawful, but since food and stomach will eventually be destroyed, none is eternally useful. The latter half of the verse corresponds to that half of the preceding verse too. The Christian is capable of rising completely above the urge of sex and yielding his body wholly to the Lord (1 Cor. 7.34).

"The body is for the Lord." This is a word having enormous import. Paul is speaking to us firstly about the issue of food. In the matter of eating and drinking the Christian is afforded a chance to prove in practice that "the body is for the Lord." Man originally fell on this very point of food; the Lord Jesus was tempted in the wilderness on this same issue as well. Numerous Christians do not know how to glorify God in their eating and drinking. They do not eat and drink simply to keep their body fit for the Lord's use but indulge to satisfy their personal desires. We should understand that the body is for the Lord and not for ourselves; hence we should refrain from using it for our pleasure. Food ought not hinder our fellowship with God since it is to be taken purely to preserve the body in health.

The Apostle mentions the subject of immorality too. This is a sin which defiles the body: it directly contravenes the principle that "the body is for the Lord." Immorality here includes not just looseness outside the marriage relationship but overindulgence within marriage as well. The body is for the Lord, wholly for the Lord, not for oneself. Thus license even in legitimate sexual intercourse is prohibited also.

The Apostle Paul's intent in this passage is to show us that any excess of the flesh must be thoroughly resisted. The body is for the Lord; the Lord alone can use it. The indulgence of any part solely for personal gratification is not pleasing to Him. Other than as an instrument of righteousness, the body is not to be used in any other way. It, like our entire being, cannot serve two masters. Even in such natural affairs as food and sex the body should be engaged exclusively to fill *needs*. While needs do require satisfaction, the body is nonetheless for the Lord and not for food and sex. Nowadays many Christians aspire to sancification of their spirit and soul, not fully appreciating how greatly sanctification in these realms depends on sanctification of the body. They forget that unless all nerve responses, sensations, actions, conduct, works, food and speech which belong to the body are utterly for the Lord, they can never arrive at perfection.

"The body is for the Lord." This signifies that though the outer flesh belongs to the Lord it is entrusted to man for him to maintain for Him. How few are those who know and practice this truth! Many saints today are stricken with sickness, weakness and suffering; God is chastening them that they may present their bodies to Him a living sacrifice. They would be healed if they yielded them completely to God. God wants them to know that the body is for the Lord, not for themselves. If they continue to live according to their wishes they shall see the scourge of God remain upon them. All who are sick should take these words seriously to heart.

"And the Lord for the body." This is an incredibly wonderful statement! We usually think of the Lord as saving only our spirit and our soul, but here it is said that "the Lord (is) for the *body*." Christians look upon the Lord Jesus as having come to save their spirit and soul alone, that the body is useless, having no value in spiritual life and not graciously provided for in God's redemptive scheme. But it is plainly enunciated here that "the Lord is *for* the body." The Lord, affirms God, is equally for the earthen vessel which man lightly esteems.

Why do believers overlook their fleshly frames? It is because they erroneously look upon the Lord Jesus as saving them merely from their sins and not also from the sickness of their body. Hence they can only resort to human methods for the cure of their physical weakness and illness. When they look into the four Gospels they find that the Lord Jesus healed more bodies than He saved souls; yet they spiritualize the affair entirely by interpreting these infirmities as being spiritual sicknesses. They may concede that the Lord Jesus did heal physical sicknesses while on earth, but they believe too that He heals only spiritual diseases today. They are willing to hand their spiritual ills over to the Lord for healing but take it for granted that they must go elsewhere for their physical ills, concluding that the Lord will have nothing to do with those. They forget that "Jesus Christ is the same yesterday and today and forever" (Heb. 13.8).

It is quite customary among today's saints to assume the attitude that God apparently has made no provision for the body. They limit the redemption of Christ to the spirit and the soul and cross out the body completely. They disregard the facts that the Lord Jesus healed physical ills in His day and that the Apostles continued to experience this power of healing in their day. No other explanation for their attitude can be put forward than that of unbelief. The Word of God, however, declares the Lord is also for the body.

This is related to what was said just before. Our body is for the Lord and simultaneously the Lord is for our body too. We see in this the joint relationship of God and man. God gives His Own Self totally to us that we may offer ourselves completely to Him. Upon offering ourselves to Him He will again give Himself to us according to our measure of committal. The Lord wishes us to know that He has given His body for us; He also wants us to know that if our body is genuinely for Him we will experience Him for it. The meaning of the body for the Lord is that we present ours wholly to Him to live for Him; while the Lord for the body implies that, having accepted our consecration, He will grant His life and power to our bodily frames. He will care for, preserve and nourish this physical frame of ours.

Aware of its weakness, uncleanness, sinfulness and deadness, it seems scarcely conceivable that the Lord is also for the body. This we shall nonetheless understand if we contemplate God's way of salvation. When the Lord Jesus was born the Word became flesh. He possessed a body. While on the cross, "he himself bore our sins in his *body* on the tree" (1 Peter 2.24). United to Him by faith, our bodies were crucified with Him as well; and thus has He released them from the power of sin. In Christ this fleshly tent of ours has been resurrected and ascended to heaven. The Holy Spirit is presently dwelling in us. Therefore may we say that the Lord is for our body—not just for our spirit and soul but for our body too.

The Lord for the body embraces several meanings: (1) It conveys the idea that the Lord will deliver the body from sin. Nearly every sin is related somewhat to it. Quite a few sins arise from special physiological causes. Feasting for example is an indulgence of one's physical taste and drinking is a catering to one's bodily lust. Many moments of anger are triggered by physical discomforts. Oversensitive nerves may cause people to be brittle and harsh. Peculiar personalities often result from a peculiar physiological make-up. Many notorious sinners physically are constructed differently from normal persons. Even so, with all these manifestations, the Lord is still for the body. If we offer ours to Him, acknowledging Him as Lord of everything and claiming His promise by faith, we shall see how the Lord can deliver us from ourselves. Irrespective of how we physiologically are made, even possessing special weaknesses, we can overcome our sins through the Lord.

(2) The Lord is additionally for our physical ills. As he destroys sin so will He heal diseases. He is for every matter related to our body; He is consequently for our sicknesses also. Diseases are but the manifestation of the power of sin in our bodies. The Lord Jesus is able to deliver us from sicknesses as well as from sins.

(3) The Lord is also for our living in the body. He will be its strength and life so that it may live by Him. He desires us to experience in our daily walk the power of His resurrection in order that our body too may live by Him.

(4) The Lord is equally for the glorification of the body. This pertains to the future. Today we attain great heights if we walk by Him, yet that does not change the nature of our body. But the day shall come when the Lord shall redeem it and transform this lowly frame into a likeness of His glorious body.

We must underscore the significance of the body being for the Lord. If we yearn to experience the Lord for the body we first must practice the body for the Lord. It is impossible to experience the Lord for the body if we use our bodies according to our wants and for our pleasure instead of presenting them for living entirely unto the Lord. Yet were we to hand ourselves over completely to God, yielding our members as instruments of righteousness and conducting ourselves in all matters according to God's order, He most surely would accord us His life and power.

"And God raised the Lord and will also raise us up by his power" (v.14). This is to explain the last clause of the preceding verse which is "the Lord for the body." The resurrection of the Lord is a *bodily* one: our future resurrection will therefore be *bodily* too. As God has already raised the body of the Lord Jesus so will He also raise ours from the dead. These two facts are equally certain. Hence this is how the Lord is for our body: He will raise us up by His power. It is yet future, nevertheless today we may foretaste the power of His resurrection.

"Do you not know that your bodies are members of Christ? Shall I therefore take the members of Christ and make them members of a prostitute? Never!" (v.15). The first question is noticeably unusually phrased. In other places, such as 1 Corinthians 12.27, it merely states "*you* are the body of Christ and individually members of it"; but only in this passage does it say "your *bodies* are members of Christ." Our whole being is indeed a member of Christ; why, then, is the body specified here? We naturally assume that our spiritual life is a member of Christ for is it not spiritual? But how can this corporeal frame be considered a member of Christ? We are verily witnessing an exceedingly wonderful truth.

We must understand our union with Christ. God does not look at believers individually; He includes them together within His view of Christ. No Christian can exist outside of Christ, because his daily strength to live is supplied by Him. To God, the union of believers with Christ is an altogether definite reality. The "body of Christ" is not just a spiritual term, it is truly a fact. Just as a physical body is joined to a head, so believers are joined to Christ. In God's eye, our union with Christ is perfect, unlimited and absolute. To word it another way, our spirits unite with the spirit of Christ (most important of all), our souls unite with the soul of Christ (the union of wills, the union of affections, and the union of minds), and our bodies unite with the body of Christ. If our union with Christ is *complete* how can the corporeal part of our being be excluded? If we are the members of Christ our bodies too are the members of Christ.

Unquestionably perfect union will not be achieved until the time of future resurrection. Even so, our union with Christ is already a present verity. This teaching is vital, for what comfort we have when we know that *the body of Christ is for our bodies.* All truths may be experienced. Do we have any physiological defect, sickness, suffering or weakness? Remember, Christ's body is for our bodies. Ours are united to His; accordingly we may draw life and strength from His body for the supply of our physical needs. Everyone who has bodily defects should stand on this union with Christ by faith and draw from His resources for their fleshly needs.

The Apostle marvels that the Corinthian believers could be ignorant of such a clear truth. Had they truly apprehended this teaching they would have encountered many spiritual experiences as well as dealt responsibly with various practical warnings; such as, if these bodies are members of Christ could we have dared make them members of a prostitute? For the Apostle right away inquires: "Do you not know that He who joins himself to a prostitute becomes one body with her? For as it is written, 'The two shall become one' " (v.16). Paul develops this doctrine of union most effectively. "He who joins himself to a prostitute becomes one body with her," that is, he becomes a member of the prostitute. A believer has been united with Christ, hence he is a member of Christ. Where will this leave Christ if this member of His becomes a member of a prostitute? The Apostle forbids such a thing.

"But he who is united to the Lord becomes one spirit with him" (v.17). In verses 15-17 we can behold the mystery of our body's union with Christ. The thought of this seventeenth verse is that if man in joining his body to that of a prostitute becomes one *flesh* and also a member of her, how could our bodies not become the members of Christ if we are united to the Lord and become one spirit with Him? To join the body to a prostitute will effect the union of the two bodies: how much more must the two bodies become one if our whole being is joined to Christ!

Paul views the first step in uniting with the Lord as becoming "one spirit with Him." This is a union in the spirit. But he does not regard the believer's body as something unrelated. He concedes that the primary union is in the spirit, yet this fusion of the spirit will consequentially cause the believer's body to be a member of Christ. This ultimately proves that the body is for the Lord and the Lord is also for the body.

The issue before us is union. The children of God ought to perceive clearly their position in Christ, how there is not the slightest gap in their union with Him. Their bodies are members of Christ through which His life may be exhibited. They could not expect much if the Lord were weak and sick; but since the opposite is true, they undeniably can obtain health, power and life from him.

We need to call to mind one point, however. We should at no time harbor the thought that because the *body* is the member of Christ we must therefore physically feel every spiritual fellowship and affair there as though we must have evidence in the body. If we must feel the presence of God in our fleshly frame—if He must take direct control of it and shake it—if the Holy Spirit must fill our frame and make His will known through it—or if the Holy Spirit must assume management of the tongue of the body and speak—then our body has supplanted our spirit in the latter's works. And the result will be that our spirit loses its operation as its work is taken over by the body. But our earthen vessel is not capable of enduring such strenuous labor, hence it often becomes weakened. Furthermore, the evil powers as disembodied spirits crave human bodies. Their chief aim is to possess man's physical frame. A Christian who has his body extended beyond its normal capacity gives opportunity to the evil spirits to work. This is in accordance with the law of the spiritual realm. Assuming that God and His Spirit will commune with him in the *body*, the Christian naturally anticipates experiencing such fellowship there. But God and His Spirit never communicate directly with one's body; God communicates through His Spirit in the believer's spirit. If a child of God persists in seeking to experience God in his body, the evil spirits shall seize the opportunity to come in and shall accord him what he naïvely seeks. The consequences can be none other than occupation by evil spirits. But as to the union of the believer's body with Christ, this fact explains how it is able to receive God's life and be strengthened. Owing to the spirit's noble position, one must be doubly cautious lest he allow his body to usurp its work!

"Shun immorality. Every other sin which a man commits is outside the body; but the immoral man sins against his own body" (v.18). The Bible considers immorality or fornication as more serious than other sins because it has a special relationship to our bodies which are the members of Christ. Need we wonder why the Apostle emphatically and persistently persuades Christians to avoid fornication? We look at it in terms of a moral uncleanness, but the Apostle stresses a far different aspect of it. No sin other than fornication can occasion our body to be united with another; wherefore this is a sin against the body. This implies that no sin but fornication can render a member of Christ a member of a prostitute. Fornication is sinning against the members of Christ. Since Christians are united with Christ, fornication becomes doubly abominable. Or to view it from another perspective: by seeing the abomination of fornication we can appreciate how very real is our body's union with Christ.

"Do you not know that your body is a temple of the Holy Spirit within you, which you have from God?" (v.19) This is the second instance the Apostle Paul asks "Do you not know?" The first occurred in verse 15 which spoke of "the body for the Lord." In this second instance he is referring to "the Lord for the body." Earlier Paul had expressed it in a general way as *"you* are God's temple" (3.16); now he says specifically that *"your body* is a temple of the Holy Spirit." It indicates that the habitation of the Holy Spirit is extended beyond the spirit to the body. We commit a signal error if we consider the body His primary dwelling place, for He dwells initially in our spirit where He holds fellowship with us. However, this does not preclude His life flowing from the spirit to make our body alive. We are deceived if we expect the Holy Spirit to descend primarily on our bodies; but we shall suffer loss, too, if we limit His dwelling place to our spirits.

We should recognize the place of the body in God's design of redemption. Christ sets apart our fleshly frames that we may be filled with the Holy Spirit and become His instruments. Because He has died, been resurrected and been glorified, He is now qualified to give His Holy Spirit to our body. As in the past our soul life permeated our body, so now His Spirit shall permeate it. His life will flow into every member, and He will give us life and power far abundantly beyond what we can think.

That our body constitutes a temple of the Holy Spirit is a sure fact; and it can be livingly experienced as well. Yet many are like the Corinthian believers who forgot this glorious possibility. Though God's Spirit does dwell in them, He seems non-existent to them. We need to exercise faith to believe, to acknowledge and to accept this fact of God. If we *draw* on this fact by faith we shall discover that the Spirit will bring not only the holiness, joy, righteousness and love of Christ to our souls, but also life, power, health and strength to our weak, weary and sick bodies. He will give to our earthen vessels the life of Christ together with the vital elements of His glorious body. When our body has truly died with Christ, that is, when it is subject completely to Him, all self-will and independent action denied and nothing sought but to be a temple of the Lord, then the Holy Spirit shall assuredly manifest the life of the risen Christ in our mortal frame. How good it is for us to genuinely experience the Lord in healing and in strengthening, in His being our health and life! If we see our tent as a temple of the Holy Spirit we shall follow Him in wonderment and in love!

"You are not your own; you were bought with a price. So glorify God in your body" (vv.19-20). You are members of Christ, you are a temple of the Holy Spirit, you are not your own. You were purchased by God with a price. Everything of yours belongs to Him, especially your body. The union of Christ with you and the seal of the Holy Spirit within you proves that your body particularly is God's. "So glorify God in your *body*." Brethren, God wishes us to honor Him there. He wants us to glorify Him both through the consecration of this "body for the Lord" of ours and also through the grace exhibited by the "Lord for the body" of His. Let us be sober and watchful lest we use our bodies for ourselves or permit them to fall into a condition as though the Lord were not for the body. Thus we shall glorify God and allow Him to demonstrate His power freely in delivering us from weakness, sickness and suffering as well as from self-interest, self-love and sin.

CHAPTER 2
SICKNESS

SICKNESS IS A COMMON occurrence in life. For us to know how to keep our body in a condition which glorifies God, we first must know what attitude to take towards sickness, how to make use of it, and also how to be healed. Because sickness is so prevalent we cannot avoid having a serious lack in our life if we do not know how to deal with it.

SICKNESS AND SIN

The Bible discloses a close relationship between sickness and sin. The ultimate consequence of sin is death. Sickness lies between sin and death. It is the sequel to sin and the prologue to death. If there were no sin in the world, there would be neither sickness nor death. Had not Adam sinned, sickness would not have come upon the earth: of this we can be most certain. Hence as with every other woe, sickness was ushered in by sin.

Human beings are made up of two natures: the noncorporeal and the corporeal. Both suffered from man's fall. The spirit and soul were damaged by sin and the body was invaded by sickness. The sin of the spirit and soul together with the sickness of the body attest that man must die.

When the Lord Jesus came to save, He not only forgave man's sin but also healed man's body. He saved bodies as well as souls. From the outset of His ministry He healed man's sickness; at the conclusion of His labor He became a propitiation on the cross for man's sins. Behold how many sick people were healed by Him during His earthly days! His hands were ever ready to touch the sick and raise them up.

Judging both by what He Himself did and by the command He gave His disciples, we cannot help but see that the salvation He provides includes the healing of sickness. His is the gospel of forgiveness *and* healing. These two go together. The Lord Jesus saves people from sins and sicknesses that they may know the love of the Father. In reading the Gospels, the Acts, the Epistles or the Old Testament, we continually witness how healing and forgiveness run parallel to each other.

We all know Isaiah 53 forms the clearest chapter in the Old Testament on the gospel. Various places in the New Testament make reference to this particular chapter when the fulfillment of its prophecies concerning the redemptive work of the Lord Jesus is in view. "The chastisement of our peace was upon him; and with his stripes we are healed" (v.5 ASV). It tells us in unmistakable terms that both the healing of the body and the peace of the soul are accorded us. This is made even plainer when we consider the two different uses of the verb "bear": "he bore the sin of many" (v.12) and "he has borne our griefs (Hebrew: sicknesses)" (v.4). The Lord Jesus bears our sins; He also bears our sicknesses. Because He has borne our sins, we need not bear them again; in like manner, since He has borne our sicknesses, we need no longer bear them either.* Sin has done damage to our soul and body, so the Lord Jesus saves both. He saves us from sicknesses as well as from sins. Believers today can offer praise with David: "Bless the Lord, O my soul; and all that is within me, bless his holy name! . . . Who forgives all your iniquity, who heals all your diseases" (Ps. 103.1,3). What a shame that so many Christians can utter but half a praise for they know but half a salvation. It is a loss to both God and man.

Let us note that God's salvation would not be complete if the Lord Jesus simply forgave our sins but did not heal our sicknesses too. How could He save our souls and yet leave

---

*Now of course there is a difference in scope between the Lord's bearing sins and His bearing sicknesses. This is enlarged upon in the author's message on sickness and healing which has been included as an addendum to Chapter 2 of this Part.—Translator.

our bodies to be tormented by infirmities? Did He not stress both while He was on earth? Sometimes He forgave first and then healed; at other times, just the reverse. He does according to what man is able to take in. In perusing the Gospels we find that the Lord Jesus performed more healing than any other works, because the Jews at that time seemed less able to believe in the Lord's forgiving them than in the Lord's healing (Matt. 9.5). Christians today, however, are precisely the opposite. In those days men believed that the Lord had power to heal sickness but they doubted His grace of forgiveness. Today's saints believe His forgiving power and doubt His healing grace. They confess that the Lord Jesus came to save people from sin, yet ignore the fact that He is equally the Savior Who heals. Man's unbelief divides the perfect Savior into two, though the truth remains that Christ is forever the Savior of man's body and soul, competent to heal as well as to forgive.

In our Lord's thought, it is not enough that a man be forgiven and not healed too. Hence, we find Him commanding, "Rise, take up your bed and go home" after His declaration to the paralytic, "Man, your sins are forgiven you" (Luke 5. 24,20). But as to ourselves, although we are people plagued by both sins and sicknesses, we count forgiveness from the Lord sufficient, leaving illness to be borne by ourselves and to be healed by other means. The Lord Jesus, however, did not want people to have to take the paralytic home still confined to a bed after his sins had been forgiven.

The Lord conceives a contrary view from us with respect to the relationship between sin and sickness. Our thought is that sin belongs to the spiritual realm, something disliked and condemned by God, whereas sickness is merely a mundane phenomenon having nothing to do with Him. On the other hand, the Lord Jesus considers both the sins of the soul and the infirmities of the body to be the works of Satan. He came "to destroy the works of the devil" (1 John 3.8), therefore He casts out demons and heals sicknesses. When Peter under revelation speaks of the Lord's *healing ministry*, he declares that He "went about doing good and healing all that were oppressed by the devil" (Acts 10.38). Sin and sickness are as intimately associated as are our soul and body. Forgiveness and healing complement each other.

THE CHASTISEMENT OF GOD

Having seen something of the Lord's thought regarding sickness, we now turn our attention to the causes of the sickness of *believers*.

"That is why many of you are weak and ill, and some have died. But if we judged ourselves truly, we should not be judged. But when we are judged by the Lord, we are chastened so that we may not be condemned along with the world" (1 Cor. 11.30-32). Paul explains here that sickness is one type of the Lord's chastening. Owing to their having erred before the Lord, believers are chastened with illness to prompt them to judge themselves and eliminate their mistakes. In chastening His children God deals graciously towards them that they may not be condemned with the world. If Christians repent of their faults God will no longer chasten them. Can we not then avoid sickness through self-judgment?

We often conclude sickness to be merely a physical problem and to have no relation to God's righteousness, holiness and judgment. But the Apostle tells us quite plainly in this passage that sickness is an effect of sin and a chastisement of God. Christians like to cite the story of the blind man in John 9 to support the contention that their sickness is not God's chastisement due to sin. Yet the Lord Jesus has not said there that sin and sickness are unrelated; He simply is warning His disciples not to condemn each and every sick person. If Adam had not sinned, that man in John 9 would never have been blind. Moreover, that particular man was *born* blind, so the *nature* of his illness is quite unlike that of a believer's sickness. The infirmities of those who are born infirm are perhaps not due to their own sins; but according to the Scriptures sickness after we have believed in the Lord is usually related to sin. "Therefore confess your sins to one another, and pray for one another, that you may be healed" (James 5.16). Sins must first be confessed and then there will be healing. <u>Sin is the root of sickness.</u>

Illness is frequently the chastisement of God employed to draw our attention to some sin which we have overlooked so that we may forsake it. God *permits* these sicknesses to fall upon us that He may discipline us and purge us from our faults. God's hand bears down on us to direct our eyes to some unrighteousness or some debt, some pride or love of this world, some self-reliance or greediness in work, or some disobedience to God. Sickness is consequently God's open judgment of sin. Yet we are not to infer from this that the one who is ill is necessarily more sinful than others (cf. Luke 13.2); quite the opposite, they who are chastened by the Lord are usually the holiest. Job is a prime example.

Each time a believer is chastened by God and becomes sick he is open to great blessing, for the Father of spirits "disciplines us for our good, that we may share his holiness" (Heb. 12.10). Sickness prompts us to recollect and examine the past as to whether there be any hidden sin, obstinacy or self-will. Then and there we can detect if any barrier exists between us and God. As we search the depths of our heart we come to realize how full of self and unlike the holiness of God has been our past life. These exercises enable us to advance in spiritual development and to obtain God's healing.

Hence the first action one should take when ill is not to scurry around in search of healing and the means of healing. He should neither be anxious nor afraid. What he should do is place himself completely in God's light for examination, having an honest desire to learn if he is being chastened because of some lack. He should judge himself. Thus the Holy Spirit shall point out to him where he has failed. And whatever he is shown, it must be immediately confessed and forsaken. If that sin *has done harm to others* then he must *do his best* to make it up, meanwhile believing that God has accepted him. He should offer himself afresh to God and be disposed to obey His will fully.

God "does not willingly afflict or grieve the sons of men" (Lam. 3.33). He will cease chastening when He realizes the objective of self-judgment is attained. God is most happy to withdraw His chastisement when no longer needed. The Bible assures us that if we judge ourselves we will not be judged. God desires us to be freed from sin and self; once that end has been reached the sickness will disappear because it has accomplished its mission. What the Christian needs to understand today is that God chastens him for a specific purpose. Accordingly, always allow the Holy Spirit to uncover what the sin is so that the aim of God may be achieved and the chastisement may no longer be necessary. Then will God heal.

Once the saint has confessed and forsaken his sin and in addition believed for forgiveness, he can trust God's promise and know without fear that He will make him well. With a conscience void of accusation he has the boldness to approach God for grace. It is when we are far away from Him that we find it hard to believe or that we dare not believe; but after sin is forsaken and forgiven through the enlightening of, and obedience to, the Holy Spirit, we have free access to God. Since the cause of the sickness has been removed, the sickness itself shall be removed. Now the sick believer has no difficulty in believing that "the chastisement of our peace was upon (Christ); and with his stripes we are healed." At that moment the presence of the Lord will be manifested abundantly and the life of the Lord will enter his body to make it alive.

Are we really aware that the heavenly Father is not pleased with us in many areas? He uses sickness to help us perceive our shortcomings. If we do not suppress the voice of conscience the Holy Spirit shall most certainly show us the reason for the chastisement. God delights to forgive our sins and heal our ills. The great redemptive work of the Lord Jesus includes both forgiveness and healing. He will permit nothing between us and Him; He wants us to live by Him as never before. Now is the time to trust and obey Him totally. The Heavenly Father does not wish to chastise. How willing He is to heal us that through seeing His love and power we may hold closer communion with Him.

SICKNESS AND SELF

All evil and adverse environment has the effect of exposing our true condition. These do not add any particular sin to us; they only reveal what is in us. Sickness is one of these environments through which we can read our true condition.

We never realize how much we are living for God and how much for self until we are sick, especially if that sickness is a protracted one. During our ordinary days we may declare with great conviction in our hearts that we will obey God with our whole heart and will be satisfied with whatever treatment we receive from Him; only at the time of sickness, though, do we discover how much of that declaration is genuine. What God wishes to accomplish in His children is that they be satisfied with His will and way. He does not want His children to murmur against His will and way because of their *own* immature feelings. For this reason God permits sickness to descend upon His dearest children time and again in order to make manifest their attitude towards His specially arranged will.

How pitiful is the Christian who for the sake of his own desire murmurs against God when under trial. He does not accept what God gives as the best for him; instead his heart is flooded with the desire for early healing. (What we mean by sickness given by God is in reality sickness permitted by God, for the one who directly gives sickness is Satan. But whatever illness befalls a Christian comes through God's permission and comes with a purpose. The experience of Job is a perfect example.) Because of this, God must prolong the sickness. He will not withdraw His instrument before He has achieved His purpose. The end in all communications between God and the believer is to bring the latter to an unconditional submission to Him, gladly welcoming any treatment from Him. God is not pleased with that person who praises Him in prosperity but complains against Him in adversity. God does not want His own to doubt His love or misunderstand His acts so easily: He wants them to obey Him even to death.

God intends His children to recognize that everything which comes upon them is given by Him. However dangerous is the physical or environmental circumstance, it is measured by His hand. Even the falling of a hair is within His will. Should a person resist what comes upon him he cannot but be resisting as well the God Who permits these occurrences. And should he develop a heart of hatred following a painful period of sickness, he cannot but be hating the God Who allowed it to happen to him. The question under discussion is not whether a believer ought to be sick but whether he is opposing God. God wants His own to forget their sickness when ill. Yes, forget their sickness and look away steadfastly at God. Suppose His will is for me to be sick and to continue to be so; am I ready to accept it? Can I humble myself beneath the mighty hand of God and resist not? Or do I covet in suffering a health which is outside God's present purpose? Can I wait until His end is fulfilled before asking in His will for healing? Or will I seek other means of healing while He is chastening me? Am I, in the time of deep suffering, striving for what He presently will not grant? These questions should pierce deeply into the heart of every sick believer.

God takes no pleasure in His children's sickness. Rather does His love make Him desire smooth peaceful days for them. But He knows the danger: in time of ease our love towards Him, our words of praise and our service for Him, are conditioned by peaceful living. He knows how easily our hearts can turn from Him and His will to His gifts. He consequently permits sickness and similar phenomena to come upon us that we may see whether we want Him or purely His gifts. If in days of adversity we seek nothing else, then it indicates we genuinely want God. Sickness readily discloses whether one seeks his own desire or the arrangement of God.

We still harbor our personal desires. Such aspirations prove how flushed with our own thoughts our daily life is. Both in the work of God and in our dealings with people, we hold tenaciously to many thoughts and opinions. God is compelled to bring us near the door of death in order to teach us the folly of resisting Him. He lets us pass through deep waters that we may be broken and may forsake our self-will—that behavior of ours which displeases Him immensely. How numerous are the Christians who ordinarily seem to follow nothing of what the Lord has said but become obedient only after their bodies are afflicted. The way of the Lord must therefore be this: He chastises after love's persuasion has lost its effectiveness. The purpose of His chastisement is to break down self-will. Every sick Christian should judge himself seriously in this respect.

Besides self-desire and self-will, what God additionally hates is a heart of *self-love*. Self-love endangers the spiritual life and destroys spiritual works. Except God expunge this element from us, we cannot run our spiritual race swiftly. Self-love has a special relationship to our body. To say we love ourselves means we cherish our bodies and our life. Hence to destroy this odious trait God often permits sickness to come upon us. Because of our love of self we are fearful lest our body be weakened; yet God weakens it; He allows us to experience pain. And when we expect to get well our sickness becomes the more serious. We wish to keep on living, but that hope appears to fade. God of course deals differently with different people—some drastically, some relatively lightly; nonetheless, the purpose of God in removing the heart of self-love remains the same. How many *strong* ones must be brought near the gates of death before their love of self dissolves: what else is left to be loved now that his body is ruined, his life is endangered, sickness has progressively devoured his health, and pain has swallowed up his power? By this time the person is actually willing to die; he is hopeless but also self-loveless. It would be the height of tragedy were he at this moment not to return and claim God's promise of healing.

The heart of a believer is far from God's. God permits him to be ill that he may forget himself; but the more ill he grows the more self-loving he becomes; he endlessly dwells on his symptoms in his anxiety to find a cure. Almost all thoughts revolve about himself! How attentive he now is to his food, what he should or should not eat! How worried he is when anything goes awry! He takes great care for his comforts and rest. He agonizes if he feels a bit hot or cold or has suffered a bad night, as though these were fatal to his life. How sensitive he is to the way people treat him: do they think enough of him, do they take good care of him, do they visit him as often as they should? Countless hours are exhausted in just this way of thinking about his body; and so he has no time to meditate on the Lord or on what the Lord may be wanting to accomplish in his life. Indeed, many are simply "bewitched" by their sickness! We never truly know how excessively much we love ourselves until we become sick!

God is not delighted with our self-love. He desires us to comprehend the far-reaching damage it inflicts upon us. He wishes us to learn in the hour of sickness how to be engrossed not in our symptoms but exclusively in Him. It is His desire that we commit our body entirely to Him and allow Him to care for it. Every discovery of an adverse symptom should warn us not to be occupied with our body but to mind the Lord.

Due to love of self the believer seeks healing as soon as he is sick. He does not perceive that he ought to rid his heart of wicked deeds before beseeching God to heal. His eyes are fixed upon healing. He does not bother to inquire why God has permitted this sickness, what he should repent of, or how he should let God's work be perfected in him. All he can contemplate is his own weakness. He longs to be strong again, so he searches everywhere for the means of healing. That he may be cured speedily, he entreats God and inquires of man. With the sick believer in such a state as this, it is impossible for God to accomplish His purpose in him. That is why some are made well only temporarily; after a while their old infirmity returns. How can there be lasting healing if the root of sickness is not removed?

Sickness is one of the methods by which God chooses to speak to us. He does not want us to grow anxious and seek immediately for cure; instead He asks us to pray obediently. What a pity it is for that person who eagerly expects to be healed while simultaneously is unable to say to the Lord, "Speak, Lord, for Your servant hears." Our sole aim is merely to be delivered from pain and weakness. We rush to find the best remedy. Sickness prompts us to invent many cures. Each symptom frightens us and sets our brain to work. God appears to be far from us. We neglect our spiritual welfare. All thoughts center upon our sufferings and the means of cure. Should the medicine work, then we praise the grace of God. But should the cure be delayed we lapse into misunderstanding our Father's love. Yet let us ask ourselves: if all we desire is to be delivered from pain, are we being led by the Holy Spirit? Do we think we can glorify God with the power of the flesh?

MEDICINE

Self-love naturally produces self-means. Instead of solving the root of the sickness in God, Christians covet cure through man's drugs. We do not intend to waste a lot of time here in arguing whether or not a believer can use medicine. Yet we do want to say that since the Lord Jesus has provided for the healing of our body in His salvation, it seems to be ignorance, if not unbelief, if we turn to the aid of man's invention.

Many debate whether or not the saints should take medicine. They seem to imply that if this question is resolved all questions are solved. But are they aware that the principle of spiritual living is not in "can or can't" but in whether or not God has so led? Our question, therefore, is: when a believer, because of self-love, depends on medicine and eagerly seeks healing, is he being guided by the Holy Spirit or is it exclusively his own activity? According to human nature, until one has experienced many adverse circumstances he is reluctant to be saved by faith; he usually strives to be saved by his works. Is it not equally true with the healing of one's body? Perhaps the struggle over divine healing is even more intense than that over forgiveness of sin. Believers will acknowledge that unless they trust the Lord Jesus for salvation they cannot gain entrance to heaven; but why, such ones will ask, must they depend on the salvation of the Lord for healing when they can employ many other medical means? So our attention is not focused upon whether medicine can be used but upon whether in using it through one's own activity he has demeaned God's salvation. Has not the world spun out sundry theories for saving man from sin? Does not the world supply many schools of philosophy, psychology, ethics and education as well as countless rituals, rules and practices to assist people to be good? Can we as believers accept these means as perfect and workable? Are we for the finished work of the Lord Jesus on the cross or for these ingenious human devices? In such a similar manner has the world invented multiplied kinds of drugs to relieve people from ailments; yet the Lord has equally accomplished on the cross that work of salvation pertaining to the body. Shall we therefore seek cure according to human methods or shall we rely on the Lord Jesus for healing?

We do acknowledge that occasionally God utilizes intermediaries to manifest His power and glory. Judging from the teaching of Scripture and the experience of Christians, however, we are forced to confess that after the fall of man our feelings seem to control our lives, which prompts us naturally to incline towards the intermediaries than towards God Himself. Hence we observe that during the period of illness Christians direct more attention to medicine than to the power of God. Although their lips may proclaim a trust in God's power, their hearts are almost totally wrapped up in medicine—as though without its help God's power cannot be released. No wonder they exhibit signs of unrest, anxiety and fear, hotly pursuing the best means of cure everywhere. These ones lack the peace which springs from trusting in God. With their hearts thus absorbed in the use and application of medicine, they turn to the world and sacrifice the presence of God. God has purposed through sickness to bring people *nearer to Him,* yet precisely the *opposite* seems to be the effect. Perhaps some indeed are able to use medicine without damaging their spiritual life, but such ones are few. Most of God's people tend to rely on intermediaries more than on Him and consequently their spiritual life is harmed through the use of drugs.

There is a vast distinction between cure through medicine and healing by God. The power of the first is natural while that of the second is supernatural. The way of obtaining the cure is likewise distinguishable: in using medicine the trust rests in human cleverness; in depending on God the confidence is in the work and life of the Lord Jesus. Even should the physician be a believer who entreats God for wisdom and for blessing in the drug used, he is nonetheless powerless to impart spiritual blessing to the one healed, for unconsciously the latter already has pinned his hope of cure on medicine rather than on the power of the Lord. Though he be healed physically, his spiritual life shall suffer loss. If the person verily trusts in God he will commit himself to His love and power. He will inquire and investigate the cause of his sickness—wherein has he displeased the Lord. So that when he is healed he shall be blessed spiritually as well as bodily.

Many argue that since medicine is given by God they certainly can use it. But this is what we want to emphasize: does God lead us to use medicine? We do not wish to debate whether or not medicine comes from God; we instead wished to inquire whether or not the Lord Jesus is given by God to His children as the Savior of their physical ills: should we seek a cure through the natural power of drugs as unbelievers or weak Christians do, or should we accept the Lord Jesus Whom God has prepared for us and trust in His name?

Trusting medicine and accepting the life of the Lord Jesus are absolutely diametrical. We grant the effectiveness of medicine and other medical inventions, but these cures are natural, short of the best God has provided for His own. Believers may ask God to bless the drugs and be cured; they may also thank God after being cured by these, regarding themselves as having been healed by God Himself; yet such healing is not the same as accepting the life of the Lord Jesus. For by so doing they are taking the easy way out, quitting the battlefield of faith. If, in our conflict with Satan, healing were the only objective to attain in sickness then we could employ any available means of cure. But should there be more important purposes than mere healing to be realized, then must we not be quiet before God and await His way and time?

We do not want to state dogmatically that God never blesses medicine. We know God has blessed many times, for He is so kind and generous. Christians who trust in medicine are nevertheless not standing on the ground of redemption. They are assuming the same position as do worldly people. They cannot testify for God in this particular matter. Swallowing pills, applying ointments, and taking injections will not afford us the life of the Lord Jesus. In trusting God we are elevated to a place higher than that of the natural. Cure by medicine is often slow and painful; the healing of God is quick and blessed.

One observation is certainly beyond dispute, which is: that were we to be healed by dependence on God, we would derive such spiritual profit from it as a cure by medicine could never accord us. When sick in bed how deeply people repent of their past lives; but once they are healed through use of medicine they drift further away from God. Yet they would not fall into such an after-effect were they to be healed like others by waiting and trusting in God. These latter ones confess their sins, deny themselves, trust in God's love, and depend on His power; they accept the life and holiness of God; and they establish a new indivisible relationship with Him.

The object lesson God purposes us to learn in sickness is to cease from all our own activity and trust Him thoroughly. How often in anxiously seeking cure we are driven on by a heart of self-love. We forget God and the lesson He wishes to teach us. For if God's children were void of self-love, would they so eagerly strive after healing?—if they have truly ceased from their activities, would they turn to the assistance of human medicine? Not at all. They would examine themselves quietly before God, seeking to understand first the meaning of their sickness, and afterwards asking *Him* for healing on the basis of the Father's love. The contrast between leaning on medical help and leaning on God's power is that in the former case the person anxiously seeks for a cure while in the latter case he calmly aspires to ascertain God's will. It is because believers are full of self-love, impetuous desire and their own strength that they so seek for a cure when sick. They would react differently were they to learn to depend on God's power. To trust in God for healing, believers must honestly confess and forsake their sins and be willing to offer themselves utterly to Him.

Many today are sick. In each of these sicknesses the Lord has a special purpose. Whenever "self" relinquishes its power, the Lord will heal. If Christians refuse to bow, if they refuse to gladly receive the sickness as the best from God, and if they search for means other than God, they will be filled with sickness again even after being cured. If they cling to self-love and are mindful of themselves all the time, God will give them increased cause to pity themselves. He will show them that earthly medicine cannot permanently heal. God intends His children to know that *a strong and healthy body is neither for the sake of pleasing one's self nor to be used in accordance with one's desires but is wholly for God.* The spirit of healing is a spirit of holiness. What we lack is not healing but holiness. What we need to be delivered from initially is not sickness but self.

When a child of God has denied the use of human means and medicine and has trusted in the Father with singleness of heart, he notices his faith waxing stronger than usual. He has launched upon a new relationship with God; he begins to live by that life he formerly did not trust. He commits his body as well as his spirit and soul to his heavenly Father. He discovers that the will of God is to manifest the power of the Lord Jesus and the love of the Father. He is led to exercise faith unto proving that the Lord redeems the body as well as the spirit and soul.

"Therefore I tell you, do not be anxious about your life" (Matt. 6.25). The Lord will care for whatever we commit to Him. If we secure instant healing, let us praise God. Should our symptoms grow more severe, let us not doubt but let us look away instead to God's promise and furnish no occasion for self-love to be revived. God may be using this very situation to extinguish the last drops of our love for self. Were we to regard our body we would commence to doubt; but if we behold God's promise we will draw nearer to Him, our faith will be increased, and healing eventually will come to us.

We must nevertheless be careful lest we fall into extremes. Though God aims for us to rely exclusively upon Him, yet once we have definitely denied our own activities and trusted Him in perfect faith, He may delight in our using some natural means to render help to our body. We mean such articles as "a little wine" prescribed for Timothy. Timothy possessed a weak stomach and was afflicted frequently with ailments. Instead of scolding him for lack of faith and failure to be cured directly from God, Paul persuaded Timothy to use a little wine for it would be beneficial to him. What the Apostle here enjoins us to use is some such element as wine, something neutral in its innate character.

From this case we may learn a lesson. We must, it is very true, believe and depend on God (even as Timothy must have done); even so, we at the same time should not go to extremes. If our body is weak we should learn to be led by the Lord to eat some singularly nourishing food. By using a little of such nourishments according to the leading of the Lord, our body shall be strengthened. Before our body is fully redeemed we continue naturally to be human beings who yet possess a physical body. We should therefore be attentive to its natural needs.

Such use of nutrients is not contradictory to faith. Only, believers need to be cautious lest they know merely these nutrients and do not trust in God.

BETTER TO BE HEALED

Some of God's saints have run to extremes. They were naturally hard and obstinate but were broken by God through sickness sent them. By submitting themselves to the purpose of God's chastisement they became most gentle, kind, soft and holy. However, since sickness has been so effective in transforming their lives, they begin to relish sickness more than health. They view sickness to be an enzyme to spiritual growth. They aspire no more to be healed but accept unnaturally instead the sickness which comes to them. They now contend that were they meant to be whole, God would step in Himself and heal them. According to their reckoning, it is less troublesome to be godly in sickness than in health, one is nearer to God in inactivity and suffering than in activity, and it is more excellent to lie in bed than to run to and fro. Consequently, they have no desire to seek divine healing. How can we help them to know that health is *more profitable* than weakness? We acknowledge that many believers do forsake their wickedness and enter upon a deeper experience during sickness; we admit that a number of invalids and infirm persons possess unusual godliness and spiritual experiences; but we must additionally confess that many Christians are rather unclear on several points.

The sick may be holy, but such holiness is a little unnatural. Who knows but what, once he was recuperated and again had the freedom of choice, he would return to the world and to himself? In sickness he is holy; in health he becomes worldly. The Lord has to keep him in prolonged illness in order to keep him holy. His holiness hinges on his sickness! Let us understand, however, that life with the Lord need not at all be restricted to illness. Never, never entertain the thought that unless one is under the yoke of sickness he has no strength to glorify God in his daily duties. On the contrary, he should be able to manifest the life of God in an ordinary daily walk. To be able to endure suffering is good, but is it not even better if one can obey God when he is full of strength?

We should recognize that healing—divine healing—is something which belongs to God. In striving to be cured by human medicine we naturally are separated from Him; but in aspiring to be cured by God we will be drawn closer to Him. He who is healed by *God* glorifies Him more than he who is always sick. Sickness can glorify God, for it presents Him with an opportunity to manifest His healing power (John 9.3); yet how can He be glorified if one remains protractedly ill? When we are healed by God we witness His power as well as His glory.

The Lord Jesus never portrayed sickness as a blessing which His followers ought to endure to their death. Hs never suggested it was an expression of the Father's love. He calls His disciples to take up the cross, but He does not allow the sick to remain ill for long. He tells them how they should suffer for Him but never says they should be sick for Him. The Lord foretells we shall have tribulation in the world, yet He does not view illness as tribulation. How truly He suffered while on earth, yet never was He sick. Moreover, on every occasion when He met a sick person He healed him. He avows that sickness comes from sin and the devil.

We must differentiate suffering from sickness. "Many are the afflictions of the righteous," notes the psalmist, "but the Lord delivers him out of them all. He keeps all his bones; not one of them is broken" (Ps. 34.19-20). "Is anyone among you suffering?" asks James. Then "let him pray" that he may obtain grace and strength; but, the Apostle continues, "is any among you sick? Let him call for the elders of the church" that he may be healed (5.13-14).

1 Corinthians 11.30-32 deals with the relationship of believers to sickness most comprehensively. Sickness is the chastening of God. If a Christian is willing to judge himself, God shall withdraw the illness. God never desires His own to persist long in it. No chastisement is permanent. Once the cause of it is removed, the chastisement itself will follow suit. "For the moment all discipline seems painful rather than pleasant; *later* . . . "—believers tend to forget God's "later"—"it yields the peaceful fruit of righteousness

to those who have been trained by it" (Heb. 12.11). Thus we find chastisement is only momentary; afterwards it will produce the most excellent fruit of righteousness. Do not let us misconstrue the discipline of God as being punishment. Strictly speaking, believers are no longer judged. The passage of 1 Corinthians 11.31 supports this statement. The concept of *law* should no longer be with us as though sin must always be answered with a corresponding degree of punishment. What we have here is not a judicial, but a family, problem.

Let us return to the positive teaching of the Bible concerning our body. One verse in Scripture which can completely overthrow the idea some have is 3 John 2: "Beloved, I pray that all may go well with you and that you may be in health; I know that it is well with your soul." This is a prayer of the Apostle John as revealed to him by the Holy Spirit, so it expresses the eternal thought of God in regard to the body of the believer. God has no intention for His children to be sick throughout their lives, unable to serve Him actively. He wishes them to be in bodily health even as their souls are well. Accordingly, we can conclude beyond doubt that prolonged illness is not God's will. He may chasten us temporarily with sickness, but He has no pleasure in protracted sickness.

Paul's word in 1 Thessalonians 5.23 additionally confirms that inordinately long illness is not God's will. As the spirit and soul are, so should be the body. God is not satisfied to have our spirit and soul sound and blameless while our body remains weak, sick and racked with pain. His purpose is to save the whole man, not just a part of him.

The work of the Lord Jesus also reveals the will of God concerning sickness, because He did nothing but the will of God. In the healing of the leper He especially unveils to us the heart of the heavenly Father towards the sick. The leper pleaded, "Lord, if you *will*, you can make me clean." Here we see a man knocking at the gate of heaven inquiring if it is God's will to heal. The Lord stretched out His hand, touched him, and said, "I will; be clean" (Matt. 8.2-3).

Healing often represents God's mind. He who thinks God is reluctant to heal does not know His will. The earthly ministry of the Lord Jesus included "healing *all* who were sick" (v.16). How can we arbitrarily claim that He now has changed His attitude?

The aim of God for today is for His "will (to) be done on earth as it is in heaven" (Matt. 6.10). God's will is carried out in heaven: is there sickness there? No! God's will is altogether incompatible with sickness. What a serious fault it is for Christians, upon having asked healing of God and having given up hope, then to utter the words, "May the Lord's will be done" as if the will of the Lord were synonymous with sickness and death. God does not will for His children to be ill. Though He sometimes permits them to be sick for their profit, His determinate counsel forever is health for His people. The fact that there is no sickness in heaven fully proves what the will of God is.

Were we to trace the source of sickness we would be doubly persuaded to seek for healing. All who were sick "were oppressed by the devil" (Acts. 10.38). The Lord Jesus described the woman who was bent over and could not fully straighten herself as one "whom Satan bound" (Luke 13.16). When He healed Peter's mother-in-law He "rebuked the fever" (Luke 4.39) in the same manner as He rebuked the demons (cf. vv. 31-41). In reading the book of Job we learn that it is the devil who caused Job's sickness (Ch. 1 & 2); but it is God Who healed him (Ch. 42). The thorn that harassed and weakened Paul was "a messenger of Satan" (2 Cor. 12.7); the One Who made him strong is God. He who has the power of death is the devil (Heb. 2.14). We know illness ripens into death, for it is one of the facets of death. As Satan has the power of death, he has the power of sickness too, for death is but the ultimate step beyond sickness.

We cannot avoid concluding from these passages that sickness originates with the devil. God *permits* Satan to attack His children because they contain some defects in their lives. If they refuse to forsake what God has demanded and thus allow illness to continue in their lives, it is as if they have forsaken what God has ordered and have welcomed sickness instead. In so doing they voluntarily place themselves under the oppression of Satan. Who is so illogical as to return to bondage after he has obeyed the revealed will of God? Realizing that sickness proceeds from the devil, we ought to resist it. We should be clear that it belongs to our enemy and hence is not to be welcomed by us. The Son of God comes to set us free, not to have us bound.

Why does God not remove our infirmity when it is no further needed? This is a question posed by many saints. Let us give heed to the principle of God's dealing with us which is always that of "be it done for you as you have believed" (Matt. 8.13). Often God wishes to make His children well, but He has to let sickness remain with them because of their unbelief and lack of prayer. If God's saints accede to sickness —nay, even welcome it—as though it would deliver them from the world and make them holier, then the Lord can do nothing except grant them what they ask. God frequently deals with His own according to what they are able to receive. God may be most delighted to cure them; yet for the lack of believing prayer this precious gift is not the portion of all.

Are we wiser than God? Should we exceed what the Bible reveals? While the sick room may at times be like a sanctuary where the inner man is deeply moved, illness nonetheless is not God's ordained will nor is it His best. Should we follow our emotional whim and disregard the revealed will of God, He can only let us have what we desire. How many of the Lord's people piously say: I leave myself in God's hand for healing or for sickness; I allow God to do what He wills. But these are generally people who use medicine. Is this committing everything to God? How contradictory is such a life! Their submission is but a sign of spiritual lethargy. In their hearts they long for health, but mere desire will not prompt God to work. They have accepted sickness passively for so long that they simply succumb to it, forfeiting all courage to seek freedom. The best for them would be for other people to believe on their behalf or for God to confer upon them the faith to believe. However, faith given by God shall not come unless their will becomes active in resisting the devil and in holding on to the Lord Jesus. Many are infirm not out of necessity but for lack of strength to lay hold on God's promise.

Be it therefore apprehended that the spiritual blessing we receive in sickness is far inferior to what we receive in restoration. If we rest on God for healing, then naturally after being cured we will continue to walk in holiness so as to preserve our health. By making us well the Lord possesses our body. Unspeakable is the joy found in a new relationship and a new experience with Him, not because of sickness cured but because of a new touch with life. In such a time believers glorify the Lord far more than in the time of ill-health.

God's children should accordingly rise up and strive after healing. First hear what God has to say through our sickness, then do as has been revealed with singleness of heart. Moreover, commit your body afresh to the Lord. If there are near you elders of the church who can anoint you with oil (James 5.14-15), then call them and follow the *injunction* of the Holy Scriptures. Or else quietly exercise faith to lay hold of the promise of God (Ex. 15.26). God will heal us.

> [*Translator's note*: It was thought profitable for the reader that the following message on sickness and healing, spoken by Mr. Nee in 1948, should be included at this point as an addendum to what has just been set forth in this section on the subject by the author. Although some duplication does appear, it was felt best to include the message in its entirety.]

There are a few matters concerning sickness we would like to consider together before God:

1. *The Relation between Sickness and Sin*

Before the fall of mankind no infirmity of any kind existed; sickness arose only after man had sinned. One can say generally that both sickness and death resulted from sin; for by one man's tresspass sin and death came into the world (Rom. 5.12). Sickness spread to all men just as did death. Though not all sin in the same way as Adam did, yet because of his transgression, all die. Where there is sin there is also death. In between these two is that which we usually call sickness. This, then, is the factor common to all disease. However, there is actually more than one cause to account for sickness coming upon people. Some sicknesses spring from sin, while others do not. So far as *mankind* is concerned, sickness does come from sin; but in relation to the *individual* it may or may not be the case. We need to distinguish between these two applications of sickness. Now it is entirely true that were there no sin there could neither be death *nor* sickness; for if there were no death in the world, how could there ever be sickness? Death arises through sin, and sickness through the inception of death. Even so, this cannot be specifically and indiscriminately applied to every individual, because while many do fall ill through sin there are others who become ill for reasons other than sin. In this matter of the relationship of sin to sickness we must therefore make a careful distinction between the application of this relationship to mankind as a whole and its application to individual men.

We will recall in such Old Testament books as Leviticus and Numbers that God's promise was, that if the people of Israel obeyed Him, walked in His way, rebelled not against His laws and did not sin against Him, then He would keep them from many diseases. These words plainly teach that many maladies derive from sin or rebellion against God. Yet in the New Testament we discover that some sicknesses are not caused by the person having committed any transgression at all.

Paul once wrote that he would deliver to Satan for the destruction of his flesh that man who had sinned by living with his father's wife (1 Cor 5.4-5). This definitely indicates that some sickness proceeds from sin. The consequence of sin is either sickness if the sin is light or death if it is serious. Judging from the words of 2 Corinthians 7 this man was not sick to the point of death because, out of godly grief, he produced a repentance which led to salvation and brought no regret (vv.9-10). Paul charged the church at Corinth to forgive such a man (2 Cor. 2.6-7). In 1 Corinthians 5 mention is made of delivering this man's flesh (not his life) to Satan; he was to be sick but was not to die.

Paul further wrote that those in the church at Corinth who ate and drank of the bread and the cup of the Lord without discerning the Lord's body had become weak and ill and some even had died (1 Cor. 11.29-30). This reveals that disobedience to the Lord was the provocation for their sickness.

The Scriptures have served sufficient notice that many (but not all) are ill because of sin. Hence the first action we must take when sick is to examine ourselves to determine whether or not we have sinned against God. By searching, many find that their illness is in fact due to sin: on a particular occasion they had rebelled against God or had disobeyed His Word. They had gone astray. Just as soon as that particular sin is found out and confessed, however, the sickness will be over. Countless brothers and sisters in the Lord have encountered such experiences. Shortly after the cause is discovered before God the illness is gone. This is a phenomenon beyond the explanation of medical science.

Sickness does not necessarily issue from sin, yet much of it actually does. We acknowledge that many diseases have their natural causes, but we equally maintain that we cannot attribute all sickness to natural reasons.

I am reminded of one brother, a professor in a medical school, who once lectured his students as follows. We have isolated many natural explanations for illnesses. For instance, a certain type of coccus causes a particular kind of disease. As medical doctors, he continued, we can determine which type of organism produces what kind of disease, but we have no way to explain why among certain equally exposed people some are infected while others remain immune. Suppose, for example, ten persons enter the same room simultaneously and are exposed to the same type of coccus. We would expect the physically weak to be infected; yet the fact may be that the weak are spared and the strong are the ones stricken. We have to acknowledge, he concluded, that aside from natural causes there is additionally the control of Providence. Personally I think well of what this brother has said. How often people grow sick in spite of every preventive measure.

I also recall what one of my schoolmates related to me about his experience at Peking Medical College. There was a certain professor in the college who was profound in learning yet short on patience. Hence he usually posed very simple questions in examinations. Once he asked why people contracted tuberculosis. This was a simple enough question; yet many failed to supply the proper answer. Most replied by writing that certain people had tubercle bacillus. All of *these* answers were marked incorrect. The professor explained that the earth was full of tubercle bacilli but that not everybody was felled by tuberculosis. It is only under certain favorable conditions, he reminded them, that these bacilli cause the disease called tuberculosis. The bacillus alone cannot cause the disease. Most students forgot the importance of these favorable conditions. Let us be aware, therefore, that despite the presence of many natural factors Christians become sick only by God's permission given under appropriate conditions.

We unreservedly believe that there are natural explanations for sickness; this has been proven scientifically. We confess nonetheless that many illnesses among God's children are the consequences of sinning against God such as in the case cited in 1 Corinthians 11. It is consequently essential to ask for forgiveness first, then for healing afterwards. We frequently can detect, soon after we have been struck down with sickness, where we have transgressed against the Lord or how we have been disobedient to His Word. When the sin is confessed and the problem resolved, the sickness fades away. This is truly a most marvelous event. Thus the initial point we need to know is the relation between sin and sickness. Generally sickness results from sin; and individually, too, it may result from sin.

2. *The Lord's Work and Sickness*

"Surely he has borne our griefs and carried our sorrows; yet we esteemed him stricken, smitten by God, and afflicted. But he was wounded for our transgressions, he was bruised for our iniquities" (Is. 53.4-5). Of all the Old Testament writings this 53rd chapter of Isaiah is quoted most often in the New Testament. It alludes to the Lord Jesus Christ, especially to Him as our Savior. Verse 4 affirms that "he has borne our griefs and carried our sorrows" whereas Matthew 8.17 declares that "this was to fulfil what was spoken by the prophet Isaiah, 'He took our infirmities and bore our diseases'." The Holy Spirit indicates here that the Lord Jesus came to the world to take our infirmities and bear our diseases. Prior to His crucifixion He had already taken our infirmities and borne our diseases; which is to say that during His earthly ministry the Lord Jesus made healing His burden and task. He not only preached, He also healed. He preached the glad tidings on the one hand, but on the other hand strengthened the weak, restored the withered hand, cleansed the leper and raised the palsied. While on earth the Lord Jesus devoted Himself to the performance of miracles as well as to the ministry of the Word. He went about doing good, He healed the sick, and cast out demons. The purpose of His work was to overthrow sickness, the result of sin. He came to deal with death and sickness as well as with sin.

Psalm 103 is familiar to many of God's children; I myself love to read it. David proclaims, "Bless the Lord, O my soul; and all that is within me, bless his holy name!" Why bless the Lord? "Bless the Lord, O my soul, and forget not all his benefits." What are His benefits? "Who forgives all your iniquity, who heals all your diseases." (vv.1-3) I wish brothers and sisters to see that sickness is coupled with two elements: death on the one side, sin on the other. We have mentioned earlier how death is the result of sin, with sickness included therein. Both sickness and death flow from sin. Here in Psalm 103 we find that sickness is coupled with sin. Because of sin in the soul there is disease in the body. Along with the forgiveness of our iniquity comes the healing of our disease. The trouble in the body is sin within and disease without. But the Lord takes both away.

There is a basic dissimiliarity, however, between God's treatment of our iniquity and His treatment of our disease. Why this difference? Our Lord Jesus bore our sins in His body on the cross. Does any sin remain unforgiven? Absolutely none, for the work of God is so complete that sin is entirely destroyed. But in taking our infirmities and bearing our diseases while He lived on earth, the Lord Jesus did not eradicate all diseases and all infirmities. For note that Paul never says "when I sin, then am I sanctified," but he does declare that "when I am weak, then I am strong" (2 Cor. 12.10). Hense sin is thoroughly and unlimitedly dealt with whereas sickness is only limitedly treated.

In God's redemption the handling of sickness is unlike that of sin. With the latter, its destruction is totally uncircumscribed; with the former, this is just not so. Timothy, for instance, continued to have a weak stomach. The Lord permitted this weakness to remain with His servant. So in God's salvation sickness has not been eradicated as totally as has sin. Some maintain that the Lord Jesus deals solely with sin and not with illness too: others conceive the scope of His treatment of disease to be as broad and inclusive as His treatment of sin. Yet the Scriptures manifestly indicate to us that the Lord Jesus deals with both sin and sickness; only His dealing with sin is limitless while that with sickness is limited. We must behold the Lamb of God taking away *all* the sin of the world—He has borne the sin of each and every person. Sin's problem is therefore already solved. But meanwhile sickness still pervades God's children.

Nonetheless, we contend that since the Lord Jesus has actually borne our diseases there should not be so much sickness as there is among the children of God. While Jesus was on earth he unmistakably devoted Himself to the healing of the sick. He included healing in His work. Isaiah 53.4 is fulfilled in Matthew 8, not in Matthew 27. It is realized *before* Calvary. Had it been realized on the cross, healing would be unbounded. But no, the Lord Jesus bore our diseases prior to crucifixion, with the result that this aspect of His work is not as unlimited as was His bearing of our sins.

Even so, numberless saints remain ill because they have missed the opportunity of being healed; they do not see that the Lord has borne our diseases. Let me add a few more words on this point. Unless we have the assurance as did Paul upon praying thrice that his weakness would stay on because it was profitable to him, we should ask for healing. Paul accepted his weakness only after he had prayed the third time and had been shown distinctly by the Lord that His grace was sufficient for him and that His strength would be made perfect in his weakness. Until we are sure that God wants us to bear our weakness, we should boldly ask the Lord Himself to bear it and take away our disease. The children of God live on earth not to be sick but to glorify God. If to be sick will bring God glory, well and good; but many diseases do not necessarily glorify Him. Consequently, we must learn to trust the Lord while sick and must realize that He bears our sickness too. He healed a great number while He was on earth. And He is the same yesterday, today and forever. Let us commit our infirmity to Him and ask for His healing.

3. *The Believer's Attitude towards Sickness*

Every time the believer falls ill the first thing he should do is to inquire after its cause before the Lord. He should not be overanxious in seeking healing. Paul sets a good example in showing us how he was most clear about his weakness. We must examine whether we have disobeyed the Lord, have sinned anywhere, owe anybody a debt, have violated some natural law, or have neglected some special duty. We ought to know that frequently our violation of natural law can constitute a sin against God, for God sets up these natural laws by which to govern the universe. Many are afraid to die; upon becoming sick they hurriedly seek out physicians, for they are anxious to be cured. Such ought not to be the Christian's attitude. He should first attempt to isolate the cause for his malady. Alas, how many brothers and sisters do not possess any patience. The moment they fall sick they search for a remedy. Are you so afraid to lose your precious life that through prayer you lay hold of God for healing yet simultaneously lay hold of a physician for drugs and an injection? This reveals how full of self you are. But then how could you be less full of self in sickness if you are filled with self during ordinary days? Those who are ordinarily full of self will be those who anxiously seek for healing just as soon as they get sick.

May I tell you that anxiety avails nothing. Since you belong to God, your healing is not so simple. Even if you are cured this time, you will be ailing again. One must solve his problem before God first; and then can be solved the problem in his body.

Learn to accept whatever lesson sickness may bring to you. For if you have dealings with God many of your problems will be resolved quickly. You will find out that often your illness is due to some sin or fault of yours. Upon confessing your sin and asking for forgiveness, you may expect healing from God. Or, should you have walked further with the Lord, you may discern that involved in this is the enemy's attack. Or the matter of God's discipline may be associated with your unhealthy state. God chastises with sickness so as to render you holier, softer or more yielding. As you deal with these problems before God you will be enabled to see the exact reason for your infirmity. Sometimes God may allow you to receive a little natural or medical help, but sometimes He may heal you instantaneously without such assistance.

We should see that healing is in God's hand. Learn to trust Him Who heals. In the Old Testament God has a special name which is, "I am the Lord, your healer" (**Ex.** 15.26). Look to Him and He will be gracious to His own in this particular regard.

The initial step which the believer should therefore take when sick is to ferret out the cause; afterwards he may resort to several different ways for healing, one of which is to call the elders of the church to pray and anoint him with oil. This is the only command in the Bible concerning sickness.

> Is any among you sick? Let him call for the elders of the church, and let them pray over him, anointing him with oil in the name of the Lord; and the prayer of faith will save the sick man, and the Lord will raise him up; and if he has committed sins, he will be forgiven. (James 5.14-15)

Make no haste in seeking a cure, but rather have dealings with God at the outset. One of the things to be done is to call for the elders of the church to anoint you with oil. This speaks of the flowing of the oil from the Head to you as one of the members of the body. The oil which the Head receives runs down upon the whole body. As a member of the body of Christ, one can expect the oil on the Head to flow to him. Where life flows, sickness is swept away. The purpose of anointing is hence to bring down oil from the Head. Through disobedience, sin or perhaps some other reason the believer has gotten himself out of the body circulation and has departed from the body protection. Accordingly, he needs to call the elders of the church to reinstate him into the circulation and life flow of the body of Christ. This is just as in the physical body; for when any of its members is out of joint the life of the body cannot flow freely into it. Thus the anointing is to restore such a flow. The elders represent the local church; they anoint the believer on behalf of the body of Christ so that the oil of the Head may flow to him once again. Let the oil on the Head come upon that member through which life has been obstructed! Our experience tells us that such anointing may raise the seriously sick up instantly.

At times one identifies the explanation for his illness to be his individualism. This may well be the chief cause for illness. Some Christians are highly individualistic. They do everything according to their own will. They do it all by themselves. If the hand of God comes upon them they grow sick, for the supply of the body does not reach such members. I dare not over-simplify these matters. The reasons for sickness can be many and varied. One sickness may be due to disobeying the Lord's command, refusing to carry out His will; another may be caused by committing some particular sin; but still another may be the consequence of individualism. Now in the case of certain individualists God overlooks and does not discipline; but especially in the case of those who know the church, He chastens them with illness if they commence to act independently. The Lord will not let these go without some discipline.

It is also possible that infirmity is the consequence of a defiled body. Should anyone defile his body, God will destroy that temple. Many are infirm because they have corrupted their bodies.

By way of summing up, then, no sickness occurs without a cause. If the Christian contracts an illness he should try to locate its cause or causes. After he has confessed them one by one before God he should summon the elders of the church so that they may confess to one another and pray for one another. The elders will anoint the sick one with oil that the life of the body of Christ may be restored to him. The influx of life will swallow up the disease. We believe in natural causes, but we additionally must affirm that spiritual causes have priority over the natural. If the spiritual are taken care of, the sickness shall be healed completely.

4. *God's Chastening and Sickness*

An amazing fact is found in the Bible: that it is relatively easy for a "heathen" to be healed, but healing for a Christian is not so easy. The New Testament overwhelmingly shows us that whenever an unbeliever seeks the Lord he is cured immediately. Now the gift of healing is for the brethren as well as for the unbelievers. Yet the Bible tells of some believers who are not healed; among them are Trophimus, Timothy and Paul. And these are the best of the brethren. Paul left Trophimus ill at Miletus (2 Tim. 4.20). He exhorted Timothy to use a little wine for the sake of his stomach and his frequent ailments (1 Tim. 5.23). Paul himself experienced a thorn in his flesh from which he suffered much and was reduced to great weakness (2 Cor. 12.7). Whatever the nature of that thorn, be it eye trouble or some other disease, it pricked his flesh. One feels great discomfort should a little finger be pricked by a thorn. Paul's, however, was a big thorn, not a tiny one. It gave him such discomfort that he could only describe his physical condition as weakness. These three are brethren par excellence, yet none was healed. They had to endure sickness.

It is quite evident that sickness is different from sin in its outworking. Sin does not produce any fruit of holiness, but sickness does. The more a person sins the more corrupt he becomes; sickness, though, bears the fruit of holiness because the chastening hand of God is upon the sick. Under such circumstances it behooves a child of God to learn how to submit himself under the mighty hand of God.

If one is ill he ought to deal with every cause of his illness before the Lord. If, after all has been dealt with, the hand of God still remains upon him, then he should understand that this illness is for the purpose of restraining him from being proud or loose or for some other purpose. He should accept it and learn its lesson. To be sick is valueless if the lesson is not learned. Sickness itself does not make a man holy, but its lesson if accepted produces holiness. Some grow worse spiritually during illness; they become more self-centered. That is why one must discover the lesson in such a period. What profit or fruit can be derived from it? Is the hand of God upon me to keep me humble as He did with Paul, "to keep me from being too elated by the abundance of revelations" (2 Cor. 12.7)? Or is it because God desires to weaken my stubborn individuality? What is the use of sickness if it does not provoke me to learn the lesson of weakness? Many are sick in vain because they never accept the Lord's dealing with their particular problems.

Do not look upon sickness as something terrible. In whose hand is this knife? Remember that it is in God's hand. Why should we be anxious over our infirmity as though it were the hand of the enemy? Know that God has measured out all our sickness. To be sure, Satan is the originator of them; it is he who makes people ill. Yet all who have read the Book of Job realize that this is only through God's permission and is completely under the restriction of God. Without God's permission Satan cannot make anyone sick. God permitted Job to be attacked with ill-health, but note that He did not allow the enemy to touch his life. Why then are we so agitated, so full of despair, so anxious to be cured, so afraid we will die when we are struck down with ill-health?

It is always well for us to bear in mind that all sickness is in God's hand. It has been both measured and circumscribed by Him. After Job had fulfilled the course of his trial his sickness was over, for it had accomplished its purpose in him—"Ye have heard of the patience of Job, and have seen the end (purpose) of the Lord, how that the Lord is full of pity, and merciful" (James 5.11 ASV). What a shame that so many are ill without realizing its purpose or learning its lesson. All infirmities are in the Lord's hand and are measured out to us that we may learn our lessons. The sooner we learn them the quicker these infirmities pass away.

May I put it bluntly: many are sick simply because they love themselves too much. Unless the Lord removes this self-love from their hearts He cannot use them. Therefore we must learn to be those who do not love ourselves. Some people can think of nothing but themselves. The whole universe seems to revolve around them. They are the center of the earth as well as the hub of the universe. Day and night are they occupied with their own selves. Every creature exists for them, everything circles around them. Even God in heaven is for them, Christ is for them, and the church is for them. How can God destroy this self-centeredness? Why is it that some maladies are hard to be cured? How intently they solicit men's sympathy! If they should spurn human sympathy their ailments would soon be healed.

A startling fact is that many are ill because they like to be ill. In sickness they receive the attention and love which they do not usually enjoy in health. They frequently become ill that they may habitually be loved. Such people need to be severely reprimanded; and should they be willing to receive God's dealing in this particular matter they shall soon be well.

I know a brother who always expected love and kindness from others. Whenever people inquired after his well-being, he habitually responded with complaints about his physical weakness. He would give a detailed report of how many minutes he suffered from fever, how long it was he had a headache, how many times per minute he breathed, and how irregular was his heartbeat. He was continually in discomfort. He loved to tell people of his distress so that they might sympathize with him. He had nothing to relate except his tale of endless sickness. And at times he wondered why he was never healed.

Now it is difficult to speak the truth. And sometimes it can be costly. One day I was inwardly strengthened to tell him candidly that his long illness was due to his love for sickness. He of course denied it. Nevertheless I proceeded to point out to him: You are afraid that your sickness might leave you. You crave sympathy, love and care. Since you cannot secure these in any other way, you obtain them by being sick. You must rid yourself of this selfish desire before God will ever heal you. When people ask how you are, you must learn to answer that "all is well." Would this be telling a lie if the night before had been ill-spent? Recall the story of the woman in Shunem. She laid her dead child on the bed of the man of God and went to see Elisha. When she was asked, "Is it well with you? Is it well with your husband? Is it well with the child?", she replied, "It is well." (See 2 Kings 4.26) How could she say that, knowing the child had died already and was laid on Elisha's bed? Because she had faith. She believed that God would raise up her child. So today you too must believe.

Whatever may be the cause, be it intrinsic or extrinsic, the sickness will be over once God has obtained His end. People like Paul, Timothy and Trophimus are exceptions. Although their sicknesses were long-sustaining, they acknowledged that this was profitable to their work. They learned how to take care of themselves for the glory of God. Paul persuaded Timothy to drink a little wine, to be careful in eating and drinking. In spite of their frailties the work of God was not neglected. The Lord gave them sufficient grace to overcome their disabilities. Paul labored in weakness. By reading his writings we can conclude easily that he accomplished as much as ten persons could have. God used this weak man to exceed ten strong persons. Though his body was frail, God nevertheless gave him strength and life. These though are the exceptions in the Bible. Some of God's special vessels may receive the same treatment. But the rank and file, especially beginners, should examine whether they have sinned; and upon confessing their sins they shall see their sickness readily healed.

Lastly, I wish you to see before the Lord that sometimes Satan may launch a sudden attack or sometimes you unwittingly may violate some natural law. Even so, you still can bring it to the Lord. If it is the enemy's assault, rebuke it in the name of the Lord. Once a sister had a protracted fever. After discovering that it was a satanic attack, she rebuked it in the Lord's name and the fever left her. If you violate a natural law by putting your hand in the fire, you surely shall be burnt. Take good care of yourself. Do not wait until you are sick before you confess your negligence. It is important to take care of your body during the ordinary days.

5. *The Way to Seek Healing*

How should men seek healing before God? Three sentences in the Gospel of Mark are worth learning. I find them especially helpful, at least they are very effective for me. The first touches upon the power of the Lord; the second, the will of the Lord; and the third, the act of the Lord.

a) The Power of the Lord: "God can." "And Jesus asked

his father, 'How long has he had this?' And he said, 'From childhood. And it has often cast him into the fire and into the water, to destroy him; but *if you can* do anything, have pity on us and help us.' And Jesus said to him, '*If you can!* All things are possible to him who believes'" (9. 21-23). The Lord Jesus merely repeated the three words which the child's father had uttered. The father cried, "If you can, help us." The Lord responded, "If you can! Why, all things are possible to him who believes." The problem here is not "if you can" but rather "if you believe."

Is it not true that the first problem which arises with sickness is a doubt about God's power? Under a microscope the power of bacteria seems to be greater than the power of God. Very rarely does the Lord cut off others in the middle of their speaking, but here he appears as though He were angry. (May the Lord forgive me for phrasing it this way!) When He heard the child's father say "If you can, have pity on us and help us," He sharply reacted with "Why say if you can? All things are possible to him who believes. In sickness, the question is not whether I can or cannot but whether *you believe* or not."

The initial step for a child of God to take in sickness therefore is to raise up his head and say "Lord, you can!" You remember, do you not, the first instance of the Lord's healing of a paralytic? He asked the Pharisees, "Which is easier, to say to the paralytic, 'Your sins are forgiven,' or to say, 'Rise, take up your pallet and walk'?" (Mark 2.9) The Pharisees naturally thought it easier to say your sins are forgiven, for who could actually prove it is or is not so? But the Lord's words and their results showed them that He could heal sickness as well as forgive sins. He did not ask which was more difficult, but which was easier. For Him, both were equally easy. It was as easy for the Lord to bid the paralytic rise and walk as to forgive the latter's sins. For the Pharisees, both were as difficult.

b) The Will of the Lord: "God will." Yes, He indeed can, but how do I know if He wills? I do not know His will; perhaps He does not want to heal me. This is another story in

Mark again. "And a leper came to him beseeching him, and kneeling said to to him, 'If you will, you can make me clean.' Moved with pity, he stretched out his hand and touched him, and said to him, 'I will; be clean' " (1.40-41).

However great the power of God is, if He has no wish to heal, His power shall not help me. The problem to be solved at the outset is: Can God?; the second is: Will God? There is no sickness as unclean as leprosy. It is so unclean that according to law whoever touches a leper becomes himself unclean. Yet the Lord Jesus touched the leper and said to him, "I will." If He would heal the leper, how much more wills He to cure *our* diseases. We can proclaim boldly, "God can" and "God will."

c) The Act of the Lord: "God has." One more thing must God do. "Verily I say unto you, Whosoever shall say unto this mountain, Be thou taken up and cast into the sea; and shall not doubt in his heart, but shall believe that what he saith cometh to pass; he shall have it. Therefore I say unto you, all things whatsoever ye pray and ask for, believe that ye receive (Gr. *received*) them, and ye shall have them" (11. 23-24 ASV). What is faith? Faith believes God can, God will, and God has done it. If you believe you have received it, you shall have it. Should God give you His word, you can thank Him by saying, "God has healed me; He has already done it!" Many believers merely *expect* to be healed. Expectation regards things in the future, but faith deals with the past. If we really believe, we shall not wait for twenty or a hundred years, but shall rise up immediately and say, "Thank God, He has healed me. Thank God, I have received it. Thank God, I am clean! Thank God, I am well." A perfect faith can therefore proclaim God can, God will and God has done it.

Faith works with "is" and not "wish." Allow me to use a simple illustration. Suppose you preach the gospel and one professes that he has believed. Ask him whether he is saved, and should his answer be, I wish to be saved, then you know this reply is inadequate. Should he say, I will be saved, the answer is still incorrect. Even if he responds with, I think I shall definitely be saved, something is yet missing. But when he answers, <u>I am saved</u>, you know the flavor is right. If one believes, then he is saved. All faith deals with the past. To say I believe I shall be healed is not true faith. If he believes, he will thank God and say, I have received healing.

Lay hold of these three steps: God can, God will, God has. When man's faith touches the third stage, the sickness is over.

CHAPTER 3
GOD AS THE LIFE OF THE BODY

We noted earlier how our body is the temple of the Holy Spirit. What arrests our attention is the special emphasis the Apostle Paul gives to the body. The common concept is that the life of Christ is for our spirit, not for our body. Few realize that the salvation of God reaches to the second after He gives life to the first. Had God desired that His Spirit live solely in our spirit so that only it might be benefited, the Apostle would simply need to have said that "your spirit is the temple of God" and not mention the body at all. By now, however, we should understand that the meaning of our body as the temple of the Holy Spirit is more than its being the recipient of a special privilege. It likewise means being a channel for effective power. The indwelling of the Holy Spirit strengthens our inner man, enlightens the eyes of our heart and, makes our body healthy.

We have also noted how the Holy Spirit makes alive this mortal frame of ours. To wait until we die before He raises us up is not necessary, for even now He gives life to our mortal body. In the future He will raise from the dead this *corruptible* body, but today He quickens the *mortal* body. The power of His life permeates every cell of our being so that we may experience His power and life in the body.

No more need we look upon our outer shell as a miserable prison, for we can see in it the life of God being expressed. We now can experience in a deeper way that word which declares that "it is no longer I who live but Christ who lives in me." Christ has presently become the source of life to us.

He lives in us today as He once lived in the flesh. We can thus apprehend more fully the implication of His pronouncement: "I came that they may have life, and have it abundantly" (John 10.10). This more abundant life suffices additionally for every requirement of our body. Paul exhorts Timothy to "take hold of the eternal life" (1 Tim. 6. 12); surely Timothy is not here in need of eternal life that he may be saved. Is not this life that which Paul subsequently describes in the same chapter as "the life which is life indeed" (v.19)? Is he not urging Timothy to experience eternal life today in overcoming every phenomenon of death?

We would hasten to inform our readers that we have not lost sight of the fact that our body is indeed a mortal one; even so, we who are the Lord's can verily possess the power of that life which swallows up death. In our body are two forces in action: death and life: on the one side is consumption which brings us nigh to death; on the other side is replenishment through food and rest and these support life. Now extravagant consumption weakens the body because the force of death is too powerful; but by the same token excessive supply reveals signs of congestion because the force of life is too strong. The best policy is to maintain these two forces of life and death in balance. Beyond this, we should understand that the weariness which believers often experience in their body is in many respects distinct from that of ordinary people. Their consumption is more than physical. Because they walk with the Lord, bear the burdens of others, sympathize with the brethren, work for God, intercede before Him, battle the powers of darkness, and pommel their body to subdue it, food and rest alone are insufficient to replenish the loss of strength in their physical frame. This explains in a measure why many believers, who before the call to service were healthy, find themselves physically feeble not long afterwards. Our bodily strength cannot cope with the demands of spiritual life, work, and war. Combat with sin, sinners, and the evil spirits saps our vitality. Solely natural resources are inadequate to supply our bodily needs. We must depend on the life of Christ, for this alone can sustain us. Should we rely on material food and nourishment and drugs we will be committing a serious blunder. Only the life of the Lord Jesus more than sufficiently meets all the physical requirements for our spiritual life, work, and war. He alone furnishes us the necessary vitality to grapple with sin and Satan. Once the believer has truly appreciated what spiritual warfare is and how to wrestle in the spirit with the enemy, he will begin to realize the preciousness of the Lord Jesus as life to his body.

Every Christian ought to see the reality of his union with the Lord. He is the vine and we the branches. As branches are united with the trunk, so are we united with the Lord. Through union with the trunk the branches receive the flow of life. Does not our union with the Lord produce the same results? If we restrict this union to the spirit, faith will rise up to protest. Since the Lord calls us to demonstrate the reality of our union with Him, He wishes us to believe and to receive the flow of His life to our spirit, soul, and body. Should our fellowship be cut off, the spirit most assuredly will lose its peace, but so will the body be denied its health. Constant abiding signifies that His life continually is filling our spirit and flowing to our body. Apart from a participation in the life of the Lord Jesus there can be neither healing nor health. The call of God today is for His children to experience a deeper union with the Lord Jesus.

Let us therefore recognize that, though phenomena do occur to us in the *body*, they are in truth spiritual matters. To receive divine healing and to have our strength increased are spiritual and not purely physical experiences, although they do take place in the body. Such experiences are nothing less than the life of the Lord Jesus being manifested in our mortal frame. As in the past the life of the Lord caused this dead spirit of ours to be resurrected, so now it makes alive this mortal body. God wants us to learn how to let the resurrected, glorious and all-victorious life of Christ be expressed in every portion of our being. He calls us to renew our vigor daily and hourly by Him. This is precisely our true life. Even though our body is still animated by our natural soul life, we no longer live by it because we have trusted in the life of the Son of God Who infuses energy into our members far more abundantly than all which the soul life could impart. We lay great stress on this "life." In all our spiritual experiences this mysterious yet wonderful "life" enters into us abundantly. God desires to leads us into possessing that life of Christ as our strength.

The Word of God is the life of our body: "Man shall not live by bread alone, but by every word that proceeds from the mouth of God" (Matt. 4.4). This substantiates the thought that God's Word is able to support our body. Naturally speaking man must live by bread, but when the Word of God emits its power man can live by it too. Herein do we behold both the natural and the supernatural way of living. God does not say that henceforth we need not eat; He simply informs us that His Word can supply us with life which food cannot. When food fails to produce or to sustain the desirable effect in our body, His Word can give us what we need. Some live by bread alone, some by it *and* the Word of God. Bread sometimes fails, but God's Word never changes.

God hides His life in His Word. Inasmuch as He is life, so also is His Word. Should we view God's Word as a teaching, creed or moral standard, it shall not prove very effective in us. No, God's Word must be digested and united with us in the same manner as is food. Hungry believers take it in as their food. If they receive it with faith the Word becomes their life. God claims His Word is able to sustain our life. When natural nourishment fails we can believe God according to His Word. Then shall we perceive Him not only as life to our spirit but as life to our body as well. Christians nowadays experience great loss in not noticing how bountifully God has provided for our earthly tent. We confine God's promises to the inner spirit and overlook their application to the outer flesh. But do we realize our physical requirement is no less needful than that of the spiritual?

THE EXPERIENCES OF THE SAINTS OF OLD

God never wants His children to be weak; His ordained will is for them to be robust and healthy. His Word affirms that "as your days, so shall your strength be" (Deut. 33.25). This naturally points to the body. As long as we live on earth the Lord promises to give us strength for it. God never presumes to grant us an extra day of life without in addition providing extra stamina for that day. Because of the failure of His children to claim this precious promise by faith, they find their vitality unequal to their days on earth. In order to provide as much energy for His children as the days He gives require, God promises to make Himself their strength. As God lives and as we live, so shall be our strength. Believing God's promise, we can say each morning upon arising and seeing the dawn that as God lives so shall we have enablement for the day, enablement physical as well as spiritual.

It was a common occurrence for the saints of old to know God as the strength of their body or to experience God's life permeating their body. We can observe this first in Abraham: "He did not weaken in faith when he considered his own body, which was as good as dead because he was about a hundred years old, or when he considered the barrenness of Sarah's womb" (Rom. 4.19). By faith he begot Isaac. The power of God was displayed in a body as good as dead. The crux of the matter here is not so much the condition of our body as the power of God in that body.

The Scriptures describe the life of Moses by saying that he "was a hundred and twenty years old when he died; his eye was not dim, nor his natural force abated" (Deut. 34.7). This is speaking beyond question about the power of God's life in Moses' body.

The Bible also mentions the physical condition of Caleb. After the Israelites had entered Canaan Caleb testified:

> Moses swore on that day, saying, 'Surely the land on which your foot has trodden shall be an inheritance for you and your children for ever, because you have wholly followed the Lord my God.' And now, behold, the Lord has kept me alive, as he said, these forty-five years since the time that the Lord spoke this word to Moses, while Israel walked in the wilderness; and now, lo, I am this day eight-five years old. I am still as strong to this day as I

was in the day that Moses sent me; my strength now is as my strength was then, for war, and for going and coming. (Josh. 14. 9-11)

To this one who followed the Lord wholeheartedly God became his strength as He had promised, so that even after forty-five years he did not diminish in vigor.

In reading the book of Judges we learn about the physical prowess of Samson. Though Samson performed many immoral acts and though the Holy Spirit may not impart such towering strength to every believer, yet one point is sure: if we depend on the Holy Spirit we shall find His power supplying all our daily needs.

From what David sang as recorded in his psalms, we can ascertain that the power of God was in David's body. Note the following passages:

> "I love thee, O Lord, my strength. . . . the God who girded me with strength and made my way safe. He made my feet like hinds' feet, and set me secure on the heights. He trains my hands for war, so that my arms can bend a bow of bronze" (18.1,32-34)
> "Jehovah is the strength of my life; of whom shall I be afraid?" (27.1 ASV)
> "May the Lord give strength to his people!" (29.11)
> "Summon thy might, O God; show thy strength, O God, thou who hast wrought for us. . . . the God of Israel, he gives power and strength to his people" (68.28,35)
> "Who satisfies you with good as long as you live so that your youth is renewed like the eagle's" (103.5)

Other psalms record also how God became strength to His Own people, for example: "My flesh and my heart may fail, but God is the strength of my heart and my portion for ever"; "Blessed are the men whose strength is in thee"; and "With long life I will satisfy him, and show him my salvation" (73.26, 84.5, 91.16).

Elihu related to Job the chastening of God and its after effects.

> Man is also chastened with pain upon his bed, and with continual strife in his bones; so that his life loathes bread, and his

> appetite dainty food. His flesh is so wasted away that it cannot be seen; and his bones which were not seen stick out. His soul draws near the Pit, and his life to those who bring death. If there be for him an angel, a mediator, one of the thousand, to declare to man what is right for him; and he is gracious to him, and says, 'Deliver him from going down into the Pit, I have found a ransom; let his flesh become fresh with youth; let him return to the days of his youthful vigor.' (Job 33.19-25)

This signifies how the life of God can be manifest in one who is near the gate of death.

The prophet Isaiah too bears testimony concerning this matter:

> Behold, God is my salvation; I will trust, and will not be afraid; for the Lord God is my strength and my song, and he has become my salvation. (12.2) He gives power to the faint, and to him who has no might he increases strength. Even youths shall faint and be weary, and young men shall fall exhausted; but they who wait for the Lord shall renew their strength, they shall mount up with wings like eagles, they shall run and not be weary, they shall walk and not faint. (40.29-31)

All this stamina is shown in the body, for the power of God is generated in those who wait on Him.

When Daniel beheld the vision of God he whispered: "No strength was left in me; my radiant appearance was fearfully changed, and I retained no strength" (10.8). But God sent His angel to increase Daniel's strength. So in recording this incident Daniel explained how "again one having the appearance of a man touched me and strengthened me. And he said, 'O man, greatly beloved, fear not, peace be with you; be strong and of good courage.' And when he spoke to me, I was strengthened and said, 'Let my lord speak, for you have strengthened me'" (10.18-19). Once more we see how God supplies power to man's body.

The Lord's children today ought to know that He does care for their body. God is not only strength to our spirit, He is equally so to our body. Even in the Old Testament time when grace was not manifested as much as it is today, the saints experienced God as strength to their outer flesh.

Can today's blessing be less than theirs? We should experience at least the same divine invigorating power as they did. If we are uninformed as to the riches of God, we perhaps may restrict them to what concerns our spirit. But those who have faith will not limit His life and power to the spirit by neglecting their application to the body.

We wish to underscore the fact that God's life is adequate not only to heal sickness but also to preserve us strong and healthy. God as our might enables us to overcome both illness and weakness. He does not heal so that we may live afterwards by our natural energy; *He* is to be energy to our body that we may live by Him and find power for all His service. When the Israelites left Egypt God promised them by saying, "If you will diligently hearken to the voice of the Lord your God, and do that which is right in his eyes, and give heed to his commandments and keep all his statutes, I will put none of the diseases upon you which I put upon the Egyptians; for I am the Lord, your healer" (Ex. 15.26). Later we find this promise wholly fulfilled as noted in Psalm 105: "there was not one feeble person among his tribes" (v.37 ASV). Let us hence understand that divine healing includes both God's curing our sicknesses and His withholding diseases from us that we may remain hardy. If we are totally yielded to God, resisting His will in nothing but believingly receiving His life as strength to our body, we shall yet prove the fact that Jehovah heals.

THE EXPERIENCE OF PAUL

If we accept the Biblical teaching that our bodies are the members of Christ, we cannot but also acknowledge the teaching that the life of Christ flows through them. The life of Christ flows from the Head to the body, supplying energy and vitality to it. Since *our* bodies are members of *that* body, life naturally flows to them. This however needs to be appropriated by faith. The measure of faith by which we receive this life will determine the measure in which we actually experience it. From the Scriptures we have learned that the life of the Lord Jesus can be appropriated for the believer's body, but this requires faith. Doubtless Christians, when first exposed to such teachings, are struck with surprise. Yet we cannot dilute what the Word distinctly teaches. An examination of Paul's experience can assure us of the preciousness and reality of the teaching.

Paul, in referring to his physical condition, remarked about a thorn in his flesh. Three times he entreated the Lord concerning this, that it should be removed. But the Lord answered him, "My grace is sufficient for you, for my power is made perfect in weakness." And in response the Apostle said, "I will all the more gladly boast of my weaknesses, that the power of Christ may rest upon me . . . for when I am weak, then I am strong" (2 Cor. 12.9-10). We need not inquire what that thorn was because the Bible does not divulge it. One point however is certain: the consequence of this thorn on the Apostle was that it weakened his body. The "weakness" here referred to is physical in nature. The same word is used in Matthew 8.17. The Corinthians were well acquainted with Paul's bodily frailty (2 Cor. 10.10). Paul himself acknowledged that when he was with them the first time he was physically weak (1 Cor. 2.3). His debility cannot be due to any lack of spiritual power, for both Corinthian letters reveal a powerful spiritual vigor in the Apostle.

From just these few passages we can gain insight into Paul's physical condition. He was very weak in body, but did he remain long therein? No, for he informs us that the power of Christ rested upon him and made him strong. We notice a "law of contrast" here. Neither the thorn nor the weakness which came from the thorn had left Paul; yet the power of Christ inundated his frail body and gave him strength to meet every need. The power of Christ was in contrast to the weakness of Paul. This power did not waft the thorn away nor did it eliminate weakness, but it abided in Paul to handle whatever situation with which his weakened frame could not cope. It may be likened to a wick which though kindled with fire is not consumed because it is saturated with oil. The wick is as flimsy as ever, but the oil supplies everything the fire requires of it.

Thus do we apprehend the principle that God's life is to be our bodily enablement. His life does not transform the nature of our weak and mortal body: it merely fills it with all its necessary supplies. As to his natural condition, Paul was unquestionably the weakest physically; as to the power of Christ which he possessed, he was the strongest of all. We know how he labored day and night, pouring out his life and energy, performing work which several strong-bodied men could not stand. How, then, could a weak man like Paul undertake such work unless it were that his mortal frame was made alive by the Holy Spirit? It is an established fact that God imparted strength to Paul's body.

How did God do it? Paul was speaking about his body when he related in 2 Corinthians 4 how he and those with him were "always bearing about in the body the dying of Jesus, that the life also of Jesus may be manifested in our body. For we who live are always delivered unto death for Jesus' sake, that the life also of Jesus may be manifested in our mortal flesh" (v.10-11 ASV). What particularly arrests our interest is that verse 11 in relation to verse 10, though seemingly redundant, is not repetitious. Verse 10 is concerned with the life of Jesus being manifested in our bodies whereas verse 11 is concerned with the life of Jesus being exhibited in our *mortal flesh*. Many are able to express the life of Christ in their bodies but fail to advance further to do so in their mortal flesh. The distinction is far-reaching. When Christians fall ill many are truly obedient and patient and voice no complaint or anxiety. They sense the presence of the Lord and exhibit His virtues in their countenance, speech, and act. Through the Holy Spirit they genuinely manifest the life of Christ in their bodies. Nevertheless, they do not appreciate the healing power of the Lord Jesus nor have they heard that His life is also for their lowly bodies. They fail to exercise faith for the healing of their bodies as they previously did for the cleansing of their sins and the quickening of their dead spirits. They are therefore powerless to manifest the life of Jesus in their *mortal* flesh. They receive grace to endure pain but do not receive healing. Verse 10 they have experienced, yet verse 11 goes untried.

How does God heal us and strengthen us? By the life of Jesus. This is most significant. When our mortal flesh is revitalized the nature of our body is not changed to immortality—it remains the same. The life which supplies the vitality to this body, however, *is* changed. Whereas in days past we lived by the power of our natural life, now we live by the energy of that supernatural life of Christ. Because His resurrection power is sustaining our body, we are empowered to perform our appointed tasks.

The Apostle did not suggest that once having lived by the Lord he would never again be weak. Not at all, for whenever the power of Christ did not cure him he would be as weak as ever. We can forfeit the manifestation of the life of the Lord Jesus in our bodies through neglect, independence, or sin. Sometimes we may be weakened through the attack of the powers of darkness against whom we have boldly advanced. Or we may suffer affliction for the sake of Christ's body if we are deeply involved with it. But only in the life of deeply spiritual persons do both of these occur. In any case, we are certain that, weak though we may yet be, God's will is never for us to be invalids unable to work for Him. The Apostle Paul was often weak, but never did God's work suffer because of his weakness. We acknowledge the absolute sovereignty of God, but Christians cannot use that as their excuse.

"Always bearing about in the body the dying of Jesus" is the basis for "the life of Jesus (to) be manifested in our body." In other words, our own life must be denied totally before that of the Lord Jesus will be manifested in our bodies. This unfolds to us the intricate relationship between a spiritual selfless walk and a sound healthy body. The power of God is used exclusively for Him. When God exhibits His life in our bodies He does so for the sake of His Own work. He never dispenses to us His life and strength that we may consume it selfishly. He does not give His energy to our bodies that we may waste it; nor does He do so to accomplish our purpose. How then will He ever bestow this power upon us if we do not live entirely for Him? Right there do we locate the reason for many unanswered prayers. Believers too often covet health and vitality solely in order to enjoy themselves. They seek God's strength for their bodies that they may dwell more comfortably, joyfully, conveniently. They want to be able to move freely without any impediment. That is why up to this very moment they are still weak. God will not furnish us His life for us to wield independently. For would we not live even more for ourselves, and would not the will of God incur even greater loss? God is waiting today for His children to come to *their* end that He may grant them what they are seeking.

What is meant by "the dying of Jesus"? It is that life of the Lord which always delivers its self up to death. The entire walk of our Lord was characterized by self-denial. Right through to His death the Lord Jesus never did anything by Himself but always executed His Father's work. Now the Apostle informs us that by his letting the dying of Jesus so work in his body the life of Jesus was manifested also in his mortal flesh. Can we receive this teaching? Presently God is waiting for those who are willing to accept the dying of Jesus so that He may live in their bodies. Who is inclined to follow God's will perfectly? Who will not initiate anything by himself? Who dares to attack the powers of darkness incessantly for God? Who refuses to use his body for his own success? The life of the Lord Jesus shall be manifested in the bodies of such believers as these. If we take care of the death side God will look after the life side: we offer our weakness to Him and He gives His strength to us.

NATURAL POWER AND THE POWER OF JESUS

If we have presented ourselves utterly to God we can believe that He has prepared a body for us. We often imagine how nice it would be had we had control over how we were made. What we most want is that our bodies shall not contain many inherent defects but possess a greater resistance instead in order that we may live long without pain or illness. But God has not consulted us. He knows best what we should have. We should not judge our ancestors for their faults and sins. Neither should we doubt God's love and wisdom. Everything which concerns us is ordained before the foundation of the world. God fulfills His excellent will even in this body of pain and death. His purpose is not for us to desert this body as though it were a burdensome weight. Rather, He urges us to lay hold of a *new* body through the Holy Spirit Who indwells us. In preparing whatever body He gives us God is fully aware of its limitations and dangers; nonetheless He wants us through painful experiences to desire a new body so that we may no longer live by our *naturally possessed* power but by the power of God. Thus we shall exchange our weakness for His strength. Even though this body of ours has not been transformed, the life by which it lives is already a new one.

The Lord delights in flooding every nerve, capillary, and cell of our body with His might. He does not transform our enfeebled nature into a vigorous one, nor does he dispense a great deal of strength to be stored in us. He wants to be the life to our mortal flesh so that we may live *momentarily* by Him. Perhaps some may think that to have the Lord Jesus as life to our body means God miraculously grants us a large measure of bodily power that we may never again suffer or be sick. But this was evidently not the experience of the Apostle, for does he not definitely declare that "we who live are always delivered unto death for Jesus' sake, that the life also of Jesus may be manifested in our mortal flesh"? Paul's flesh was frequently weakened, but the strength of the Lord Jesus continuously flowed into him. He lived momentarily by the life of the Lord. To accept Him as life for our body requires *constant trust*. In ourselves we cannot meet any situation at any time; but by trusting continually in the Lord we receive moment by moment all the necessary strength.

This is what is meant by the words spoken by God through Jeremiah: "I will give you your life as a prize of war in all places to which you may go" (45.5). We are not to deem ourselves safe and secure because of our own inherent strength; we must instead commit ourselves to the life of the Lord for every breath. In this alone is safety, for He alone ever lives. We do not possess any *reserve* power which enables us to move as we wish; each time we need strength we must draw from the Lord. A moment's drawing is good for that moment's living; there is no possibility of holding a little in reserve. This is a life completely united with, and exclusively dependent upon, the Lord. "I live because of the Father, so he who eats me will live because of me" (John 6. 57). Precisely there is the secret of this life. Were we able to live independently of the life-giving Lord, we would renounce this heart of utter reliance and live according to our own will! And would we not then be like those of the world, wasting our strength? God wants us to have a constant trust as well as a constant need. Just as the manna long ago had to be gathered daily, so our bodies must momentarily live by God.

By walking in this fashion we will not limit our work by any inherent power nor will we always be anxious because of the body. If it is God's will, we must dare to walk this way, however much man's wisdom may consider it risky. For God is our strength; and we are but waiting to be sent. In ourselves we have no power to undertake any task, yet our eyes are upon the Lord. We are absolutely helpless, nonetheless through Him we shall go forth and conquer. Alas, how many of us are too powerful in ourselves! We know not how to distrust our strength that we thereby may know how to trust in Him. His strength is made perfect in our weakness. The more helpless we are (this pertains to attitude), the better is His power demonstrated. Our strength can never cooperate with the Lord. If we try to reinforce His strength with ours we shall reap nothing but defeat and shame.

Since the Lord demands such a trust in Him, this practice should not be limited to the naturally weak situation in us but should include the naturally strong in us too. Perhaps some Christians who currently can boast robust and healthy bodies assume they need not seek this experience until they become weak. This is a misjudgment, for both the naturally weak and the naturally strong require the life of God. Nothing we receive in the old creation is satisfactory to Him. Were believers deeply taught by the Lord they would lay down their own power to accept God's, even should their bodies be strong and seemingly have no need for His life. This is not a *choosing* of weakness with their will but is rather a *disbelieving* in their own strength just as they distrust their own talents. Such consecration will preserve them from self-exaltation founded on natural energy—a common ill among many servants of the Lord. They will not dare move beyond what He orders. They will act as the naturally weak do; without the strengthening of the Lord they dare not move one step. They will refrain from overworking and avoid careless living, just as though they were weak naturally.

In such a way of life it is imperative that "self" be imprisoned by the Holy Spirit; otherwise we certainly shall be defeated. Some genuinely admire the self-denying life but are unable to cease completely from their own energies. Hence they disregard God's purpose and move along according to their desire. They may reap the temporary admiration of men but their bodies shall finally collapse. God's life refuses to be enslaved to man's will. That work which He has not ordered He shall never give His strength to supply. If we should become active outside the realm of God's will we shall discover the life of God is apparently leaking away and that our fragile body must undertake the task. In order to live by Him we must not be presumptuous; we should begin to move only upon being assured that it is truly God's will. Solely through obedience will we experience the reality of His life for us. Else would He ever give us His strength to rebel against Him?

THE BLESSING OF THIS LIFE

Were we to receive the life of the Lord Jesus to be the life of our body, we would today experience our bodies being strengthened by the Lord as well as our spirits being prospered by Him.

As far as our knowledge is concerned we already realize that our body is for the Lord; yet because of our self-will He is unable to fill us completely. But now we commit our all to Him that He may deal with us in whatever way He wishes. We present our bodies a living sacrifice; therefore we control neither our life nor our future. Now we truly understand what is meant by the body for the Lord. What worried us before cannot now shake us. The enemy may tempt us by reminding us that this way is too risky or that we are being too unmindful of ourselves; even so, we are not frightened as we used to be. One thing do we know: we belong to the Lord absolutely: nothing can therefore befall us without His knowledge and permission. Whatever attack may come is but an indication of His special purpose and His unfailing protection. Our bodies are no longer ours. Every nerve, cell, and organ has been handed over to Him. No more are we our own masters, hence we no longer are responsible. If the weather abruptly changes, this is His business. A sleepless night does not make us anxious. No matter in what unexpected way Satan assaults, we remember the battle is the Lord's and not ours. Then and there the life of God flows out through our bodies. At such an hour others might lose peace, grow despondent, become worried, and desperately seek some remedial measure; but we quietly exercise faith and live by God, for we know we henceforth live not by eating, drinking, sleeping, and so forth, but by the life of God. These things cannot hurt us.

Understanding now that the Lord is for his body, the Christian is able to appropriate all the riches of God for his needs. For every urgent requirement there is always His supply; his heart is accordingly at rest. He does not request more than what God has supplied, but neither is he satisfied with anything less than what He has promised. He refuses to use his own strength in any matter to help God ahead of His time. While worldly people are anxiously running for help because of the suffering and pain of the flesh, he can wait calmly for God's time and God's riches due to his union with

Him. He holds not his life in his own hand but looks for the Father's care. What peace this is!

During this period the believer glorifies God in every respect. He takes whatever may happen as an opportunity to manifest His glory. He does not use his own ways and thus interfere with the glory which is due God. But when the Lord stretches out His arm to deliver, then is he ready to praise.

The aim of the child is no longer the blessing from the Father. God Himself is far more precious than all His gifts. If healing would not express God then he does not want to be healed. Should we merely covet the Father's protection and supply, should we cry out only for deliverance from temptation, we already have fallen. God as our life is not a business proposition. Those who genuinely know Him do not beg for healing but always seek the Father. If health might lead him astray and take away from God's glory, he would rather not be healed. Believers continually should remember that whenever our motive is to covet God's gifts rather than God Himself, we already are beginning to falter. Should a Christian live perfectly for the Lord he will not be anxious to seek help, blessing, or supply. He will instead commit himself unconditionally to God.

CHAPTER 4
OVERCOMING DEATH

The experience of overcoming death is not unusual among saints. By the blood of the lamb the Israelites were protected from the hand of the death angel who slew the first-born of Egypt. In the name of the Lord David was saved from the paws of the lion and the bear and also from the hand of Goliath. By casting some meal into the pot Elisha drove death out of it (2 Kings 4.38-41). Shadrach, Meshech and Abednego suffered no harm in the fiery furnace (Dan. 3.16-27). Daniel witnessed God shutting the mouths of the lions when he was thrown into their den. Paul shook off a deadly viper into the fire and experienced no harm (Acts 28.3-5). Enoch and Elijah both were raptured to heaven without tasting death—perfect examples of death being overcome.

It is God's aim to bring His children through the experience of overcoming death now. To triumph over sin, self, the world, and Satan is necessary; but victory is not complete without a corresponding triumph over death. If we wish to enjoy a complete victory we must destroy this *last* enemy (1 Cor. 15.26). We will leave one foe unconquered if we fail to experience the triumph over death.

There is death in nature, death in us, and death from Satan. The earth lies under a curse; it is therefore ruled by that curse. If we desire to live victoriously on this earth, we will have to ovecome the death which is in the world. Death is in our body. On the day we are born it begins to work in us; for which of us from that day onward does not commence traveling towards the tomb? Do not view death merely as a "crisis"; it is pre-eminently a progressive matter. It is already in us and is gradually and relentlessly devouring us. Our release from this earthly tent is but the crisic consummation of the protracted working of death. It can strike at our spirit, depriving it of life and power; it can strike at our soul, crippling its feeling, thought and will; or it can strike at our body, rendering it weak and sick.

In reading Romans 5 we find that "death reigned" (v.17). Death not only exists, it also reigns. It reigns in the spirit, in the soul, in the body. Although our body is still alive, death already is reigning in it. Its influence has not yet reached its zenith, but it is reigning nonetheless and pushing its frontiers so as to engulf the whole body. Various symptoms which we discover in our body demonstrate how much its power is upon us. And these lead people to that ultimate demise—physical death.

While there is the reign of death, there is also the reign of life (Rom. 5.17). The Apostle Paul assures us that all who receive the abundance of grace and the free gift of righteousness "reign in life," a force which far exceeds the operative power of death. But Christians today have been so occupied with the problem of sin that the problem of death has virtually been forgotten. Important as the overcoming of sin is, the overcoming of death—a related problem—should not be neglected. We know Romans Chapters 5 to 8 deal very distinctly with the matter of overcoming sin, but it gives equal attention to the question of death: "the wages of sin is death" (6.23). Paul deals with the consequence of sin as well as with sin itself. He not only contrasts righteousness and trespasses but also compares life and death. Many Christians stress overcoming the various manifestations of sin in their character and daily life, yet they fail to emphasize how to overcome the result of sin, namely, death. The Apostle, however, is used by God in these few chapters to discuss not so much sin's manifestations in daily life as sin's consequence which is death.

We must see clearly the relationship between these two elements. Christ died to save us not only from our sins but from death as well. God is now calling us to subdue both these phenomena. As sinners we were dead in sins, for sin and death reigned over us; but the Lord Jesus in His death for us has swallowed up our sin and death. Death at first reigned in our body, but being identified with His death we have died to sin and been made alive to God (6.11). Because of our union with Christ "death no longer has dominion over him (us)" nor can it bind us anymore (6.9,11). The salvation of Christ replaces sin with righteousness and death with life. Since the main objective of the Apostle in this portion of Scripture is to deal with sin and death, our acceptance cannot be complete if we absorb only half the theme. Paul describes the full salvation of the Lord Jesus in these terms: "the law of the Spirit of life in Christ Jesus has set me free from the law of sin and death" (8.2). Granted we have a great amount of experience in overcoming sin, yet how much have we experienced the overcoming of death?

Having received the uncreated life of God in our spirit, we who have believed in the Lord and are regenerated undeniably have as a result some experience in triumphing over death, but must our experience be limited to just this little measure? How much can life overcome death? Unequivocally most of the Lord's saints have not enjoyed the full extent of this particular experience which God has provided for them. Must we not confess that death works more potently in our body than does life? We ought to be as attentive to sin and death as is God. We must overcome death as well as sin.

Since Christ has conquered death, believers *need not* die though they *may* yet die. It is the same as the fact that Christ condemned sin in the flesh so that believers *need not* sin any more even though they *may* yet sin. If a Christian's goal is not to sin then not to die should likewise be his goal. As his relationship with sin is regulated by the death and resurrection of Christ, so must his connection with death be regulated by them. In Christ the Christian has conquered completely both sin and death. Hence God now calls him to triumph over these two experientially. We usually assume that since Christ has conquered death for us we need not pay any further attention to it. How can we then exhibit the victory of the Lord experimentally? To be sure, there is no basis for our victory apart from that of Calvary; yet to not claim what Calvary has accomplished for us is certainly not the way to victory. We do not conquer sin by being passive, neither can we conquer death by disregarding it. God desires us to be serious about overcoming death; that is, through the death of Christ we actually must overcome the power of death in our body. We heretofore have subdued many temptations and also the flesh, the world, and Satan; now we must rise up to defeat the power of the last enemy.

If we determine to resist death in the same way we have resisted sin, our attitude towards the former will be changed completely. Mankind is marching towards the tomb, and because death is the common lot of the entire fallen race, we naturally tend to adopt a submissive attitude. We have not learned to rise against it. Despite our knowledge of the soon return of our Lord and the hope of not passing through the grave but being raptured to heaven, most of us still prepare to wait out death. When the righteousness of God works in us we abhor sin; but we have not allowed God's life to so work in us that we equally begin to hate death.

To overcome death believers must alter their attitude from one of submission to one of resistance towards it. Unless we cast off our *passive* approach we will not be able to overthrow death but will be mocked by it instead and finally come to an untimely end. Numerous saints today misapprehend passivity for faith. They reason that they have committed everything to God. If they ought not to die, He verily shall save them from it: if they ought to die, then He doubtless shall allow them to die: let the will of God be done. Such a saying *sounds* right, but is this faith? Not at all. It is simply a lazy passivity. When we *do not know* God's will, it is fitting for us to pray: "not my will, but thine, be done" (Luke 22.42). This does not mean we need not pray *specifically*, letting our requests be made known to God. We should not submit passively to death, for God instructs us to work together actively with His will. Except we *definitely know* God wants us to die, we must not passively permit death to oppress us. Rather, we must actively cooperate with God's will to resist it.

Why should we adopt such an attitude as this? The Bible treats death as our enemy (1 Cor. 15.26). Consequently, we must resolve to oppose it and subdue it. Since the Lord Jesus has faced and overcome death on earth for us, He wants us personally to conquer it in this life. We should not petition God to grant us strength to put up with the power of death; we should petition instead for might to overthrow its power.

As death has come from sin, so our victory over death has come from the work of the Lord Jesus Who died for us and saved us from sin. His redemptive work is closely related to death—"Since therefore the children share in flesh and blood, he himself likewise partook of the same nature, that through death he might destroy him who has the power of death, that is, the devil, and deliver all those who through fear of death were subject to lifelong bondage" (Heb. 2.14-15). The cross is the basis for victory over its power.

Satan has this power, which power he derives from sin: "as sin came into the world through one man and death *through sin,* and so death spread to all men because all men sinned" (Rom. 5.12). But the Lord Jesus invaded the domain of death and through His redemptive act removed its sting which is sin, thus disarming Satan of his power. By Christ's death, sin lost its potency, and so death was deprived of its power too. Through the crucifixion of Christ we henceforth shall overthrow the power of death and lift its siege around us by claiming the victory of Calvary.

Three different ways are open for Christians to overcome death: (1) by trusting we will not die until our work is finished; (2) by having no fear of death even should it come because we know its sting has been removed; and (3) by believing we will be delivered completely from death since we shall be raptured at the Lord's return. Let us ponder these one by one.

DEATH AFTER OUR WORK IS FINISHED

Unless a Christian plainly knows his work is finished and he no longer is required by the Lord to remain, he should by all means resist death. If the symptoms of death have been seen already in his body before his work is done, he positively should resist it and its symptoms. He should believe that the Lord will undertake in what he has resisted, for He has work for him yet to do. Hence before our appointed task is discharged we can trust in the Lord restfully even in the face of dangerous physical signs. In cooperating with the Lord and resisting death we will soon see Him work towards the swallowing up of it by His life.

Notice how the Lord Jesus resisted the jaws of death. When people tried to push Him down a cliff He passed through the midst of them and went His way (Luke 4.29-30). On one occasion "Jesus went about in Galilee; (but) he would not go about in Judea, because the Jews sought to kill him" (John 7.1). On another occasion the Jews "took up stones to throw at him; but Jesus hid himself, and went out of the temple" (John 8.59). Why did He thrice resist mortality? Because His time had not yet come. He knew there was an appointed hour for the Messiah to be cut off; He could not die in advance of God's appointed moment nor could He die at any other place than at Golgotha. We too must not die before our time.

The Apostle Paul likewise had the experience of resisting death. The powers of darkness pressed for his premature departure; yet he overcame them in each instance. Once when he was imprisoned with death as the possible outcome, he confessed as follows:

> If it is to be life in the flesh, that means fruitful labor for me. Yet which I shall choose I cannot tell. I am hard pressed between the two. My desire is to depart and be with Christ, for that is far better. But to remain in the flesh is more necessary *on your account*. Convinced of this, I know that I shall remain and continue with you all, for your progress and joy in the faith. (Phil. 1.22-25)

Paul was not afraid to die, nevertheless before the work was done he knew by faith in God he would not die. This was his victory over death. And towards the end, when he said "I have fought the good fight, I have finished the race, I have kept the faith," he also knew that "the time of (his) departure (had) come" (2 Tim. 4.7,6). Before our race is fully run we must not die.

Peter knew the time of his departure too: "I know that the putting off of my body will be soon, as our Lord Jesus Christ showed me" (2 Peter 1.14). To concede—by a sizing up of our environment, physical condition, and feeling—that our time has come is an error on our part; we instead need to possess definite indications from the Lord. As we live for Him, so must we die for Him. Any call for departure which does not come from the Lord ought to be opposed.

In reading the Old Testament we find that all the patriarchs died "full of years." What is meant by this phrase? It means they totally lived out the days appointed them by God. God has apportioned each of us a particular age (John 21). If we do not live to that age we have not conquered death. How are we to know the span appointed us? The Bible offers a general yardstick—"the years of our life are threescore and ten, or even by reason of strength fourscore (Ps. 90.10). Now we are not suggesting that everybody must live to be at least seventy, for we cannot encroach on God's sovereignty like that; but in case we receive no registration of a shorter period, let us accept this number as standard and repulse any earlier departure. By standing on the Word of God we will see victory.

NO FEAR IN DEATH

In speaking of overcoming death we do not mean to imply that our body shall never die. Though we believe "we shall not all sleep" (1 Cor. 15.51), yet to say that *we* will not die is superstitious. Since the Bible suggests the common span of life as seventy years of age, we can expect to live that long if we have faith. But we cannot hope to live forever because the Lord Jesus is our life. We know God frequently has His exceptions. Some die before the age of seventy. Our faith can only ask God that we do not leave before our task is finished. Whether our life be long or short, we cannot perish like sinners before half our appointed days are over. Our years should be sufficient enough to accomplish our life work. Then when the end does come we can depart peacefully with the grace of God upon us, as naturally as the falling of a fully ripened melon. The book of Job describes such a departure in this manner: "You shall come to your grave in ripe old age, as a shock of grain comes up to the threshing floor in its season" (5.26).

Overcoming death does not necessarily mean no grave, for God may wish some to overcome it through resurrection just as our Lord Jesus did. In passing through death believers, like their Lord, need have *no fear of it*. If we seek to overcome the jaws of death because we are afraid or unwilling to die, we already are defeated. It may be that the Lord will save us from death altogether by rapturing us alive to heaven; we nonetheless should not ask for His speedy return out of a fear of mortality. Such apprehensiveness shows we are defeated already by death. Let us come to see that even should we go to the grave we are merely walking from one room to another room. There is no justification for unbearable inward pain, fear and trembling.

We originally were "those who through fear of death were subject to lifelong bondage" (Heb. 2.15). The Lord Jesus, however, has set us free and therefore we fear it no more. Its pain, darkness and loneliness cannot frighten us. An Apostle who had experienced victory over death testified that "to die is gain. . . . My desire is to depart and be with Christ, for that is *far better*" (Phil. 1.21,23). Not a wrinkle of fear could be detected there. The victory over death was actual and complete.

RAPTURED ALIVE

We know that at the return of the Lord Jesus many will be raptured alive. This is the last way of overcoming death. Both 1 Corinthians 15.51-52 and 1 Thessalonians 4.14-17 discuss this way. We realize there is no set date for the

Lord's coming. He could have come at any time during the past twenty centuries. Hence believers always could cherish the hope of being raptured without passing through the grave. Since the coming of the Lord Jesus is currently much nearer than before, our hope of being raptured alive is greater than that of our predecessors. We do not wish to say too much, but these few words we can safely affirm; namely, *should* the Lord Jesus come in our time, would we not want to be living so as to be raptured alive? If so, then we must overcome death, not letting ourselves die before our appointed hour so that we may be raptured alive. According to the prophecy of Scripture, some believers shall be raptured without going through death. To be thus raptured constitutes one more kind of victory over death. As long as we remain alive on earth we cannot deny we may be the ones to be so raptured. Should we not therefore be prepared to overcome death completely?

Perhaps we *will* die; nonetheless, we are not necessarily under any obligation so to do. The words the Lord Jesus variously proclaimed make this teaching crystal clear. On the one hand our Lord asserted: "he who eats my flesh and drinks my blood has eternal life, and I will *raise* him up at the last day" (John 6.54). On the other hand, yet on the same occasion, Jesus also affirmed this: "This is the bread which came down from heaven, not such as the fathers ate and died; he who eats this bread will *live for ever*" (v.58). What the Lord is saying is that among those who believe in Him, some will die and be raised up while others will not pass through death at all.

The Lord Jesus expressed this view at the death of Lazarus: "I am the resurrection and the life; he who believes in me, though he die, yet shall he live, and whoever lives and believes in me shall never die" (John 11.25-26). Here the Lord is not only the resurrection but also the life. However, most of us believe Him as the resurrection, yet forget that He also is the life. We readily admit He will raise us up after we die, but do we equally acknowledge that He, because He is our life, is able to keep us alive? The Lord Jesus explains to us His two kinds of work, yet we only believe in one. Believers throughout these twenty centuries shall have experienced the Lord's word that "he who believes in me, though he die, yet shall he live"; certain others shall enjoy in the future His other word that "whoever lives and believes in me shall never die." Thousands and thousands of believers already have departed in faith; but God says some shall never die—not some shall never be raised again, but, some shall *never die*. Consequently we have no reason to insist that we first must die and subsequently be resurrected. Since the coming of the Lord Jesus is nigh, why should we die beforehand and wait for resurrection? Why not expect the Lord to come and rapture us that we may be delivered totally from the power of death?

The Lord indicates He will be resurrection to many but also life to some. Marvelous though it is to be raised from the dead, as was the experience of Lazarus, this by no means exhausts the way of victory over death. The Lord has another method: "never die." We are appointed to walk through the valley of the shadow of death; on the other hand God has erected a floating bridge for us that we might go directly to heaven. This floating bridge is rapture.

The time of rapture is drawing near. If anyone desires to be raptured alive he here and now must learn how to overcome death. Before rapture, the last enemy must be overcome. On the cross the Lord Jesus entirely overcame that enemy; today God wants His church to experience this victory of Christ. We all sense we are living in the end time. The Holy Spirit is presently leading us to wage the last battle with death before the rapture comes.

Realizing his days are numbered Satan exerts his utmost strength to block Christians from being raptured. This explains in part why God's children are being assaulted so fiercely in their bodies today. Due to the severity of these physical attacks, they seem to breathe into themselves the air of death, thereby relinquishing any hope of being raptured alive. They do not perceive this is but the challenge of the enemy, aimed at hindering their ascension. However, should they receive the call of rapture, they naturally soon come to possess a combative spirit against death. For they sense in their spirit that death is an obstacle to rapture which must be overcome.

The devil is a murderer (John 8.44). The purpose of Satan's work against the saints is to kill them. He has a special tactic for the last days: to "wear out the saints" (Dan. 7.25). If he can add just a little anxiety to the believer's spirit, increase just a trifle the restlessness in his mind, cause the saint to lose sleep one night, eat less the next time and overwork still another time, then he has made inroads with his power of death. Although a single drop of water is powerless, continuous dripping can indisputably wear a hole in a rock. Being well acquainted with this truth, Satan incites a little worry here, a little anxiety there, or a little neglect elsewhere to literally wear out the saints.

Sometimes the devil directly attacks believers and causes them to die. Many deaths are assaults such as these, though few recognize them for what they are. Perhaps it is merely a cold, sunstroke, insomnia, exhaustion or loss of appetite. Perhaps it is uncleanness, wrath, jealousy or licentiousness. Failing to perceive that the power of death is behind these phenomena, the full victory for Christians is jeopardized. Were they to recognize them as the assaults of death and resist aright, they would triumph. How often saints attribute these to their age or to some other factor and miss the real import of it all.

The Lord Jesus is returning soon. We must therefore wage a total war with death. Even as we fight against sin, the world and Satan, so must we fight against death. We should not only *ask* for victory; we should also lay hold of it. We should claim the triumph of Christ over death in all its fullness. Were we to review our past experience beneath the light of God we would discover how many times we have been assailed by death without our knowledge. We endlessly attributed happenings to other causes and thereby lost the power to resist. If we had recognized certain events to have been the assaults of death, we would have been strengthened by God to have experientially overcome death. In that case our experience would have been like passing over broken bridges and torn-up roads: for in that experience all our surroundings appear to demand our death—yet we *cannot die*: time and again we despair of life, still *we cannot die*: we ask ourselves why we *now* must die, for though the battle fiercely escalates, we do not feel like dying: we seem instead to cry out—I do not *want* to die! What is the implication of this kind of experience? Simply that God is leading us to fight our last battle with death before we are raptured. These assaults are designed for no other purpose than to frustrate our being raptured alive.

We should clamp shut the wide-open gates of hades with the victory of Christ. We should stand against death, forbidding it to make any inroad in our bodies. Resist everything possessing the disposition of death. View sickness, weakness and suffering with this attitude. Sometimes the body may not be conscious of anything, yet death is at work already. Anxiety in the spirit or sorrow in the soul may produce death as well. God is now calling us to the rapture; accordingly, we must subdue whatever might hinder that event.

God places His children in various circumstances which impel them hopelessly and helplessly to commit their lives by a thread of faith into the hand of the Lord. For his hand is their only hope. And during such a period it is as though they were crying out, "Lord, let me live!" Today's battle is a battle for life.

Murderous evil spirits are working everywhere. Unless the saints resists and pray they shall be defeated. They shall die inescapably if they continue to remain passive. Should you pray "Lord, let me conquer death," He will respond with "If you resist death, I will let you conquer it." Prayer alone is futile if the will is passive. What you should say is: "Lord, because of your conquest over death, I now resist all its onslaughts. I am determined to conquer death immediately. Lord, make me victorious."

The Lord will enable you to overcome death. So lay hold of the promises God has given you, ask for life, and trust that nothing can harm you. Do not concede to the power of death, or else it will touch you. For instance, you may be staying in a disease-infected area; yet you can withstand all diseases and not permit anything to come upon you. Do not allow death to attack you through sickness.

No longer can we wait passively for the Lord's return, comforting ourselves with the thought that we will be raptured anyway. We must be prepared. As in every other matter, rapture requires the cooperation of the church with God. Faith never lets affairs follow the line of least resistance. Death must be singularly resisted and rapture must be claimed wholeheartedly. Faith is necessary, but that does not mean passively deserting responsibility. If we only believe mentally that we can escape death yet passively continue to submit ourselves to its power, how are we benefited?

MORTAL SIN

The Bible mentions a kind of mortal sin or "sin unto death" which believers may commit (1 John 5.16). The death here does not point to spiritual death, for the eternal life of God can never be extinguished; nor can it be an allusion to "the second death" since the Lord's sheep cannot perish. It necessarily signifies the death of the body.

Now let us especially notice what the essence of mortal sin is. To do so will enable us to know how to keep ourselves away from it so that (1) our flesh may not be corrupted, (2) we may not forfeit the blessing of being raptured before death, or (3) we may still finish the Lord's appointed work before our days are fulfilled and we die, if He should tarry and we must pass through the grave. May we say that because of their negligence in this matter quite a few of God's children have had their years shortened and their crowns lost. Many of God's workers, had they given attention to this, might yet be serving the Lord.

The Word has not spelled out concretely what this sin is. It only assures us that such a sin is possible. From the Scripture records we understand that this sin varies according to people. A particular sin for some is mortal, yet to another person it may not be a sin unto death, and vice versa. This is because of differences in grace received, light accepted, and position attained among different believers.

While the Bible never identifies this sin, we can nevertheless observe that any sin which results in death constitutes a mortal one. The people of Israel committed such a sin at Kadesh (Num. 13.25-14.12). Although they had tempted the Lord many times before (14.22), He always simply forgave them. But this time, though He still forgave them after they refused to enter Canaan, He additional caused their *bodies* to fall in death in the wilderness (14.32).

At the waters of Meribah Moses was provoked to speak "words that were rash" (Ps. 106.33): this was his "mortal sin": he died outside Canaan. Aaron committed the same offense as Moses and he likewise was forbidden to enter the holy land (Num. 20.24). The man of God who journeyed from Judah to Bethel disobeyed the commandment of the Lord with regard to eating and drinking; in so doing he committed his mortal sin (1 Kings 13.21-22). In the New Testament we learn how Ananias and Sapphira were punished with death because they committed what for them was their mortal sin, because they attempted to lie to the Holy Spirit by keeping back part of the proceeds from their land (Acts 5). The man in Corinth who lived with his father's wife was guilty too of this kind of sin, forcing the Apostle Paul to pronounce judgment by telling those at Corinth "to deliver this man to Satan for the destruction of the flesh" (1 Cor. 5.5). Not a few of the brethren in Corinth died because they were guilty of profaning the body and blood of the Lord (1 Cor. 11.27,30). They had committed the sin unto death.

To overcome mortality we must persistently overcome sin, for the former results from the latter. If we wish to live till our days are accomplished or till the Lord returns, we should be careful not to sin. Negligence in this has driven many to the grave prematurely. The mortal sin is not any particular terrifying transgression, because it is nowhere fixed or specified. Such a sin as fornication, of which the Corinthians were guilty, may be counted as mortal; but so too may rash words such as Moses uttered become a sin unto death (for note how the Scriptures characterized Moses: "now the man Moses was very meek, more than all men that were on the face of the earth" Num. 12.3; therefore no sin could be overlooked in this man's life).

Now is the day of grace. God is full of grace. So let our hearts be comforted. Do not allow Satan to accuse you, hinting that you have committed the mortal sin and hence must die. Although the Bible does not encourage us to pray for others who have sinned this mortal sin, God will forgive us if we judge ourselves and genuinely repent. The man in 2 Corinthians 2.6-7 is believed by many to be that very one who had lived with his father's wife. In 1 Corinthians 11.30-32 we also are reminded that even though we may have committed the sin unto death, we can nevertheless escape death if we judge ourselves truly. Therefore never permit any sin to reign in your body lest it become your mortal sin. Our flesh can be weakened, yet we must never lose the heart of self-judgment. We must judge our sin without mercy. It is true that we can never attain to sinless perfection in this life, but frequent confession and trust in God's grace are indispensable. God will yet forgive us. Those who seek victory over death need to remember this.

> Then he declares to them their work and their trangressions, that they are behaving arrogantly. He opens their ears to instruction, and commands that they return from iniquity. If they hearken and serve him, they complete their days in prosperity, and their years in pleasantness. But if they do not hearken, they perish by the sword, and die without knowledge. The godless in heart cherish anger; they do not cry for help when he binds them. They die in youth, and their life ends in shame. (Job 36.9-14)

THE TEACHING OF PROVERBS

The Proverbs is a book about the believer's practical daily walk. It teaches much on the ways of keeping one's life. We shall center our attention around its instruction concerning the way to overcome death.

"My son, do not forget my teaching, but let your heart keep my commandments; for length of days and years of life and abundant welfare will they give you" (3.1-2)
"It will be healing to your flesh and refreshment to your bones" (3.8)
"Let your heart hold fast my words; keep my commandments, and live" (4.4)
"Hear, my son, and accept my words, that the years of your life may be many" (4.10)
"Keep hold of instruction, do not let go; guard her, for she is your life" (4.13)
"For (my words) are life to him who finds them, and healing to all his flesh" (4.22)
"Keep your heart with all vigilance; for from it flow the springs of life" (4.23)
"He who commits adultery has no sense; he who does it destroys himself" (6.32)
"He who finds (wisdom) finds life and obtains favor from the Lord" (8.35)
"By (wisdom) your days will be multiplied, and years will be added to your life" (9.11)
"Righteousness delivers from death" (10.2)
"The fear of the Lord prolongs life, but the years of the wicked will be short" (10.27)
"In the path of righteousness is life, but the way of error leads to death" (12.28)
"The fear of the Lord is a fountain of life, that one may avoid the snares of death" (14.27)
"A tranquil mind gives life to the flesh, but passion makes the bones rot" (14.30)
"The wise man's path leads upward to life, that he may avoid Sheol beneath" (15.24)
"He who ignores instruction despises himself" (15.32)
"In the light of a king's face there is life" (16.15)
"He who guards his way preserves his life" (16.17)
"He who keeps the commandment keeps his life; he who despises the word will die" (19.16)
"The fear of the Lord leads to life" (19.23)
"The getting of treasures by a lying tongue is a fleeting vapor and a snare of death" (21.6)
"A man who wanders from the way of understanding will rest in the assembly of the dead" (21.16)
"He who pursues righteousness and kindness will find life and honor" (21.21)

As the Spirit of God leads us to overcome death we discover new meanings to these verses. We are accustomed to viewing "life" as a kind of terminology. But when we have been enlightened we begin to realize our physical life shall be extended if we fulfill God's conditions. And contrariwise, should we disobey these commandments our life shall gradually fade away. For instance, God exhorts you to "honor your father and mother that it may be well with you and that you may live long on the earth" (Eph. 6.2-3). Now if we disobey, our years on earth shall be cut short by sin. God wishes us to hearken to His words, to possess wisdom, to seek righteousness and to keep our hearts, that we lose not our life. If we would have life we must learn to obey.

THE POWERS OF THE AGE TO COME

We are told that in the future kingdom the Lord Jesus is to be the sun of righteousness with healing in its wings (Mal. 4.2). And "no inhabitant will say, 'I am sick'" (Is. 33.24). At that time we *believers* will enjoy what the Scriptures foretell: "the perishable puts on the imperishable, and the mortal puts on immortality, (and) then shall come to pass the saying that is written, 'Death is swallowed up in victory'" (1 Cor. 15.54). To Christians, the characteristic of the kingdom age is that there is no more weakness, sickness or death, because our bodies will have been redeemed and Satan trodden under foot.

We are equally instructed by the Scriptures that we may foretaste the powers of the age to come now (Heb. 6.5). Though our bodies yet wait to be redeemed, we today through faith can taste in advance the powers of the coming age in having no weakness, no sickness, and no death. This is a very deep experience, but if the Christian meets God's requirements and fully trusts in His Word, he is able to enjoy such an experience. Faith is timeless: not only can it draw upon what God has done for us in the past, it can claim as well what God will do for us in the future.

Paul the Apostle describes the change in our bodies in this manner: "while we are still in this tent, we sigh with anxiety; not that we would be unclothed, but that we would be further clothed, so that what is mortal may be swallowed up by life. He who has prepared us for this very thing is God, who has given us the Spirit as a guarantee" (2 Cor. 5.4-5). The word "guarantee" here connotes the idea of "down payment"—a payment to guarantee future payment in full. The Holy Spirit in us is God's guarantee that "what is mortal is swallowed up by life." Though we have not experienced this victory fully today, we nonetheless do experience it partially for we possess the Holy Spirit as the down payment. The giving of the Spirit is that we may foretaste the future triumph of life.

"Now (God) has manifested (himself) through the appearing of our Savior Christ Jesus, who abolished death and brought life and immortality to light through the gospel" (2 Tim. 1.10). Life and immortality, declares the Apostle, are the common portion of all who receive the gospel. Wherefore the question arises, how far is the Holy Spirit able to lead a believer into possessing his portion? Death has been abolished; consequently, believers ought to experience something of this. Now this age is soon to be over; with the rapture in view the Holy Spirit intends to bring believers to experience more of possessing this possession.

Let us believe it is possible to foretaste the powers of the age to come. When Paul exclaims, "Thanks be to God, who gives us the victory through our Lord Jesus Christ" (1 Cor. 15.57), he is pointing to the *present* and he is concerned with the problem of *death*. Although he is referring to future total victory over death, even so he is not content to leave such an experience entirely to the future. He claims we may overcome through the Lord Jesus now!

God has among His principles this one—that what He intends to do in a certain age He first exhibits in a few. What all will experience in the millennium, the members of Christ should currently be experiencing. Even in past dispensations there were people who experienced in advance the powers of the coming age. How much more must the church today have the experience of Christ's victory over death. God desires us to thrust through the boundaries of hades now. The Lord calls us to overcome death for His body's sake. Unless we conquer the last enemy our battle is not concluded.

Let each of us therefore seek the Lord's mind concerning our future. We entertain no superstitious concept that we will not die. But if now is the end time and the coming of Christ will tarry no more but will be consummated in our lifetime, then we should exercise faith to lay hold of God's Word and trust that we shall not die but shall see the Lord's face alive. And let us who thus hope in Him purify ourselves as He is pure. Moment by moment let us live for Him and draw upon His resurrection life for the needs of our spirit, soul and body.

"By faith Enoch was taken up so that he should not see death" (Heb. 11.5). Let us likewise believe. Believe that death is not necessary, that rapture is certain, that the time will not be long. "Now before (Enoch) was taken he was attested as having pleased God" (Heb. 11.5). How about us?

Oh how excellent is the future glory! How perfect is the salvation which God has prepared for us! Let us arise and go up. May "heaven" so fill us that the flesh finds no ground nor the world holds any attraction! May the love of the Father so be in us that we hold no more communication with His enemy! May the Lord Jesus so satisfy our hearts that we desire none else! And may the Holy Spirit create in each believer the prayer, "Come, Lord Jesus!"